Kashmir
in
Sunlight & Shade

Kashmir in Sunlight & Shade

A DESCRIPTION OF THE BEAUTIES OF THE COUNTRY, THE LIFE, HABITS AND HUMOUR OF ITS INHABITANTS, AND AN ACCOUNT OF THE GRADUAL BUT STEADY REBUILDING OF A ONCE DOWN-TRODDEN PEOPLE

By

C. E. TYNDALE BISCOE, M.A. (CANTAB.)

WITH AN INTRODUCTION BY

MAJOR-GEN. L.C. DUNSTERVILLE, C.B., C.S.I.

GYAN

Published by

Gyan Publishing House
5, Ansari Road
Daryaganj, New Delhi-110002
Phone: 011-47034999, 9811692060
E-mail: books@gyanbooks.com

Distribution Network
gyanbooks.com
India, USA, Canada, UK, Australia, France

ISBN : 978-81-212-6709-0 (PB)
First Published, 1922

2nd Impression 2022

Printed at: Gyan Press, Delhi.

KASHMIR IN SUNLIGHT & SHADE
Author: C. E. TYNDALE BISCOE

KASHMIR

IN

SUNLIGHT & SHADE

A DESCRIPTION OF THE BEAUTIES OF THE COUNTRY, THE LIFE, HABITS AND HUMOUR OF ITS INHABITANTS, AND AN ACCOUNT OF THE GRADUAL BUT STEADY REBUILDING OF A ONCE DOWN-TRODDEN PEOPLE

BY

C. E. TYNDALE BISCOE, M.A.(CANTAB.)

AUTHOR OF "MEN IN THE MAKING," &c.

WITH AN INTRODUCTION BY

MAJOR-GEN. L. C. DUNSTERVILLE, C.B., C.S.I.

AUTHOR OF "THE ADVENTURES OF THE DUNSTER FORCE"

WITH 28 ILLUSTRATIONS & A MAP

1922

Photo by] [*G. W. Millais.*

MULBE MONASTERY.

A Lama on the look-out.

INTRODUCTION

AN intimate friendship of many years may perhaps give me authority to express my admiration for the author of the present volume as a *man* and as a *worker*. His reluctance to undertake the task, the outcome of natural modesty, was with difficulty overcome, and I gladly seized the opportunity which was offered to me, of prefacing his lively account of Kashmir and its people with a few words which may perhaps be inadequate, but at any rate are actuated by sincere feelings of the deepest regard and highest admiration.

My natural tendency is to employ the space at my disposal in a eulogy of the author and his methods, but I know him well enough to feel that he would wish to be spared my superlatives, and I will leave it to the readers to express their own feelings. Having, however, known him, and the land in which he works, for so many years, and having had many first-hand opportunities of admiring his system, I must allow myself just a few words to introduce this apostle of cheerful and happy Christianity to those of the public who may not know him.

"In all things be men" sums up the fundamental idea in his teaching of Christianity, for true manliness entails virtue and rejects vice.

A born optimist, who regards dangers and difficulties as so many hurdles to give the racer the pleasure of leaping, a strong, forceful character with unshakable ideals and an unswerving determination to move without hesitation towards those ideals, a striver with a strong sense of humour and good sportmanship, and an indomitable courage, both moral and physical; such are briefly the traits that have enabled this indefatigable missionary to realise the remarkable success that has attended his lifelong efforts.

Although it is not the case that a large proportion of his pupils have definitely decided to accept Christ, it is nevertheless beyond doubt that the majority of his staff and boys leave the school having learnt to lead lives more nearly following the teaching of Christ than those of many professing Christians.

As an instance of this I give the following example which I have not hitherto told to Mr Tyndale Biscoe.

I was walking with a rather corpulent companion in Kashmir some years ago when we came to a small stream about ten yards across and about two feet deep. I had on rough shooting boots and putties, and I do not mind getting my feet wet, so I crossed without further ado. My friend, however, disliked wet boots and looked about for some way out of the dilemma. A rather frail-looking Kashmiri arrived at this juncture, and my heavy friend suggested in rather rough language that he should act as a beast of burden and convey his bulky form over the water. Without hesitation the Kashmiri obeyed the request, crouching before the heavy gentleman to enable the latter to place himself comfortably on his shoulders. With legs rather bending beneath his burden the docile carrier crossed the stream and placed my companion dry-shod on the opposite bank.

Translating his gratitude into pecuniary form the Englishman offered a silver coin to the late beast of burden and was surprised to receive the following answer in very good English:—"No, thank you, sir. I am one of Mr Tyndale Biscoe's masters and I am glad to have helped you."

I have never seen anyone so dumbfounded as my friend, and as we continued our walk he appeared to me to be thinking rather deeply.

Readers of this book will notice that it is one of Mr Tyndale Biscoe's characteristics to reach his objective by the most direct means possible, ignoring or brushing aside all obstacles as of small moment so long as he does attain his goal.

L. C. DUNSTERVILLE,
Major-General.

THE CRONK,
PORT ST MARY,
1921.

AUTHOR'S NOTE

I MUST express my thanks to my headmaster, Mr Shanker Pandit, B.A., who has allowed me to draw upon his knowledge of the ancient history of Kashmir, and of the various rites and ceremonies, both of Hindus and Mohammedans, with respect to birth, death, marriage, etc. What my friend Shanker does not know concerning his country is not worth knowing.

Mr R. E. Shorter, photographer in Sialkote and Kashmir, has most generously placed the whole of his huge collection of photos at my disposal, and a beautiful collection it is, the work of many years.

Mr Geoffrey Millais, the son of the late Sir John Millais, R.A., who inherits the talents of his father for making pictures, also Vishn Nath Pandit, the first Kashmiri to start a photographic business, and my brother, George Tyndale Biscoe, have given me their permission to make use of any of their photographs, and I thank them most sincerely for their kindness.

CONTENTS

CHAPTER I

PAGE

My First Journey into Kashmir 17

CHAPTER II

Beautiful Secluded Valleys 39

CHAPTER III

The Towns in the Valley 55

CHAPTER IV

The Kashmiris 60

CHAPTER V

Kashmir, Ancient and Modern 67

CHAPTER VI

Character of the Kashmiris 77

CHAPTER VII

Mohammedans and Hindus 95

CHAPTER VIII

Mosques, Temples and Shops 113

CHAPTER IX

Streets and Bazaars 119

CHAPTER X

Trades, Lepers and Beggars 126

CHAPTER XI

Fashions in Dress 137

CHAPTER XII

Brahmans and Sadhus 142

Contents

CHAPTER XIII

PAGE

HINDU CUSTOMS 153

CHAPTER XIV

BOAT-BUILDING 169

CHAPTER XV

EXPEDITIONS 182

CHAPTER XVI

A TRIP TO LADAKH 197

CHAPTER XVII

A TRIP TO LADAKH (*continued*) 210

CHAPTER XVIII

A TRIP TO LADAKH (*continued*) 216

CHAPTER XIX

KASHMIR MEDICAL MISSION 234

CHAPTER XX

EDUCATION 253

CHAPTER XXI

A KASHMIR MISSION SCHOOL 260

CHAPTER XXII

A KASHMIR MISSION SCHOOL (*continued*) . . . 272

CHAPTER XXIII

A KASHMIR MISSION SCHOOL (*continued*) . . . 289

CHAPTER XXIV

A KASHMIR MISSION SCHOOL (*continued*) . . . 299

INDEX 310

LIST OF ILLUSTRATIONS

Mulbé Monastery . . . . . *Frontispiece*

PAGE

Nanga Parbat 56

A Village Industry 62

Pilgrims Returning from the Mountains . . . 63

A Canal in the Dal 84

The Common Task of Women 96

Women Water-Carriers 96

Leaving School 97

Enemies of the Gods 97

Fateh Kadal 114

H.R.H. the Maharajah's Soldiers of the Old Army . . 115

Fishing on the Jhelum 115

Saffa Kadal 120

List of Illustrations

	PAGE
Milkmen bound for the City	134
A Brahman Woman	144
A Brahman Marriage	160
Women at the Mill and Spinning-Wheel	160
One of the Three Glaciers at Sona Marg	161
Four Ladies of Ladakh	206
A Buddhist Abbot and his Chelas or Pupils	212
Lamayuru Monastery	218
Floating Gardens on the Dal	219
High Street at Leh	222
A Winter Scene	223
Lama Actors in their Religious Plays	224
The Frances Aberigh Mackay Memorial School for Girls	225
Men in the Making	225
A Ghat at the C.M.S. Girls' School	262
A School Regatta	263

KASHMIR
IN SUNLIGHT & SHADE

CHAPTER I

MY FIRST JOURNEY INTO KASHMIR IN 1890

WE have for the last thirty hours been well shaken in the mail train from Karachi, our port of disembarkation, and are now amidst the salt range nearing Rawal Pindi; the engine is puffing and snorting, sending out volumes of smoke and sparks in its endeavour to drag its heavy load up the zigzags, through these bare, rugged red hills mounting up ever higher and higher. The country has been cut up into most curious castle-like shapes and in the dusk you fancy yourself passing through an uninhabited and bombarded city. These steep nullahs and gullies have been carved and scoured out by the heavy rain of the monsoons. At last as we round a sharp corner our attention is attracted to a most wonderful silver line touched here and there with various colours, such colours as we have never before seen, and as we try to unravel the mystery we suddenly become aware that we are looking at the sunrise upon the everlasting snows of the Himalayas; we just drink in to the full that which we cannot describe in words, a sight never to be forgotten, and every time we see this heavenly vision of purity the same indescribable thrill goes through one.

Daylight comes on apace, and we soon notice our travelling companions fastening up their bedding (for in India we always carry about our bedding with us) and putting their traps in order, which warns us that we are nearing Rawal Pindi. And now comes the town in sight, with its streets of white, flat-roofed houses and towers, Mohammedan white-domed mosques and minarets and shining Hindu temples. On the opposite side of the train we see white tents and barracks, which show us that we are at one of the great military stations of North India. The name tells us that it is a village of satyrs, *pen*= village, *Rawal*= semi-demi-god.

As the train draws up at the long platform with its usual jerks and squeaks, half-naked men are to be seen rushing about, wildly gesticulating, hither and thither, for are they not passengers who have been sitting about the station-yard since last night in hopes of finding room in the cattle pens, or third-class carriages, for the compartments are divided by iron bars and there is no glass in the windows? Most of them seem to have with them all their earthly possessions, piles on their heads and under their arms, with a child or two thrown in; they no sooner shove their way half through the carriage door than they are pushed out again by those inside, a most entertaining sight. Policemen clothed in blue tunics and yellow pants add to the row and amusement by pulling or shoving those would-be travellers in or out of the carriages as it seemeth good in their own eyes. Some of them make quite a good thing out of these pushings and shovings.

One night at Amritsar station I was waiting for a train, so could give my undivided attention to those yellow-breeched gentlemen. One man in particular had attracted my attention by his energy in the push-and-shove game, and as Easterns do not usually do things for nothing, I watched him quietly. He was apparently now resting from his labours and was leaning with his back against a sardine-packed cattle-pen carriage. One hand was twiddling his moustache, that was certain, but it was the other hand that I could not see which was of interest to me.

I strolled quietly up and down the platform near this carriage and soon discovered his little game, for those passengers, who happened to be Jhats (Sikh farmers), were all engaged in untying the corners of their puggarees and taking therefrom silver coins and placing them in that greedy, grasping, open hand; then if the stream of coins ceased a quiet turn of the head of this arm-of-the-law and a hungry, hurry-up-quick eye, or the word "Jaldi!" ("Quick!") hissed between his teeth, set the silver stream flowing again.

I thought that this fine person might like to see that two could play the same game, so I quietly came up beside him and leant against the carriage at the open window and, like him, with a careless, bored expression on my face, twiddled my moustache with my left and thrust my right hand with open palm inside, and, like him, shot in a hungry, fierce glance upon those patient and frightened Zemindars. The officer of law and order was amazed at my action, and looked at me from my sola topi (sun-hat) to my boots, and then quietly walked away, very uneasily twiddling his moustache with both hands, and when he had got amongst the crowd he turned round to see this extraordinary sight, a sahib looting the poor.

I took no notice of him, but continued to act the Indian constable. Then I quietly withdrew my hand from the window and put the money that I had taken into my pocket as he had done, and walked away in the opposite direction. I then turned round and came back to the carriage and returned the money and thanked the Jhats for their kindness. They first of all were astounded and looked at one another for an explanation of this extraordinary proceeding. Then as I salaamed to them and laughed, they saw it was a joke, and they all laughed timidly at first, and then as the crowd which had assembled in front of the carriage saw the joke also, they all roared with laughter, and scores of eyes were upon the red, blue and yellow constable, who was glad to escape. I could tell you scores of similar yarns, but I just tell this one to show how the natives oppress one another when they get a chance, and to show what enormous difficulties confront the English police officers in their Herculean efforts to administer justice in India. There is a certain class of politician who is continually trying to belittle the work of the British officer and bringing scorn, as they think, upon our administration in India by showing up the evil practices of the Indian police, but those who know India at all know that these revelations only go to show still more the need of more Englishmen to prevent the Indian bullying his brother. Englishmen have their faults, and plenty of them, but it is not in their line to oppress and bully the poor and defenceless, thank God!

Well, here we are drawn up at Pindi station and passengers are calling for coolies to carry their luggage; there they are, a host of them ready to carry a minimum of luggage for a maximum of bakshish, each man choosing the lightest load, which he puts on to his head, or gets his pal to help him up with. To the new-comer all this is most entertaining and amusing, and he forgets about his own baggage as he watches the comic operas around him.

In my compartment is a political officer who understands his Eastern brother well, and in consequence has coolies in plenty to pick up his loads when other passengers are shouting "coolie" in vain. The trick is quite simple. Instead of calling "Coolie ider ao!" in an angry tone, you say "Ider ao tum badmash!" ("Come here, you blackguard!")

in a firm voice, with a spice of jocularity thrown in and a twinkle in your eye, and give the men a good smack on their backs as they bend to lift your loads, then you will have as many coolies as you desire. I have always been most grateful to this officer for teaching me this trick, which has stood me in good stead all through my pilgrimage in this wonderful and amusing country.

Our Eastern brother is a naturally good-tempered and easy-going gentleman, who responds to pleasant and cheery treatment. If, on the other hand, you lose your temper with him you will never get willing service and often have unnecessary trouble. Treat the Indian well and you will never find better servants or more trusty friends.

Whilst I am drinking in these new experiences and enjoying this lively scene of hurtlings and jabberings, a cleanly dressed man with a bright red waistband forces his way through the crowd and puts a letter in my hand; it comes from the army chaplain of Rawal Pindi, inviting me to put up with him according to the usual custom of Anglo-Indian hospitality, to make his home my home for as long as I like, and to trust myself and belongings to his servant's guiding.

Coolies soon have all my packages poised on their heads and we all march in stately fashion out of the station, where we see hackney carriages of all sorts, from the first-class pair-horsed landau called "feton ghari" at one rupee per hour to the two-wheeled bamboo cart at three annas per hour. I select a second-class four-wheeler called a "tikka ghari," which is somewhat similar to a London growler in shape, but it is drawn by a pair of lean ponies. A London four-wheeler is not in it for shaking and rattling. The Indian sun has cracked and warped the wood so that nothing fits, hence it is impossible for two persons to carry on a conversation inside it.

The luggage is soon hoisted on the top, and now comes the paying. Like all new-comers, I pay the coolies too much, and then trouble or amusement begins. The coolies look at the coins and say, like the London cabby, "What is this?" and crowd round me demanding more pay. The chaplain's servant comes to my rescue and drives them off, and they depart grinning and jabbering in their delight at having looted a foreigner. Our Jehu starts off at the gallop and keeps his pair at that pace for most of the way by free use of the whip and tongue, as he squats cross-legged on the box. At the bungalow of the Padre Sahib I, a perfect stranger, am greeted as if I were an old friend, with every possible kindness. The first thing suggested is the bath, for every bedroom has a bathroom attached, and soon I hear the swish of water as it comes pouring out of the goatskin or "mushak" carried by the indispensable water-carrier, "bhishti," or heavenly man, which he verily is in this sun-baked land. As soon as I am clean and refreshed my host comes in to say that he trusts I have come for a long stay, at any rate I must not think of moving on at present, as the road to Kashmir is broken by avalanches, etc., etc., and that it would be wicked to go on without seeing the Station, etc. So I settle myself down for a day or two, and that afternoon we have an unexpected entertainment, for a host of locusts makes its appearance and puts an end to our game of lawn tennis; however, we get exercise and more than we bargained for, in our efforts to stop the inrush of the advance guard with our rackets. They come so thick and fast on the wind that they blind us and we are obliged to beat a hasty retreat indoors.

Next day we see all the country pink, fields, hedges, trees; everything green has been devoured and locusts have taken full possession. The crows, which have done their level best to lessen the host, sit on the roofs, surrounded by these pink and yellow insects, with beaks wide open, trying to breathe, as they are utterly and wholly stodged; they now and again just pick up a nice young one which crawls temptingly at their feet, but they are obliged to leave it, alas! as there is no room inside. One felt quite sorry for them. We soon hear the news that the trains have been stopped by them, as their squashed bodies on the rails act like grease, and the zigzags up the salt range of yesterday become unzigzagable.

This invasion becomes so serious that the troops are ordered out to fight these hosts and if possible to stop their onward march and save the crops. The soldiers dig trenches some miles in length across the locusts' line of march or flight, and in front of each trench a corresponding line of fires are kept burning so that as the locusts pass their wings become singed and they fall into the pits and receive decent burial at the hands of the troops; but, as a matter of fact, they came in such myriads that the fires were extinguished, and hence the country was eaten up by them. They finally went north and perished on the everlasting snows.

Well, all good things have to end some time, and so did my visit to the kindest of hosts, Padre Griffith and his wife. The tonga is at the door and all is ready for the 200-mile journey through the mountains to Srinagar, the capital of Kashmir.

While the servants are loading the tonga and the babu is taking my rupees and writing me out a receipt (and I may say that this came in very handy, for some months after the journey I was requested to pay twice for this particular ride), let us overhaul our chariot. It is a two-wheeled cart built very low and very strong and possesses good springs, fortunately. It holds four persons counting the driver and five if you count the sais, who usually stands or squats on the step or splash-board with his dirty shirt (for our Eastern brother wears his shirt outside his trousers) flapping in your face, so that you get full benefit of his smell. Above your head is a strong canvas hood, around which is piled the luggage from the splash-board upwards till it meets on the top and is securely fastened by ropes. Travellers should see that the luggage is securely fastened, for it has happened several times to my knowledge that such interesting luggage as dispatch-boxes and dressing-bags have been dropped off at convenient places on the road, never to return.

At the time of which I am writing it was the custom to put one pony in the shafts and fasten on a second outside of the off shaft, and this particular harnessing was one of the great causes of galling, from which the ponies suffered to a terrible extent. This harnessing, I am glad to say, has been done away with and the curricle has been fitted on instead. This consists of a short pole and cross-bar, the pole between the ponies and the cross-bar fastened to the top of the ponies' backs.

The tonga is as useful and comfortable a cart as could be well desired for a mountain road.

The last good-byes have been said, and we start off at full speed and rush straight into the Padre's gate-post and pull up dead with a mighty jerk. No harm is done, however, to the cart, but the gate-post looks a bit drunk, and we speed on, kicking up clouds of dust as we go full speed ahead, the Afghan driver cursing and whipping the ponies, howling and yelling with all his might at all carts and passengers ahead of us.

After a mile or two at this pace the ponies are lathered into a foam and we slacken down; then out comes the cracked bugle, which brays on all possible occasions, in season and out of season, and you wish the driver and his horn at Jericho. But all the same this bugle is a necessity, for the bullock-cart drivers, and camel and donkey drivers seem to have buffalo-hide ear-drums. They always keep the middle of the road, the only part that is metalled, and will not hear till the ponies' heads are almost into their carts; and then they get terribly excited, and twist the tails of their oxen round and round frantically in their efforts to escape the whip of the angry driver, who slashes vigorously and viciously at them as he anathematises them and all their female relations. If you see a bullock without a tail you now know the reason. Of course these continual blockings and the necessary sharp pull-ups, and the lashings and swearings and clouds of dust, are wearying, and you are relieved when the five-mile stage arrives and you have a minute or two of quiet whilst the ponies are changed. You are then able to get out and stretch your legs, whilst the driver saunters up to the stables and squats down to have his whiff from the public hookah and discuss the news, such as who the passenger is and how many rupees he hopes to get out of him, etc., etc.

While our Jehu inhales his smoke at the first stage we will have a look at the well where a valuable horse met its death.

Leading into the well is a narrow staircase for travellers to descend and slake their thirst. This particular horse, being allowed to roam, found this stairway and, being very thirsty, managed to squeeze itself down to have a drink, and had such a long drink that when it wished to return it found itself fixed, as it was no longer the same shape as when it entered, and there it ended its days.

A blast from the horn tells me that the tonga is ready to start, so I take my seat and off we dash at full speed with a pair of half-broken-in ponies. Dust envelops us.

More blasts of the cracked horn, more swearing and more bullocks have their tails screwed, and so on till the next stage; and so we go on all day. We climb up to Murree, 8000 feet, and down to Kohala, 2000 feet, when the shades of night are upon us; and glad I am to find myself in peace at the dak bungalow post-house, 62 miles from Pindi.

Kohala is the last rest-house on the British road. Facing us on the other side of the Jhelum, which roars beneath us, is Kashmir. The river is spanned by a fine suspension bridge.

As we look on those grand mountains let us look back to the time when it came into possession of the present rulers.

Kashmir, being one of the most lovely countries of the world, very naturally became the desire of all who visited it, and the poor Kashmiri has been the servant and slave of various dynasties.

In 1750 it came under the most cruel and worst of all, the rule of the Afghans. Those who would not give up their Hinduism for Mohammed were done to death, and thousands were tied up in sacks and drowned in the rivers and lakes.

In 1819 the Kashmiris called in the aid of the Sikhs, who drove out the Afghans and ruled with almost as cruel a hand as did the Afghans.

Again in 1846 the country came under the rule of the Rajputs, for when the British arms conquered the Sikhs we made over this lovely country to Maharajah Gulab Singh, who owned the neighbouring country of Jummu, for the paltry sum of three-quarters of a million pounds, to be his and his heirs, as an independent possession. In consideration for this transfer, Gulab Singh was to hand over annually to the British Government one horse, twelve perfect shawl goats and three pairs of shawls, and further was to bring all his troops to join ours when necessary for maintaining order in the territories adjoining his border.

When the Maharajah Gulab Singh died his son, Ranbir Singh, became Maharajah, and on his decease his eldest son, Pratab Singh, now Sir Pratab Singh, G.C.S.I., took his seat on the gaddi (throne) in the year 1885. He governs his country with the help of a state council composed of native officials, not from Kashmir but from India. Most of them are men lent by the Indian Government and hold various appointments, such as Public Works, Revenue, etc.

A British Political Officer is always in residence at Srinagar in the summer, and Jummu, the second capital, in the winter, who acts the part of adviser to his Highness. At the time of this narrative, Colonel Parry Nisbet, who had rendered most excellent service to the country, was retiring, and Colonel Prideux came into Residence in his place.

In the East everyone rises early and obeys the cheering notes of the cock, as church or town hall clock do not exist in this country. In the midst of one's dreams one hears the soft tones of the bearer saying, "Sahib, Sahib, Chhoti hazari taiyar hai!" ("Small breakfast is ready!") —and a few minutes later one hears that cracked bugle. Jehu is anxious to be off, for he has heard that the road is broken in several places by landslips, which will delay our journey later on. So we are soon off again and rattling over the suspension bridge, but not before paying the toll to the gate-keeper.

Some years later when cycling over this bridge I was stopped by the tollman, who demanded the toll. I asked why. He answered: "Pay the hire for your gari." I said: "It is not a gari." He ran his fingers up the list and then said: "It is a horse." I said he was wrong again.

He looked puzzled. Then a gleam came upon his face, and he pointed to the word "perambulator." I protested again. Lastly he tried "pedestrian." But I assured him that my feet never touched the ground. So I passed free.

But alas! when I returned some months after and was cycling past him cheerfully he cried "Stop!" and produced his list and pointed directly to the word "bicycle—2 annas." So he had me at last.

All went well till about the third stage, when in harnessing in the fresh pony, which objected mightily, I noticed that its chest was absolutely raw, the breast-band having literally taken off all the skin, so I naturally told the sais to take it away and fetch another; but the man laughed at me and proceeded to harness it in, and not until I became militant did he desist and take the pony away. The driver would not assist me, but instead sided with all the stable hands, who evidently made jokes at my expense by their excessive laughing and pointed gestures. They then one and all sat down and smoked their hookahs, evidently intending me to understand that the tonga would remain there; so I adopted their attitude and sat down also and lit my pipe and determined to sit them out.

I suppose they saw that I was determined, and no doubt the Afghan driver had learnt partially the lesson I had taught him the previous day over the excessive whipping of the ponies, so they finally bestirred themselves, and a pony less galled than the one I had refused was put in.

Some of these poor ponies are so galled and raw that they will not start until a fire of straw has been lit under them. I only saw them try that trick once.

This galling sometimes sends them mad, and the poor beasts in order to save their raw chests come broadside on, going long distances like crabs, and dash themselves into the rocks.

A friend of mine was driving down the Murree hill and one of the ponies became utterly unmanageable, no doubt from this cause, and kept jumping on the low parapet wall, and finally made a wild plunge over the wall, pulling with him the other pony and tonga. The three Europeans managed to jump out in the nick of time most marvellously, and they stood on the road aghast, watching the ponies, tonga-driver and sais going straight to death—the driver, a brave fellow, as most of them are, sticking to his duty, the sais dumbfounded, standing on the splash-board, until with a terrific smash they went straight into a huge rock. And that was the end of all except the sais, who was pitched clear of the rock and was picked up senseless, and after three days brought back, as it were, to life, and lived to tell the tale.

One could fill a book of thrilling stories of this road, terrible deaths and marvellous escapes; and so these excitements must continue until the animals are properly looked after and the hill-sides cease slipping down, or until motor vehicles supersede the tonga and the cart, and so relieve the poor animals of their burdens, which I am glad to say is now taking place.

Well, the fresh ponies are harnessed in, and off we go full speed as usual until we finally reach Domel, where the clear blue waters of the Krishen Ganga join the muddy brown stream of the Jhelum; and while we sit in the verandah of the pretty dak bungalow waiting for tiffin let me pass on to you a yarn or two of this wonderful mountain road.

About the year 1888 Colonel Parry Nisbet, an officer of the right type, was sent by the Viceroy to Kashmir as British Resident to help the Maharajah to carry out the many needed reforms in his country, and amongst them to push on this cart road from India to Srinagar, the capital of Kashmir, which from Rawal Pindi would be about 200 miles.

At that time Russia was menacing our frontier in the Hindu Kush, and it was necessary that we should have a road for our troops in order to resist if necessary any attack from that quarter.

This matter was urgent, so Colonel Parry Nisbet called to him the Kashmir state engineers, who were then finishing the first section of the road, from Kohala to Domel, a distance of 21 miles. He asked them to let him know how long they would take to finish the road to Baramulla, a distance of 78 miles, at the entrance of the valley, from which place the river is navigable. They answered that as the first section had taken them five years to make, this section would take them twelve years.

The Colonel answered that that would not do at all, the road must be finished in two years. The Kashmir engineers said that this was an impossibility, to which he replied that he would in two years' time drive into Baramulla.

As the Kashmir state was unable to push on this work, Colonel Nisbet called in the aid of Mr Spedding, a contractor, and he brought in with him a band of capable engineers and several hundreds of Pathans and other coolies and took the work in hand at once; and although the difficulties to be overcome were enormous, this party of Englishmen with their stalwart coolies accomplished their task, so that Colonel Nisbet did what he said he would do, for he drove in a carriage and pair all the way to Baramulla within the two years. This army of Afghan coolies was by no means an easy lot to manage, for amongst them were many deserters from British regiments, and several were murderers hiding from the law, and most of them no doubt had done their various murders for the honour of their respective families.

My First Journey into Kashmir

It would have been difficult to collect a finer lot of scoundrels than this army which had been brought together for driving this road through the mountains.

The English engineers had some amusing times with them.

A young man straight from Cambridge was in charge of a few score of these half savages, and at the commencement of his command the head of a certain gang flatly refused to obey his officer, and to show his determination picked up an iron bar, threatening to brain him, but before the iron bar reached its mark our hefty savage had an English fist so smartly planted in his face that he measured his length on the road.

These Pathans have some good qualities, amongst them good temper and admiration for courage, so the result of that little contretemps was most satisfactory, for Appleford was honoured and obeyed by his good-natured scoundrels till the road was finished.

I will relate one other incident which led still further to the respect of the Pathan coolies for their officers. On pay-day at the end of each week the head gangers were given the pay to distribute to their men, but when it was discovered that these men did not pass on the wages in full to them, the engineers arranged for the payments to be made in public, so that the coolies could see that the sahibs did not hold back their payments, and the piles of rupees were placed on the table for the gangers to take off. The ganger would come to the table and take off the rupees to distribute to his men, but in so doing he would hold one hand just under the table, so that as he slid the pile of rupees to the edge of the table to pick them up he would let one or two rupees drop into his hand below the table and would pocket them. In this way he hoped that the men would see that it was not he, but the sahibs, who had given short money. But again the young sahibs were level with them, for one of them would sit near the table whilst the money was being handed out in piles, and would keep his eyes on a line with the top of the table and so catch out these dishonest gangers, and make them give up to their coolies the money they had secreted. Thus day by day these rough hill-men learnt to honour and trust their English officers, and in consequence put their backs into their work, and so the road was finished in a marvellously short time.

We must get on; it is past midday and there are many miles before us, and possibly the road broken. The cracked bugle brays louder and louder, which shows that our Afghan Jehu is anxious to be off. The ponies plunge and kick a good deal, which means, probably, that the poor animals are badly galled. Crack goes the whip, the ponies plunge forward and the tonga is brought up sharp on a rock. The driver loses his temper and hits and swears at the ponies, cursing all the ponies' female relatives that he can think of. The sais is now at their heads trying to quiet the ponies, but they will not pull. He coaxes and then hits and then coaxes again, but all of no avail. He then brings a rope and ties it to the ear of one of the ponies and tries to pull it along. I make him take this off, and instead we all get hold of the tonga and shove at the wheels. The ponies, finding the load easier, bound forward and we are off, and the ponies keep it up till the driver with much difficulty pulls them up, as we come charging round a sharp corner into a long string of laden camels. The camel drivers, wakened up from their sleepy walk by the lash of Jehu's whip, bustle the camels to the roadside, and we are off full tilt again; but shortly we pull up with a jerk as one of the wheels strikes a boulder—the road is blocked with a small landslip. We three set to work and make a path for the tonga, and are off again, till we are pulled up again for a similar reason, but are fortunate to find coolies close at hand who at the promise of bakshish help us to clear the obstruction.

These particular coolies were carrying down apples to Rawal Pindi. It is simply wonderful what heavy loads these men pick up when carrying for themselves, for each man had on his back from two to three maunds (a maund is 80 lb.). Each man carries a stick in shape of a cross without the head-piece. They do not walk, but trot for about fifty yards, and then place their stick under their load at the back and spread their legs apart so that the weight of the load is on the stick; they rest for about one minute and then trot the next fifty yards, and so in this way they get the two to three maunds of apples two hundred miles in about twelve days.

Very differently does the coolie work for someone else. This you can see for yourself as you drive along the road. If any man is doing a bit of road-mending there will be sure to be at least four or five men watching him, and when he is obliged to do any shovelling there has to be a second man in front with a rope attached to the shovel to pull as the man behind shoves, just as you have in England two men to a heavy lawn-mower.

All along the road one is entertained with most amusing sights, from the sleeping forms of the bullock-cart drivers (who are supposed to be guiding their animals), wakened up by the lashes of my driver's whip as he curses them for blocking up the road, to the Kashmiri bania (shop-keeper), riding on his caparisoned pony, with his bags full of all sorts of eatables tied round his saddle. When the dashing tonga appears round a corner his steed takes fright and dashes off, having just deposited his fat master like a bundle of rags on the road, and scattering rice and raisins, etc., all along the King's highway.

We ourselves are now brought to a standstill, and no mighty blowing of the bugle will remove the obstacle in front of us, for there before us is a road which is no road, for it is covered with the debris of an avalanche.

I want the driver and sais to start cutting a road for the tonga with our feet and hands shoving the boulders over the precipice, but they say it is useless, that it is the will of Allah that they should wait. However, force of example conquers and they are soon pitching boulders down the kud. We have only been at it for half-an-hour or so when to our joy we see some English travellers with thirty coolies. The Englishmen at once order the coolies to help us; the ponies are led over the slip, the luggage is unshipped and coolies hoist the tonga on their shoulders and carry it bodily across to the road on the other side.

I am so pleased to have surmounted the difficulty that I pay the coolies handsomely, with the result that these men, who before had been quite mild and submissive, crowd round me and demand more pay, and become a nuisance, when down comes my driver with his whip and curses, and they all fly like chaff before him. Again we start, and are once more hurtling down the road, making men and animals fly to the sides as we dash past; and so we speed on till we find ourselves at Hatti Bungalow, long since burned down.

Here I welcomed the companionship of a dog; although he was a Kashmiri dog, he understood English, which those around me did not; at least he understood my language whilst he shared my dinner.

Next morning when it is pitch dark I am roused from my slumbers by the soft voice of the bearer saying

"Sahib, Sahib!" through the keyhole of my door, which I know means my tea and toast are ready, and a few minutes later I hear the cracked bugle again, and before long am again sitting beside my Afghan Jehu and trying to explain to him that I want to reach Baramulla, the last stage, before night. On this stage of the road we see several rope bridges crossing the River Jhelum, which roars unceasingly all day and night, and you wish for a little quiet.

These bridges consist of three ropes made of hazel twigs, slung from stout poles from one side of the river to the other. One rope is for the traveller's feet and the one on each side, four feet above the foot-rope, for his hands; all three ropes are joined together about every six feet by V-shaped branches. These bridges are wonderfully strong though they look so frail, and when there is a wind on you imagine what a spider must feel like on its web in a gale. Women generally cross on the backs of men and are blindfolded.

You also see the one-strand bridge made of leather. On this rope is poised a V-shaped stick upside down, with a loop of rope at each extremity of the V, through which you put your legs and hang on with one hand to this stick, and with the other you pull a lanyard which runs through a pulley on the opposite side.

The impetus with which you descend to the sag of the rope takes you some of the way up, and the rest of the journey is accomplished by the aid of this lanyard. The villagers take sheep, goats and sometimes ponies across on this rope. They tie their four legs together and they hang from this V-shaped runner and are hauled across. There have, of course, been many deaths in these crossings, as the villagers go on using them till they break, and sometimes there are five or six persons on the ropes when they break, and they drop into the raging torrent and are dashed to pieces on the rocks.

We go cantering on very steadily till twelve o'clock, when Jehu, who is a strict Mohammedan, must say his prayers; and a fine figure he is as he stands, bends, kneels and finally touches the ground with his forehead, going through the prescribed attitudes of prayer.

I wish he was as kind as he is religious, for if so the poor ponies that he drives would have an easier time, and there would be fewer broken bones of sheep and goats, etc., from the wheels of his chariot as it hustles along.

The sun has sunk behind the great mountains some time ago and darkness is creeping down into the valley, and still we are many miles from Baramulla. Jehu tells me that we cannot reach Baramulla to-night. I insist on his going on. He goes one more stage and when the ponies are taken out refuses to have others put in. I show him that I am determined to get to Baramulla and commence walking off in that direction; soon I hear the tonga wheels behind me and once more take my seat, Jehu pretending to be very angry. The road has been cut up a great deal by bullock carts, and deep ruts and boulders scattered on the road give us terrific joltings, and at last the tonga goes down one side with a great bang and we are fixed; the ponies do their best but cannot move the vehicle. We all get out in the pitchy darkness and grope for the wheels, and try turning them, to no avail. Matters look gloomy, as we are all fairly well played out, when two men turn up, so with their help we free the tonga wheels and are off once more; and before long we see lights, and then more, and then a crowd of men with torches, and we find ourselves driving into the last stage. "Baramulla!" says Jehu, and he throws the reins on the smoking ponies' backs and we crawl out. I find myself surrounded by jabbering, noisy people such as one sees at the railway stations in the Punjab, only more so. It seemed to be pitch dark but for the flaring torches, which made the darkness more intense.

These men threw themselves on to my luggage and began running off with it. I, thinking that I had fallen among robbers, let out left and right until I got back all my belongings. Jehu took this opportunity of using his whip and voice again, and landed out right and left also, for he despises the Kashmiris. Amidst this babel, I see a man dressed in a sort of dirty night-gown garment holding out to me a letter, and just as I am going to take it from him, Jehu snatches it from the man and knocks him straight on his back with his fist. It is now my turn to go for Jehu, and make him give up the letter, which I find is addressed to me from one of my fellow-missionaries, saying that they have sent this man with a boat to bring me up to Srinagar, a distance of sixty miles by river. Jehu had knocked down this man because he had quickly arranged with some other man to take me in his boat, money having no doubt passed between them.

Having secured all my belongings, with the aid of the torches, I march off to the engineer's bungalow, kindly put at my disposal as there was no dak bungalow, and here I part with my Afghan driver, who had caused me much amusement and much annoyance, but which was the greater I cannot say. My Jehu was certainly a good-tempered, amusing, hard- and light-hearted scoundrel. I have been driven by many Jehus since that day, but never a one like that first Jehu. I have never seen him again, and I think it is quite possible that he is numbered among those brave men who have driven to death on that road with their chariots, as he was a strong believer in "Kismet."

My First Journey into Kashmir

I spent a quiet and very cold Sunday in Baramulla. It was the beginning of December. On Monday morning I boarded my doonga, which the crew, consisting of two men and a woman, towed up-stream. We reached Sopor, on the Wular Lake, fifteen miles, by three o'clock.

At this place the crew tied up, and refused to cross the lake, saying that they were afraid of the storms. I, thinking this was merely an excuse, urged them to proceed. At this juncture a Kashmiri Brahman headmaster of the State School came to my assistance. He had been a student in the Mission School at Srinagar. He told me that Srinagar by road was only thirteen miles distance, so I determined to leave the boat and ride to the city, and the man procured a pony for me.

When the boatmen discovered that I had determined to leave them they relented, and promised to brave the storm, but should they be drowned their blood would be on my head. I told them that I was ready to accept the responsibility, and to proceed. So we started onwards. It was just as well that I did not accept the pony and try the road, for the distance to the city was really twenty-six miles, as the headmaster meant "kos" when he said miles, for a kos is two miles; also the road was only a path and I certainly should not have reached Srinagar that night.

We crossed the lake safely before dark and tied up. The rest of the journey up the river took two days.

Although it was snowing and bitterly cold I could not keep in the boat, on account of the smoke from the kitchen quarters and the fleas. So, great was the relief when Srinagar hove in sight, and later on warm was the welcome that I received from my fellow-missionaries, and the Srinagar community in general.

CHAPTER II

BEAUTIFUL SECLUDED VALLEYS

UP to the present we have been looking at the large central valley of Kashmir, with its river meandering down the centre, to which is attached the three beautiful lakes. As you travel up the river you see side valleys opening into the main valley in all directions, down which rushing snow-fed rivers make their way to the main stream, Father Jhelum. It is up these beautiful secluded valleys the visitors wander every summer like nomads in their tents and select their own camping grounds, under the shade of great walnut-trees, or higher up under the pines, for these valleys are clothed with pine-trees from 7000 feet to 10,000 or 11,000 feet; after that grow the birch-trees up to 12,000 feet; then juniper, and after that grass and bare rock to the snows, at 15,000 feet and upwards.

In the pine-forest belt you come upon large grassy downs, called "margs," on which the hill-folk feed their flocks and herds.

One special marg has been selected for the hill station, called Gulmarg, on which wooden bungalows have been built by the State and by private individuals. Gulmarg is 8000 feet above sea-level and is twenty-eight miles distant from Srinagar, the capital, to which it is connected by a good cart road, with the exception of the last three miles of steep ascent through the pine forest, which must be negotiated by pony, dandy or on foot.

Gulmarg has grown into the usual hill station, with its

club and gymkhana, which includes tennis courts, cricket ground, polo ground and two golf courses, one for men and one for women, which are probably the best in India.

I can remember the time when the European residences were only a few rough huts.

I shall never forget the chaplain's hut in heavy rain: there was no dry spot under the roof. The chaplain's wife had to sleep with mackintoshes over her bed and all the umbrellas that she could muster. She put the children to sleep under her bed, for that was the only spot where they could sleep in the dry.

The church in the winter was used by the cowherds for their cattle, as it was the only hut besides the Residency and another which withstood the weight of the snow on the roof, as it was built in more solid fashion. It was a long barn-like building, with a row of stout pine pillars down the centre supporting directly the ridge-pole of the roof, so every summer there had to be a good deal of spring cleaning.

Gulmarg has moved on considerably since those days, for quite a pretty stone building has taken the place of the cowshed. It has had to be repaired several times on account of the damage done to the walls by earthquake shocks. It is about to have its first stained-glass window, presented by the churchwarden, Mr Willie Mitchell, the oldest living European inhabitant of Kashmir.

Pretty wooden chalets have taken the place of the log huts, and Messrs Nedou & Sons have a large hotel in which they can accommodate one hundred visitors, with the addition of pitched tents around. There are beautiful walks round about Gulmarg among the pine forests, through which you get most glorious views of the valley, 3000 feet below, with its river and lakes catching the sunlight, and then the everlasting hills stretching away in the distance, range beyond range; and there stands that great giant Nanga Parbat, meaning "the naked mountain," 26,700 feet, towering above its lesser brethren, also clad with the everlasting snow.

Gulmarg means a meadow of flowers, and so it used to be, but they have more or less disappeared, on account of the work done on the golf links, and other works of civilisation, but there are scores of other margs untouched by the hand of man, clothed with carpets of flowers of all colours and hues, true paradises to all lovers of flowers. On these margs roam droves of ponies, herds of cows and buffaloes, and flocks of sheep and goats without number. The Mohammedans explain the extraordinary ugliness of the buffalo by the old legend that Adam was watching Allah make the animals, and became so interested in the proceeding that he asked Allah to allow him to try his hand at it: he was given permission, and the buffalo was the result.

One has to be careful when one is passing a cow buffalo with calf, for they are apt to charge pedestrians, and sometimes kill them. A friend and I were attacked once on a hill-side suddenly. We were coming to camp after a heavy day's climbing, and our feet were heavy and slow, when we, to our surprise, saw a cow buffalo making for us at full speed. We stood still, hoping that our firm attitude and the human eye would make the beast change her mind, but in our case both failed, and we had to take to our heels, one to the right and the other to the left. To my disgust she preferred to hunt me, and my friend must have enjoyed the play. I soon saw that she could run me down, so I took shelter behind a large bush of wild indigo, hoping to get a chance of dodging and so regain my breath. As the brute was not out for play of that kind, she charged straight at me through this bush, which was fortunately down-hill, and that charge, on account of her great weight, took her down the slope before she could pull up, and so gave me time to dash for another bush and hide. I hoped that I had eluded her, but no, she saw me, and was after me again. I was heartily wishing that she would now prefer paying attention to my friend, and so give me a breathing space, when unexpected deliverance was at hand. The cowherd had heard her bellowings and snortings and came running up full tilt with a big stick, with which he gave her some mighty whacks, which had the desired effect, so my friend and I were able to continue our march to camp and to our much-needed refreshment.

The cowherds, or gujars, as they are called, live a very simple life in log huts away from the haunts of men. Some of their huts are made only of large slices of bark stripped off the pine-trees. They stick these strips up on end, so that their homes resemble Red Indian wigwams.

One often visits these gujars' huts in the hope of procuring milk, but they nearly always say they have not any, which strikes one as very churlish behaviour considering the great herds of cattle that are feeding on the margs around them; but they have their reasons, for they have in the past suffered so much from having had their milk and butter taken from them without payment by the native officials, and also sometimes by the servants of travellers, who do not look after them properly. Also they keep their milk for butter, which they turn into "ghi" —*i.e.* clarified butter—a most beloved food of the Indians. Every autumn travelling merchants visit these gujar encampments and take away their stock of ghi, which is put into goatskins and carried on pack-ponies to the Punjab. The gujars always keep with them large fierce dogs, a very different beast to the pariah dog of the villages. They are used by them for protecting their flocks and herds from the bears and panthers which are ever on the watch for them.

These gujars show much pluck when defending their property, and are thus unlike Kashmiris of the valley. In order to keep themselves fit for the day of battle they practise lifting heavy weights. You will often see outside their huts huge dumb-bells; they are sections of pine-logs weighing from 50 lb. to 100 lb.—in order to get a grip they scoop out a handle which they can grip with one or two hands—and these great logs they brandish about in order to make muscle.

When a bear or panther attacks their flocks or cattle they first turn their dogs on to them, and while the beasts are busily engaged in fighting with the dogs the gujars join in with axes, and ropes with which to lasso them.

There are two kinds of bear in Kashmir—the brown, generally known as the red bear, and the black. The red bear is of rather larger build, and lives on the higher margs, and is not so fierce as the black bear, which roams about in the forests and lives nearer the dwellings of men, subsisting chiefly on fruit, and on the crops of maize, to which he does much damage.

The red bear when caught young makes an interesting pet. A friend of mine had one for several years who used to follow him like a dog all over the country, and often caused consternation to travellers who met him in these runs when he became separated from his master.

I shall not forget my first introduction to him. I was paying a morning call upon a friend. I had only just arrived in the garden when a full-grown bear appeared from behind a bush, and immediately mounted on his hind legs and came towards me. I remembered that I had been told that the human eye is a match for any wild beast (though my little affair with the buffalo had weakened my faith a degree or two), so I drew myself together and fixed him with my eye, but alas! he would not look at me properly, and came steadily on, and I feared he intended to be affectionate, and what could I do? To turn my back and run would not be British or dignified, but I had to do something and that quickly, for he was upon me and I could almost feel his breath. Fortunately I remembered that animals like having their heads scratched, so I said "Good bear," and scratched the nearest part of his body to me, which was his nose, but kept my eyes on those terrible claws and muscular arms which might encircle me at any moment.

I tried hard not to let him know that I was not exactly delighted at meeting with him alone. What was I to do next? I could not imagine, for I could not eternally scratch his nose. Fortunately all things have an end in this life, and so did the nose-scratching, for deliverance was at hand in the shape of his master, who hoped that I admired his bear, as I evidently showed that I did by the attentions I was paying him. He little knew what my real thoughts had been a few seconds before.

On another occasion this bear was chained up to a tree outside his master's tent when his master was aroused by terrible shrieks. On coming outside to see what was up he saw a Kashmiri lying on the ground shrieking with terror and calling out that he was dead, which is the common expression when they are frightened. He, poor man, when passing the tent had all of a sudden seen the bear and, not realising that he was chained up, lost his head, thinking his last hour had come. Bruin no doubt had got on his hind legs to welcome him. This poor fellow knew nothing of the trick of fixing the wild beast with the human eye. Black bear can be very unpleasant strangers to meet, for specimens of their handicraft can often be seen in the hospital wards. They seem to take a special delight in changing the shape of the face of the men or women that they happen to meet.

One hears some very interesting stories from time to time from those who have escaped with their lives. The bear generally goes straight for the face, and with one blow smashes it in, and sometimes takes out an eye with the blow. He then comes up to the fallen victim to see if he is really dead. If the man does not move, the bear, thinking he must be dead, gives him a bite somewhere on the body and then goes off to dig a hole in the ground, as a dog does for a bone that he does not then need, and men say that on account of this would-be burial they owe their escape.

I have not myself witnessed the scene so cannot vouchsafe for the truth of this statement.

Bears at times are very human in their habits, for when they have been shot in the body in a place which they can reach with their fore-paws they will scrape up grass and earth with which to stop up the wound, very much in the same way that I have seen Kashmir coolies do when they want to stop the bleeding of a wound.

Black bear are flesh-eating animals in Kashmir. Some years ago my little boys were out for a walk with their governess close to our hut in the forest, when they came upon a black bear who had just felled an ox and was on its back and had commenced eating its hump, while the ox was still alive. Some villagers came to the rescue and tried to drive the brute off, but so pleased was he with his meal that he faced the men and charged them when they came near him.

I kept a young black bear for some time and also a Himalayan monkey. It was very amusing to watch the two playing together. Sometimes the monkey would ride on the bear's back; at other times the bear would walk about with the monkey in his arms, he licking the monkey's face, while the monkey returned the compliment by relieving the bear of unwelcome visitors on his head. The bear, however, developed an unpleasant temper and was a source of danger to the children, so we thought it better to turn him into a rug. I was sorry, for I had hoped he might have become a companion like my friend the red bear, but I did not then know that their insides differed as did their skins, one being brown and the other black. One black bear I know of who liked man's society.

Some years ago the village carpenter was making for me a dug-out canoe out of a large pine-tree in the forest and for several afternoons a black bear used to come and lie down near the old man as he worked, for company, I suppose. The carpenter himself was not at all unlike a grizzly bear, for he was covered with black hair, such as I have never seen before or since, though I have seen some very hairy Kashmiris; also his movements were very slow and quiet, which was in keeping with the forest beasts around him. Most of the Kashmiris are very much afraid of bears, but this man had, I suppose, lived so much in their company that he was used to them, so they lived on friendly terms, as was the custom in the days when they were not hunted as they are now.

An old Padre told me that when he was in Kashmir as a young man and was travelling up the Sindh Valley he counted no less than eighteen black bears, which he passed in his march up; they were up on the fruit trees enjoying themselves, and did not attempt to move from the branches they were on. Even now they are plentiful in certain parts, especially in Poonch State in the autumn, when they come after the acorns. When the Raja has a big drive and several guns taking part, the party have on more than one occasion slain thirty bears in one day.

Panthers are uncanny sort of beasts and do unceasing damage to the flocks and herds. We had a lady panther for a neighbour near our hut in the forest for several years. This hut had been lent to us as a continual loan by our friend, Mr C. M. Hadow. Many of our friends came up at different times to hunt her, but always without success. She would never allow herself to be caught by the common trick of a tied-up dog or goat as a decoy.

One year she cleared off all the dogs from the neighbouring villages, which was a great blessing for us, as these dogs are persistent and clever thieves, and keep one awake at night by their continual barking as they prowl about for food. Panthers prefer dogs to any other animal; they will come right up to one's verandah or tent to pick up a dog, as has happened to several of my friends, but my dogs have so far escaped capture.

One night when the servants were as usual having their dinner in their quarters just outside our hut the last remaining dog but two of the neighbourhood was lying outside the door waiting for scraps; the servants heard a squeal and saw the panther picking up the dog, which was the size of a collie. He just chucked it across his back and jumped over the fence with it and was off.

The following night the last dog but one was lying beside the dhobi as he, with a hurricane lantern by his side, was eating his dinner under a tree close to the kitchen, when the panther made her appearance and repeated her trick of the night before to her entire satisfaction.

The next night we were prepared for her visit with our fire-arms, and as no dog visited our quarters that evening we put a kid in a basket and hung it from the branch of a tree out of the reach of the panther. We were aware of the presence of Spots by the occasional slight crackling of leaves, but she never showed herself.

Then we did some thinking, and came to the conclusion that the panther might know all about humans' tricks on land, but might be ignorant of water and boats. So as our hut was on the banks of a small lake, one of our party took ship with a shikari and hid among the reeds, some fifteen yards or so from the shore, where a kid had been tied. The moon arose and sailed up the sky, but there was no sign of the panther. At last the shikari's patience gave out, and he advised the removal of the goat to another place, so they went ashore; and as the shikari was in the act of placing the kid on his shoulders the panther's patience also gave out, for she made a spring for the kid but missed her prey as the shikari sprang aside. The man with the gun was at that moment stepping over a fallen tree and was not ready, for all happened so suddenly, so again our friend Spots escaped. Then a renowned sportsman said that he would surely be successful if he came to this place in the winter, as he would be able to follow her tracks in the snow.

He came, therefore, in the winter, found the pug marks in the snow and followed them patiently day after day for over a week. On his last day he was hard on the trail when he discovered that he was walking in a circle, and it dawned upon him that the panther was playing the old Red Indian trick, that she had come behind him and was tracking him, so he hid and waited. He had not long to wait, for he spotted two eyes looking at him over a rock at some little distance, but before he could get a shot Spots had disappeared, so again she came out top.

We began to think we were honoured with no common panther, but one with super intelligence, with a touch of the human mind, which the following event will bear out.

It was a Sunday evening in August, when one is glad to see the sun sink behind the mountains and be refreshed by the cool breeze as the wind from the mountain snows makes its way through the upper valley to the plain below. I was returning home from a walk with two children and two dogs. My boy Eric had run ahead with the dogs, though I had just warned him to keep near me with them, on account of the panther's love for dogs, so the little girl and I were running to catch him up. We had just come to a small clearance in the forest when the little girl grasped me tight by the leg and exclaimed: "Oh! daddy, look!" pointing to the left, and then I saw the panther in full cry, with her long tail sticking up and her nose on the ground, coming straight for the path we were on. It was all a matter of seconds. We stood absolutely still. She did not spot us till about six yards distant. She then drew herself up and stood stock still, glaring at us with glassy eyes, the hair on her back and her tail standing erect. Then commenced a staring match. Who could hold out the longest? The time seemed to be interminable, but I felt sure that if my eyelids would not play me false I should win. I know that I did not breathe and I do not think the panther did either. We all three behaved like stuffed animals, for little Pamela played her part splendidly, not moving a muscle. I knew she was trusting me, and I realised how impotent I was to protect her if the enemy attacked us. At last the spell was broken by the panther, whose eyes gave out first. I knew then that I had won the first round, but what was to follow? My adversary put her chin upon her fore-paws, bending low, as if she were salaaming, and then turned her face round upon us and treated us to a broad Cheshire cat grin, which seemed to say: "What sport this is! What shall we do next?" She then leapt up a great height and came down such a bang that she shook the ground. She then turned a somersault, and again, sprang up, and yet again, and repeated the performance over and over again, as if for our entertainment. Then once more she drew herself up to her full height, looking straight at us as she had done at first, and then once more dropped her chin on to her fore-paws, salaaming, as it were, again, turned her face to us with a parting grin, and was off bounding into the forest to the same spot where we had seen her emerge, and lo! our visitor was gone.

You can imagine our feelings while this beast entertained us, and our relief when the show was over. We would not have missed the experience for anything, and were most grateful to our friend Spots for having decided on acting a comedy instead of a tragedy on that Sunday evening.

I should fancy she must have been in an especially happy frame of mind, having possibly already dined satisfactorily, or possibly having come across the track of some friend of hers whom she particularly wished to meet. Anyway she was happy. It was providential that she just missed Eric with the dogs, who was ahead of us, for then the panther could hardly have helped selecting a tragedy for the evening performance, for a meal of English dogs would have been irresistible.

I came across the lady again on two occasions, one of them at even closer quarters, which is, I think, worth telling.

My wife was ill one night, and I started at midnight to get medical aid. As I knew the path through that bit of forest so well I never carried a lantern, but my wife was very anxious that I should do so, so I gave in, and took a hurricane lantern. It was a dark night. I was passing the stables, which is a two-storey building, with an outside stairway leading to the saddle-room, when I imagined I saw a man sitting on the stairs, swaying slowly from side to side. I naturally jumped to the conclusion that it must be the sais, who was ill, and was swaying from side to side in pain, most probably in his lower chest, so I went up and asked what was the reason. I had not finished my sentence when I felt a wind on my cheek and then a shaking of the ground at my feet. My sais had disappeared suddenly from view, stomach-ache and all. I then realised that I had been talking to my old friend of the jungle, only a hungry friend this time, for she had climbed the stairs and was swaying slowly from side to side as she sniffed our dogs under the saddle-room door, for we put them there at night to be out of harm's way.

The moral of this story is, husbands, obey your wives, for I hardly think I should have returned with my face intact if I had not been carrying the lantern, for it is considered the height of folly to startle a panther at any time, or to corner him in the dark, and more especially when he is hungry and on the point of commencing his late dinner.

I fear we shall never know for certain the end of our jungle friend, who ate up our thieves and stopped them keeping us awake at night, but as the dogs in the neighbouring villages once more increased to most amazing numbers, we conclude that she is either hunting in other Kashmir jungles, or, what is more probable, has joined her ancestors in happy hunting grounds elsewhere.

There are many other animals in these forests which one occasionally comes across in the early dawn or late evening.

There are wild pig, for instance, which one is apt to mistake for bear in the dark, as they crush their way through bushes and undergrowth. Jackals are always plentiful.

The lynx is said to hunt with the panther, no doubt in order to get same pickings from the kill. Pine-martens very seldom show themselves, but one continually sees where they have been feeding by the debris under the fir-trees.

The brown short-tailed Himalayan monkey may be seen all over the forests, as they live in such large communities; they are most entertaining to watch, swinging themselves from tree to tree with such a babel of voices, and especially noisy are they when they have their young. If they scent danger you see them calling to their youngsters to hurry up while they make for the pine-trees; the tiny ones mount their parents' backs and are soon out of reach up the trees. They make very interesting pets.

They can be caught by a very simple trap. An earthenware jar full of rice is put in their path, the jar must have a narrow neck, so that the monkey's hand can slip in easily when empty, but when the hand is full of rice it is unable to withdraw it. The monkey, finding this ready meal, eats greedily, but on the approach of a human being he takes a large handful, intending to make the most of his last chance, and he is unable to withdraw his hand; he has not enough sense to let go his last handful, and so is caught.

The first monkey I had was quite a companion. She rode on horseback with me, but whenwe galloped she became alarmed, and would climb on to my shoulder or my head, and hang on to any handy projection to steady herself, such as my nose and my ears, which was not pleasant. She would go boating and swimming with me, and was wonderfully obedient. I let her loose in the garden, and she would come down from the trees when I called her. But I failed to teach her honesty: she preferred stolen food to that given her freely. As an example. We were living in a house-boat on the lake and were expecting friends to tea, so that cakes were plentiful. Sundri, for that was her name—the Kashmiri for a beautiful woman—came out of the house-boat front door with a sponge cake in each hand and one in her mouth, a madeira cake under one arm and a plum cake under the other. As soon as she saw that I had seen her she made straight for the roof, and commenced climbing the ladder to the upper deck. She could only use her legs and elbows, as both hands and armpits were fully occupied with the cakes. She however reached the top safely with her burden, trying hard the while to cram the cakes into her mouth, grieving sadly that her mouth would not stretch any more. She was caught before the madeira and plum cakes had reached her mouth, and then punishment followed—viz. a ducking in the lake—which she took in good part, knowing that she deserved it, and also that she had swallowed three extra nice sponge cakes, so bore no ill will.

Sundri would sit for any length of time in the perambulator with our little boy, the two embracing one another, she making a cooing sound all the while, as she no doubt imagined him to be her own son. She hated the child's bearer, for he was the wicked man who interrupted their happiness by taking his charge away for meals or to bed. I generally had to come to the rescue, to put a stop to the awful swearings and the possible bitings which might follow as the tug-of-war was in progress between Sundri and the bearer. She, like most monkeys, hated being laughed at, and remembered those for evil who had opened their mouths at her, but responded to all who treated her with respect and took her seriously.

The Kashmir forests are just full of interest, for one never knows what interesting animal, bird or insect one may meet with in one's walks, and especially if one has leisure to sit down under the shadow of a tree, bush or rock, and in perfect stillness remain with eyes and ears open.

There is one drawback to the forest as far as I am concerned, and that is the presence of the ankhor (*Rhus acuminita*) tree. It has very graceful and vivid green foliage, but its juice is poisonous. It affects some people far more than others. I have on three occasions been ill for three weeks from having touched it by accident. After touching that tree, every part of my body which my hand touched came out in huge blisters, and the irritation was intense and caused fever. No medicine seemed to be of any use, so it had to run its course. Some Kashmiris suffer badly from it. I am told that they make use of it when they wish to punish an enemy. In climbing up a hill through brushwood one is apt to put one's hand on the trunk to help oneself up, or vice versa in descent to use it as a break on one's too rapid progress. I wage war with my enemy, and cut them down whenever possible.

CHAPTER III

THE TOWNS IN THE VALLEY

STANDING on these glorious pine-clad mountains, and seeing through a clearing in the forest the whole Vale of Kashmir stretched before one's feet, one thinks of Moses on Mount Pisgah viewing the Promised Land. For truly Kashmir is a land of milk and honey. Margs on your right and left provide grass in abundance for the cattle, and flowers galore for the bees. In front of you, in the plain below, you see clumps of trees, under which the villages nestle, surrounded by the rice-fields, now shining in the sunlight like a great sea, the villages being the islands; and beyond, you see the city of Srinagar, with its Hindu temple domes catching the sun's rays, and the Dal Lake green with its floating and other gardens and the great hills beyond, and above them ranges of snow mountains; and above all, the range near Gilgit, where Nanga Parbat stands out head and shoulders above other rocky giants.

In the valley there are only four places worthy of the name of towns: Srinagar, Baramulla, Sopor and Islamabad. Srinagar, the capital, lies in the centre of the valley, with a population of 130,000. Baramulla lies in the south-west, where the River Jhelum leaves the valley through a deep gorge, and thence becomes a foaming torrent as it drops 3000 feet to the plains of India.

Baramulla has a population of six or seven thousand, and is *the* town of export, as it is here that the river-borne traffic from this spot leaves the valley—by road chiefly, on bullock carts down the Jhelum Valley road, usually a journey of ten days, to Rawal Pindi in the Punjab.

The chief exports are fruits, such as apples, pears and walnuts; hides and grain of various sorts (but rice is not allowed to be exported); woollen homespun, skein-silk from the huge State silk factory, carpets and Yarkandi felts.

Timber, chiefly railway sleepers of deodar, floats past Baramulla on the river to Jhelum, and a rough passage it is, for the river falls 4000 feet in its journey of two hundred odd miles.

The ancient name of the town Baramulla, which is called Varamul by the natives of the country, was Varahmul. This locality has enjoyed great sanctity since early times as the dwelling-place of Vishnu in his incarnation of Adivaraha, or primeval boar. The legend connected with the sacred site is related in the *Nilamata*. An abstract of this legend may be given here. Shankasura (a conchiferous demon) had carried away the terrestrial globe, with all the sacred Vedas. The Devas (gods) were in great distress for the loss of Prithvi (goddess of the earth) and the eternal Vedas. They implored Vishnu to save the earth and their inspired books. Vishnu, in the form of a great boar, dived after the monster and killed him. He brought up the earth, with all the Vedas. The place where he rested after the great exploit became known as Varahmula (the abode of the boar). This legend preserves an indirect reference to the Great Flood, the submersion of the earth and its final reappearance after the waters of the globe had subsided.

The ancient temple of Varaha, which stood near the site of the present Kotitirtha, at the western extremity of the town and close to the river-bank, seems to have been

Photo by] [R. E. Shorter.

NANGA PARBAT.

The mountain is 26,700 ft. high.

one of the famous shrines of Kashmir. The ancient lingas and sculptures found at the Kotitirtha may have originally belonged to this temple. This shrine and its sacred image of the Varaha were destroyed by Sikandar Butshikan. About ten miles up-stream to the east is Sopor, with its population of 9000, which has not changed from the day that I first saw it in 1890.

Very picturesque it is, as it is situated on both sides of the river, which is here two hundred or more feet in width, and spanned by a drunken-looking cantilever bridge made of deodar (the tree of God) logs. The Mohammedan mosques, with their grass-covered roofs and wooden minarets, and the tin-covered domes of Hindu temples add much to its interest. The streets are very narrow, filthy and evil-smelling in the extreme.

It is the chief port of the Wular Lake, so possesses a good market for the products of the lake: fish, singara nuts and waterfowl. In the autumn sportsmen come here to spin for the masheer, a fish which runs to a great size, the record fish being 54 lb.

The drawback to this place is the mosquitoes, the air being thick with them, so much so that it is difficult to eat one's food without swallowing them. The fishermen are, as a rule, too keen on their sport to worry about them, and sometimes they are rewarded by really good sport; or the unexpected may happen.

An officer was fishing at this place when some boatmen came in from the lake saying that they had seen a bear swimming in the lake, and asking him to come and shoot it. He at first refused to believe their story, but finally agreed to go with them with his rifle, when after some time the boatmen spotted their quarry, for true enough it was a bear which was swimming across the lake, a distance of at least four or five miles at this point. But he was not allowed to finish his swim, which I think was not quite playing the game.

This reminds me of a somewhat similar event which happened in the Dal Lake, near the city, some time ago. I fear I have already written at too great a length about our wild animals, but as this is rather an extraordinary event I may be excused.

Two British officers were encamped at Naseem Bagh, which is one of the camping grounds on that beautiful lake, when some boatmen came to them in great excitement, saying that they had seen a panther on one of the small garden islands and asking them to come and shoot it. The officers naturally thought this panther was in the boatmen's imagination only, for no one had heard of a panther coming down so near the city in summer-time, as they have plenty of food on the hills. However, the boatmen promised to show them the panther, so these officers went with them. When the party arrived near this small island garden, not far from the mainland, one of the boatmen took the two officers in a small boat. As the boat glided under the willow-trees they saw the panther, who was cornered, waiting for them. One officer was standing up in the prow of the boat with his rifle, the other was in the centre, and the boatman steering with his paddle in the stern.

They had come upon the panther before they were aware, and the boatman was unable to stop the way of the boat. The panther sprang at the boat and hit it so hard that the officer in the bow and the boatman in the stern were pitched into the water, while the officer in the centre with difficulty kept his balance, as the panther was struggling, being half in the boat and half in the lake. The other officer and the boatman, who had disappeared under the water, happened to come to the surface at the same moment, when, in their excitement, they each mistook the other for the panther, and both dived to escape from a mauling. In the meantime the officer in the boat managed to put a bullet through the head of the poor beast, who was making a gallant fight for his life.

Islamabad, a town of 10,000 inhabitants, is at the east end of the valley. It is 48 miles up-stream from Srinagar, but only 33 by road, and is noted for its hot sulphur springs and tanks of sacred carp belonging to the Hindu temples situated on the banks. These springs are most useful for those suffering from that unpleasant skin disease vulgarly called the "itch." As this particular disease affects nearly every Kashmiri, these springs are much in favour. This town is also known by its Hindu name of Ananth Nag, which means "the place of many springs." It used to be one of the chief cities of the shawl trade, but now its chief industries are embroidery work and making floorcloths and curtains out of the disused woollen blankets, and very effective they are. The carpenters also turn out a good deal of highly coloured wooden articles which look like lacquer work, but is really wood coloured and then highly polished by the use of the lathe. They make very elegant spinning wheels, candlesticks, bowls and cups, etc.

CHAPTER IV

THE KASHMIRIS

BEFORE our visit to the capital, Srinagar, it would be as well to know something of the character and general look of the inhabitants of that very picturesque and dirty city.

The Kashmiris are of the Aryan stock, and are as a rule quite good-looking. The women are considered to be beautiful. I must say that I have not myself seen many beauties, but possibly if they were clean and wore becoming garments I might have reason to change my opinion. Also most of the upper-class women are never seen in the streets, and I am told by the ladies who visit the zenanas that some of the women are really beautiful. Many people think that the Kashmiris belong to the lost tribes of Israel, as many of them have such Jewish noses, also their love of money and of getting the better of their neighbours is very strong.

Their complexion is fair as compared with their Indian neighbours; those living in towns are fairer than the country folk. Some of them might easily pass for Europeans. The Hindu women and boys have generally refined features, quite of Greek type. Many have rosy cheeks and pink complexions, and a few have blue eyes and auburn hair; but auburn hair is not a popular colour, and they dislike any remark on the fact. One especially notices their fair complexion when they are with Indians or Eurasians—*i.e.* those of mixed birth, now known as Anglo-Indians.

A certain scene impressed itself on my mind in this respect. It was that of an Anglo-Indian and his servant. This Anglo-Indian, who happened to be exceptionally dark, was walking to his office on a hot day. His servant, a Kashmiri, who was scarcely distinguishable from a fair European, for he had blue eyes and pink cheeks, and a bright, happy face withal, was walking behind holding up an umbrella to shade the dusky gentleman's face from the sun, and carrying his books. Many of the dwellers in this land are very keen to keep up their position and consider it *infra dig.* to be seen carrying anything, and also like to be followed about by a servant, according to Eastern custom.

What amusement the Pandit officials used to afford one every morning in days gone by, when the head of a department was making his triumphal march from his house to his office, at the gentlemanly pace of the ox, two miles an hour, followed by his subordinate clerks and servants. I have counted as many as thirty marching at this funereal pace in order to show that they were gentlemen, and that time was no object. They all walked in single file, as one clerk was greater in position than the other and therefore could not walk abreast. The head official would be walking in front, with his lower chest well to the fore, and as he swaggered along he would chuck his words behind him to those following. Sometimes he would condescend to call one up to him, and he would come before the great man with his hands in the attitude of prayer, and head at the correct angle of obeisance. Most of this small army of followers, I was told, were dependents of the household, and were poor relatives living on the rich man's bounty, who paid for their ke[illegible] by swelling his retinue and thus bringing honour and conferring dignity upon the great man and his house. The days of slow progression are fast departing, as it is being discovered that time is valuable.

I was on one occasion on a journey with my Brahman munshi; we were riding ponies. It was a lovely day, and my pony seemed to be aware of this fact, and we were just going sixteen to the dozen, when I became aware that the munshi was not enjoying this headlong pace as much as I was, for he was crying out for me to stop. So I reined up, and then up came the Brahman munshi, red in the face and breathing hard. "Oh, Sahib," he said, "why do you ride like this, for kings always ride slow?" "Yes," I said, "they may do so, but I am not a king. So come on."

However, the munshi was almost in tears, so I had mercy on him, and we rode at a more gentlemanly pace, but not quite that of the kings' pace of which he was thinking.

In physique the dwellers in towns naturally differ much from those in the country and in the mountains. In the towns the people are weak and undersized, partly from their indoor occupations, such as weaving and embroidery work, where they sit all day in stuffy, small rooms, or are clerks bending over their desks, who never think of taking exercise after office hours by joining in games. They have no hobbies with which to fill their spare time.

But especially are they a weak lot on account of the filthiness of the towns and fetid air, which make them sickly and anæmic. Then their morals are not high, to say the least of it; the most of them suffer from bone or skin diseases. Epidemics of various kinds play havoc among them. Everyone has small-pox, with the exception of the few that have been vaccinated; every fifth person

Photo by] [*R. E. Shorter.*

A VILLAGE INDUSTRY.
Making Cloth.

The woman in this illustration is weaving the cotton "sheet" the Kashmiri likes to wear draped about his shoulders when he wishes to go anywhere in full dress,

Photo by] [*Vishu Nath.*

PILGRIMS RETURNING FROM THE MOUNTAINS.

Crossing the valley may be seen a procession of Hindu pilgrims who had met in Srinagar from all parts of upper India and who having now accomplished the journey to the sacred cave of Amarnath are returning to their distant homes. Great hardships are suffered by the older and infirm on this mountain pilgrimage, but its performance brings great "merit."

is pitted with small-pox on some part of his body, and many are blinded from it.

Every four or five years cholera in epidemic form sweeps them off in hundreds, and sometimes in thousands, during the summer months. Typhoid is rampant in the city, and now consumption is increasing and taking toll of the population.

With the advance of education the people are gradually learning that sickness is caused by germs and not by the will of Allah, or in the case of Hindus by the caprice of their various gods and goddesses. For example, when small-pox attacks a family, they seem rather pleased than otherwise, as they say the goddess has deigned to visit their humble dwelling. This is one of the reasons why the Hindus object to vaccination. It will be a slow business to alter the conditions of the towns in the matter of sanitation, as the people themselves are against improvement. Their answer to any change is always the same —namely, "Our fathers and forefathers were always very happy and contented under the existing order of things, so why should not we be satisfied?" A certain Health Officer, who had been to England for his medical training, and was out to do his duty, being keen on his work, came to me one morning very much upset, for there was an especially filthy alley leading from the main street to the river which was much frequented. He wished to have it paved with bricks so that it could be flushed with water and kept clean.

The Brahman priests of the neighbourhood had come to him and ordered him to desist, using the usual forefather argument. So as the Health Officer stood firm to his resolve they threatened that, if he attempted to pave the alley, they themselves would lie down flat on the road and he would have to lay the bricks over them. The doctor was certainly in a fix. My advice to him was to carry on, for the priests would soon have had enough of bricks. But he shook his head, saying that he dared not do that. So the Brahman priests won the day, and that alley remains what it always has been, a latrine for the priests and their families, a pestilential spot. It is not easy to hurry the East.

In the villages the habits of the people are the same as those of the towns, only as more fresh air is obtainable the health and physique of the people is better. One's nose always tells one from afar that one is nearing a village, and the people love to have it so.

The outdoor life of the villagers is, of course, a healthy one, and their bodies become strong from constant labour, but in the winter they also suffer much from disease, as they shut themselves up in their houses and froust. They keep their cows in the lower rooms, and block up every hole and cranny with mud and straw to keep out any fresh air, consequently the room becomes so hot that the moisture literally drips from the ceiling. The family sit in the room above; thus the heat of the cows, coming up from below, keeps them happy and comfortable all the winter, and with no extra expense. Truly, those in the West, with coal at such a fabulous price, have something to learn from the East. Yet, notwithstanding the unhealthy conditions of the villagers in the winter, the peasants are physically strong.

In the autumn-time, on the Jhelum Valley road, before bullock carts came into use, you would see hundreds of coolies carrying the great weight of from two to three maunds each (a maund = 80 lb.) of apples on their backs, a journey of 200 miles. Each man carries a stout stick about two and a half feet in length with a cross-bar. So when he wishes to rest he places this stick behind him under his load. By this method he can rest his load without trouble. Their custom is to trot with their load about fifty yards at a time and then rest: in this manner their load of apples would reach Rawal Pindi in twelve days. The women make muscle through their daily occupations, by grinding at the mill and husking their rice with pestle and mortar. The mortar is a hollowed trunk of a tree about two feet high and a foot and a half wide at the top. The pestle is a beam of wood about five feet long cut thin in the middle, so that it can comfortably be held with one hand. It is heavy work, and it takes from an hour to an hour and a half to husk the rice for one meal. Then besides their housework they have work in the fields as well. It is a hard, healthy life and they thrive on it.

The coolies and other hard workers employ an ingenious method for refreshing themselves when they are fagged out. The tired man will lie prone on the ground on his stomach, and call his pal to massage him. This is done by his pal walking up and down on the top of him very slowly. He begins at his heels and walks up his legs and back, to his neck, digging his toes into the muscles of his legs, his back and neck, as he slowly moves up and down him. The man who is prone keeps grunting as the toes of his pal do their work. After a few minutes of this operation he gets up and shakes himself, and then does the same kindness for his pal. After this they both shoulder their loads and go off in good spirits. I have never tried this particular form of massage, but I have had experience of other forms of their massage which they so willingly perform on one, and I have found it most refreshing.

Those who live in the mountains, especially those on the frontier states, such as Gilgit, Hunzar and Nagar, are a fine type of men, hardy mountaineers, and of quite a different stamp to the Kashmiri of the valley. They are born sportsmen, hunting the ibex among their native rocky haunts, and have become like the ibex in agility and hardiness.

CHAPTER V

KASHMIR, ANCIENT AND MODERN

AS we have now seen something of the beautiful country, and have a nodding acquaintance with the people of the valley and the hills, it may be well to look backwards into their past history, so that we may understand something of their character. Kashmir fortunately possesses an ancient history, and a civilisation more ancient than our own. There are many legends of prehistoric times when the Vale of Kashmir was a vast lake and was inhabited by a great snake.

Here is one of their legends.

According to the earliest traditional account this lake occupied the place of Kashmir Valley. A demon called Jallodbhava (water-born) resided in this lake. This demon caused great distress to all the neighbouring countries by his devastations. At last Kashyapa Muni implored Shiva to help him to kill the demon. His prayer was granted, and he succeeded in getting the demon killed, with the help of the gods, near Kaunsar-nag. Shiva made an exit near Baramulla with his trident, the water rushed out and the land thus produced became inhabitable.

At first men dwelt in it for six months only in the year and left Kashmir for the six months of winter, when it was occupied by peshachas (demons).

Ultimately the people, through Nilanaga's favour, got rid of these demons, on condition that the people performed certain rites and ceremonies for the good of these demons, during winter months, and thus the country became inhabitable throughout the year. These rites are still performed by the Hindus of Kashmir. They are:

1. *Kechi Mavas.*—It occurs in the month of January. A sort of pudding, or polao, is cooked, and in an earthen tray is placed in the middle of the compound for the demons. A line is drawn round the whole house with lime. It is believed that these demons have no power to step over this magical line.

2. *Gada Bata.*—The Hindus cook rice and fish in the dark fortnight of January. A big bowl full of rice and fish, both cooked and uncooked, is placed in the uppermost storey of the house. A lamp is kept burning and no one is allowed to sleep in that place. The cats generally enjoy a good feast. In the morning the members of the family go up to inspect the place, and they are satisfied to see the bowl empty, thinking it has been eaten by the demons.

3. *Kawa Punim.*—This ceremony is generally performed in the month of February. Rice is cooked and formed into balls. These balls of rice are placed in a kind of big spoon made of twigs and grass, and are put in a prominent place in the house for the goblins in the shape of crows. The children recite this lullaby: "Come! O you crows which are very fond of pudding; bathe in the waters of Gangabal; put on a teka of brown clay, bring your she-crows with you, perch yourselves on the eaves of our houses and enjoy a good feast."

Geological observations prove the former existence of a great lake. The lacustrine deposits are undoubtedly found in the karewa plateaux everywhere. Ancient Kashmir has long been under the sway of various *bona fide* rajas. The first raja that appears on the pages of documentary tradition is Adgonand, who ascended the throne in 4249 B.C., at a time when Egypt was ruled by demigods. He was succeeded by his son Danudar, who was killed by the Yadhus, the tribe to which Krishna belonged.

Buddhism was introduced into Kashmir by Asoka in 308 B.C. The founder of this religion was Sakhi Muni Gaotam, later on called Buddha. He was a prince of a secluded kingdom near Nepal, and lived about the time of the "Captivity of the Jews." Raja Jaluki, the grandson of Asoka and the conqueror of Bactria, spread this faith all over the country. Buddhist missionaries were sent to India to teach them "The Way."

The Tartars invaded the valley about the commencement of our era. Three of their kings are supposed to have ruled simultaneously. They are: Hushka, who founded Aushkar near Badgam; Zashka, who founded Zukar near the Nasim Bagh, and Kanishka, who founded Kanspur. These kings were very popular in Kashmir.

Kashmir was under the rule of white Huns during the first half of the sixth century, about the time of the conquest of England by the Saxons. Their king, Mehrakula, was notorious for his cruelty and violence. Buddhism declined during the time of Shankracharya in the eighth century.

The Mohammedan adventurers began to invade the country in the beginning of the eleventh century. Mahmud of Ghuzni invaded Kashmir in 1015, via Tosa Maidan, but was repulsed by the Kashmir troops. The famous historian Albruni was present with Mahmud. The first Mohammedan king of Kashmir was Renchan Shah, who ascended the throne in 1341. He was a Tibetan, and had come to Kashmir in childhood. He wanted to become a Hindu, but the Brahmans would not admit him to their religion, so he was forced to receive the tenets of Islam from a Mohammedan fakir named Bulbul Shah, whose ziarat is still in existence, and a part of the city, Bulbul Lanker, is still called after his name. Renchan Shah afterwards forced the haughty Brahmans to become Mohammedans. This Renchan Shah was a contemporary of Edward III. of England.

From the time of Renchan Shah up to the time of Sultan Qutub-ud-Din Kashmir enjoyed considerable peace. During the reign of this sultan, in A.D. 1395, Syid Ali Hamdani, commonly called Shah Hamdan, arrived in Kashmir. This man had fled from Hamdan, a town in Persia, to save himself from the hands of the Mogul Emperor Tumerlane. The story of this event is thus briefly told:

Tumerlane, like many Oriental monarchs, was in the habit of going round his capital cities at night, in disguise, in order to find out for himself the condition of his subjects and their opinion about him.

One night he stood outside the house of a very poor man. His children were weeping for want of food and his wife was in a very miserable condition. In her plight she implored her husband to go out and beg food for the children, but the man, being a respectable person, was unwilling to beg. Tumerlane, overhearing their conversation, was sorry for them, and quietly threw a few gold mohurs into the house.

In the morning the woman of the house was overjoyed to find the pieces of gold lying on the floor. Her husband bought some food and fed his children, his wife and himself.

His neighbours, seeing them eating good food, guessed that they might have stolen the money. They brought a charge of theft against this poor man, and being Syids—*i.e.* descendants of Ali, the son-in-law of the Prophet—they would have very easily succeeded in getting him punished and tortured. But happily the King came to know about this so-called theft; so he summoned both the parties before him. The accused told him the whole truth, which of course the King knew himself. The Syids contradicted his statement, and declared on oath that they had really been robbed of the money. The King was furious, and he ordered a horse of seven metals to be made. He made it red-hot and ordered all the Syids to ride it in order to prove that they were truly Syids, because according to Mohammedan tradition fire cannot harm the Syids. In this way those Syids who obeyed the order of the King were burnt to death, and those who disobeyed him were killed by his soldiers. But Syid Ali Hamdani managed to escape this ordeal, and he fled to Kashmir. It was through his and his son's instigation that the Hindus of Kashmir were ruthlessly persecuted by Qutub-ud-Din and his successor, Sikandar the Idol Breaker. Hundreds were converted to Islam by force, hundreds of those who refused were put to the sword. Sikandar destroyed all their sacred places and monuments of historical importance. With the material he built mosques and ziarats in various places. Shah Hamdan is believed to be a great saint by the Sunni Mohammedans of Kashmir, and his ziarat, which was originally built by Qutub-ud-Din, is still seen below the Third Bridge, in the city.

Sikandar's son, Ali Shah, who ascended the throne in 1435, and who was the contemporary of Henry VI. of England, completed the work of destruction which his father had undertaken. During his reign hundreds of Hindus committed suicide. Scores set fire to their own houses and burnt themselves and their families alive, and many drowned themselves in different wells to save their dharama (religion). Some tried to escape with their children to foreign countries, but their movements were watched and the passes were guarded, so they killed themselves by throwing themselves over precipices.

Those who were left to their fate and were still alive enjoyed some respite during the reign of Ali Shah's son, Zain-ul-Abidin. He was a good and humane ruler. It was he who induced the Hindus to study Persian and accept Government posts. So during his time the Hindu community was split into two sections—those who accepted Government posts and those who still clung to their own shastras. The former, from that time, were called Karkuns (Government servants) and the latter Peruhets (priests). It was Zain-ul-Abidin who introduced the art of weaving Kashmir shawls and making paper. Up to his time the Hindu scribes used to write their scriptures on birch-bark.

From his time to the time of Akbar the Great, Kashmir was ruled by different Mohammedan kings, both native and foreign. During their rule the poor Hindus, the victims of their wrath, were more or less harassed and embarrassed. They pillaged their houses, oppressed them without scruple and insulted them without compunction. Akbar was the contemporary of "Queen Bess" of England. He conquered Kashmir in 1587. He built the wall round Hari Parbat Hill in the city. Throughout the Mogul period the Hindus enjoyed some security of person and property. They were entrusted with high Government posts. It was Akbar who was pleased with their erudition and intelligence and gave them the surname of Pandits (learned men).

During the reign of his son Jahangir, who laid out many lovely gardens and villas in Kashmir, the Subadar of this place was enamoured by the beauty of a Hindu girl. When he could not obtain her consent without making trouble he had resource to a clever trick, as he thought. He persuaded an old Mohammedan woman to appear veiled before his court and she, personating the aforesaid Hindu girl, professed her love for the Subadar and was ready to marry him, but was prevented by her father under the influence of his co-religionists. The Subadar obtained a rewayet (order) from the mullahs permitting him to marry the girl without her father's consent. He then sent troops to the house of the innocent girl to seize her by force and bring her to his harem. His orders were promptly executed. The father of the girl was a discreet person. He made no fuss but, through his daughter, requested the Subadar to wait six months, which he readily agreed to, from the fear of the King. Meanwhile her father quietly set out for Agra, to Jahangir. When he reached the palace he rang the bell which Jahangir had attached to his private chambers and told the Emperor the whole story of this villainy. Jahangir, ease-loving as he was, at once mounted his famous dromedary and, attended by a few of his bodyguard, journeyed to Kashmir in disguise. When he reached Srinagar he went straight to the house of the Mohammedan woman who had personated the Hindu girl, and pretending to be a foreigner, and giving her some pieces of gold to prepare some food for him, he made her relate the whole story. The Emperor spent the night in her house. In the morning he put on his Court dress and went to the imperial palace. It was at once rumoured that the Emperor was there. The Subadar and other high officials, in consternation, presented themselves and paid their homage to their liege lord.

The Emperor as usual asked them if all was well, and while this conversation was proceeding, the Hindu, as prearranged, submitted his complaint against the Subadar. As a matter of course the Subadar tried to convince the King that the kafir (infidel) had told abominable lies and put before the King the futwa (decree) of the mullahs. The King at once summoned the woman in whose house he had passed the night. The woman at once recognised her guest and she, without any hesitation, divulged the whole secret before all the courtiers. The Subadar was dumbfounded. The Emperor summoned all the mullahs. They too could do naught but confess their crime. Then and there Jahangir struck off the head of the sinful Subadar with his own hand. He arrested all the mullahs and had them led in chains to a place outside Akbar's wall, round Hari Parbat, and there had them blown to pieces from a big gun. They were buried, without any funeral rites, in the same place. From that time the place received the name of Mullah Khah. Jahangir's son, Shah Jahan, built many palaces and laid out many gardens in the Happy Valley. His son, Aurangzeb, who ascended the throne in 1658, and who was the contemporary of Charles II., James II. and William III. of England, again began to persecute the Hindus in Kashmir and elsewhere.

Kashmir remained under the tyranny of the Mogul Subadars up to the year 1751, when it was conquered by Ahmad Shan Durani, who assassinated his own master, Nadir Shah, soon after 1738. With this murderer and his Afghan successors returned the evil days of the Hindus.

It remained for these Afghans to continue the work of spoliation and slaughter already begun. They collected all the religious scriptures of the Hindus. With these they constructed a bund, called Mussuth, which is still extant. When they were tired of killing so many people with the sword, they put them into bags and drowned them in the Dal Lake. The place where these atrocities were committed is still called Batta Mazir (the graveyard of the Hindus).

Their houses were ransacked, they were freely tortured to accept Islam, and their women were taken away from them and used as concubines. Numbers of the poor Hindus died of ill-usage or slew themselves to avoid it. They were not allowed to put on their turbans. If they appeared in a public street any Mohammedan could ride on their backs and force them to carry him a certain distance. This was called Khos.

This reign of terror lasted till 1820, when Ranjit Singh, the Raja of the Punjab, conquered Kashmir, and rescued the remaining handful of the Hindus from the claws of their oppressors. To take revenge the Sikhs in their turn persecuted the Mohammedans. During this time the Mohammedans could not freely offer prayers.

After the first Sikh war Kashmir was ceded to the British, who sold it to Maharajah Gulab Singh in 1846. The grandson of this Raja is the present Maharajah of Kashmir.

His Highness the Maharajah General Sir Pratab Singh, who ascended the Gadhi in the year 1886, is ruler over a large tract of country the size of England and Scotland, which includes, besides the Vale of Kashmir, Jummu, Poonch, Ladakh, Baltistan and all the states included in the Gilgit Agency, with a population of over three millions. His Highness is aided in the government of his state by three ministers—the Chief, Revenue and Home Minister, men who have been selected by the Indian Government and approved of by his Highness.

Then there is the British Resident, who is the King's representative and has the assistance of other British officers. One is his personal assistant. There are also the Resident of Poonch State, the Resident of Ladakh and Baltistan and the Agent of Gilgit, which includes all the mountain states, Chilas, Hunzar Nagar, etc. Since the year 1890 there have been thirteen Residents. On my arrival here Colonel Parry Nisbet was the Resident, and a great personality he was, for it was through his tact and energy that the Jhelum Valley cart-road was cut along the mountain-sides from Domel to Baramulla, a magnificent piece of engineering, the work of the State Engineer, Mr Alkinson, and carried through by Spedding & Co., contractors.

The Resident's position is not altogether an easy one, for it is one requiring much tact, patience and courage.

It would be invidious to single out those who have done especially good work. Some of course have possessed stronger characters than others, and have consequently left their mark for good on the country, and their memory in the hearts of the people.

There are also British advisers in the various departments of the State, such as the Army, P.W.D. Accountants, Land Settlement, etc.

The heir to the Gadhi is General Prince Sir Hari Singh, K.C.S.I., son of the late Sir Raja Amar Singh, who was a man of power. The young Prince is a sportsman, and possesses a keen sense of justice and plenty of common sense.

CHAPTER VI

CHARACTER OF THE KASHMIRIS

TO write about the character of the Kashmiris is not easy, as the country of Kashmir, including the province of Jummu, is large and contains many races of people. Then, again, these various countries included under the name of Kashmir are separated the one from the other by high mountain passes, so that the people of these various states differ considerably the one from the other in features, manners, customs, language, character and religion.

The people of Jummu province are Dogras, cousins of the Rajputs, and talk Punjabi. As their country is on the lower slopes of the mountains, and not in the plains, the people are a sturdy race and good fighters. The Maharajah's army is chiefly composed of these men, and our Indian army contains many Dogra regiments. The Kashmiri Dogra regiments behaved splendidly in the East African campaign, and won a great name for themselves. Jummu is the winter capital of his Highness Sir Pratab Singh, K.C.S.I., etc., Maharajah of Jummu and Kashmir, and not to be confused with Sir Pratab Singh, Maharajah of Idar, whose name and picture figured so often in the papers during the war. This town is situated on the top of a high cliff overlooking the River Ravi, a most imposing-looking town from a distance on account of its many temple domes sparkling in the bright sunlight. Jummu is strongly Hindu. The late Maharajah wished to make his capital a second Benares, which is the Mecca of the Hindus. The Dogras are Kishatrias, or the soldier caste, next below the Brahmans in caste. The people of Poonch state are very similar in build and physique to the Dogras; they are sturdy mountaineers. Poonch state gave more recruits for the Indian army than any other part of the Indian Empire. They are Mohammedans. The people in the country of Ladakh, or Lesser Tibet, are Mongolians, and Buddhists by religion, sturdy, hard-working and cheery people.

I have already mentioned the inhabitants of the mountains on the frontier, so now, having cleared the ground somewhat, we can discuss the character of the inhabitants of the valley. It is with these people that the Europeans who visit this country are chiefly concerned: servants, coolies, boatmen, shopkeepers, clerks, merchants, etc.

So when people speak of the Kashmiri they have these particular classes of people in their minds. To call a man a "Kashmiri" is a term of abuse, for it stands for a coward and a rogue, and much else of an unpleasant nature. For instance, when giving a servant a character, a man whom you are dismissing and could not possibly recommend, you write: "This man is a good specimen of a Kashmiri." Everyone understands that such a man is not fit for employment.

I had written a character for an unsatisfactory scholar who bothered me for a "chit." I wrote in it that this young man was an excellent specimen of a Kashmiri Pandit. A few days later his elder brother called upon me and begged me to write another chit for his brother as he could not obtain employment with that chit. On asking him his reason for thinking so, he said: "You have written that 'he is an excellent specimen of a Kashmiri Pandit.' Everyone knows the meaning of this and will not employ him." So I answered his request, and in place I wrote, "This young man has a slice of the 'reynard' in him." So the brother left comforted.

I hate having to write thus of the Kashmiri, as I am really very fond of him. I can name scores as my friends. Many have stood by me in dangers and difficulties, and a few have suffered for me, and I know many who have risked their lives in saving life, from drowning and other causes, so that I look upon them as heroes and true gentlemen, and all the more so on account of their adverse surroundings and environments. Yet, to be truthful, and I do not believe in writing lies, I must say that the ordinary Kashmiri such as I have known for thirty years is a coward, a man with no self-respect and deceitful to a degree, and I perhaps may write with a clear conscience, for I have told this to all classes of them to their faces times without number, and, to give them all credit, they never resent it, because they know it is true. Instances of cowardice, deceit and villainy I could give *ad nauseam*, and so can everyone who knows Kashmir.

But why are they so different from the people living around them? Because they happen to live in one of the most beautiful countries on earth, and therefore other people have coveted it. Kashmir has been conquered and reconquered by invaders, who have murdered, oppressed and enslaved their ancestors, and so ground the life and heart out of them that their better selves have been crushed. It is quite possible that if we Britishers had had to undergo what the Kashmiris have suffered in the past we might have lost our manhood. I recall instances in my own school life when boys have been severely bullied and so lost their manhood, for their better self had been crushed out of them. But, thank God, it has been otherwise with us and other

Western nations, for to us instead has been given the opportunity of helping some of the weaker peoples of the world, and the Kashmiri among them. May we ever be true to our trust.

Gradually are the Kashmiris rising from slavery to manhood, though the growth is naturally very slow at present, but they are on the upward road; I shall later on prove to you that ere long they will find themselves, and I trust become once more a brave people, as they were in the days of old when their own kings led them forth to battle.

I am writing of things as they are, and hence I shall have to speak unpleasant truths maybe, for I am no believer in veiling the truth or playing to the gallery.

The Kashmiris have a virtue, a very important one—viz. the saving grace of humour. Sir Walter Lawrence, who was such a blessing to the tillers of the soil when he was the Land Commissioner thirty years ago, was on tour in the district, and on entering a village he saw a man standing on his head. On asking him the reason for taking that uncomfortable position, the man said that his family matters were in such an utter muddle that he did not know whether he was standing on his head or on his feet. I did not hear the end of the story, but I feel certain that the Commissioner Sahib put him right side up and helped him to find himself, for he had great sympathy with these downtrodden cultivators of the soil. They are all Mohammedans, and all the officials in those days were Hindus.

My wife and I were travelling one summer in the valley and having arrived at a village toward evening we pitched our tents. Then we sent for the "Chowkidar" of the village to ask him to supply us with the usual necessaries, the most important being milk for our baby boy, who was making his wants known in the manner usual to babies. The Chowkidar appeared carrying his spear with a flag upon it, this being his wand of office. I told him of our needs, and asked him to let us have some milk for the child as soon as possible. He answered, saying that he was very sorry but there was not a drop of milk in the village. So I asked him what the babies of his village drank, and he said: "They always drink water." So I told him not to be a fool, but to bring the milk. He answered: "How can I, for there are no cows in the village?" At that moment I happened to catch sight of one of the cow tribe feeding on the village green. I said to him: "What animal is that?" pointing to it. "Can it be a bear?" "No, Sahib," said he, "it is not a bear, it is a cow; but all our cows are out of milk." I then said to him: "Well, what about eggs?" To this he replied: "There are no hens in the village." At that moment a cock crew, so I asked him: "What noise is that? Is that the voice of an eagle?" "No," said he. "True, O Sahib, it is a cock's voice." "Well, then, be off quick and bring us eggs." "I am very sorry," said he, "I cannot do that either, for all the fowl in this village happen to be cocks." And he added: "We have nothing in this village."

By this time I was getting impatient, as our baby boy was crying and my wife anxious to give him his tea, so I said to the Chowkidar: "Look, what bird is that?" pointing up to a kite soaring overhead. As his eyes went aloft I seized the spear out of his hand and turned it on that part of his person which he uses when he happens to sit down, saying at the same time: "Milk! Eggs!" The scene changed immediately, for the Chowkidar was off at full speed to the village, shouting "blue murder," and I hard at his heels until we entered the village gate, where I posted myself with the spear and told him to look sharp. I had not long to wait, for within ten minutes he was back, loaded with milk, eggs and chickens, and grinning from ear to ear as he motioned me to return to the camp, whilst he came on behind carrying the provender, so immediately all was peace and happiness. The baby enjoyed his tea, my wife's anxiety was dissipated, the Chowkidar and I laughed together over our little contretemps, and all went like a marriage bell whilst we remained under the trees of that village, for the Chowkidar and I understood one another.

On a country road leading up a short, steep hill I overtook a party of fourteen coolies carrying sacks of grain on their backs. They were evidently very tired, for they were groaning as they trudged along; it was towards evening and they had been at this hard labour all day. So I went up to one of them who was an undersized man who seemed to be more fagged than the rest, and asked him if he was tired. He said: "Yes, very tired and ready to die, if not already dead." So I told him to get on my back, as I would carry him on my back up the hill. He stared at me, opening his mouth and eyes very wide, and shook his head. However, I insisted, and made him get on my back with his load, for I was then young and fit. I carried him to the top of the hill and then deposited him and his load, whereupon the whole gang, who had trudged up the hill with me, put their loads on their cross-bar sticks behind, placed their legs apart and roared and roared with laughter, and when they had recovered their winds started off again, laughing loudly, and continued to do so till out of hearing, their tiredness forgotten. Kashmiris can laugh, and it does one good to hear them.

When a Kashmiri slips up and falls in the street he will as often as not join in the laughter of those around. I think it is a fact that we always feel inclined to laugh when we see a human fall, but never when an animal does so, and not so often when we ourselves come down a cropper.

Now that we have seen a little into the insides of the Kashmiris, we will visit their great town, and see them at their daily occupations, and their ordinary everyday life on the river and in the streets.

Srinagar, or Sirinagar, which means "the City of Wealth," is a most picturesque town, stretching for three miles on both sides of the River Jhelum, the divided town being united by seven bridges.

The usual remark of visitors when they approach the city by river is that it looks like a town that has been bombarded, or has suffered from earthquake, as so many of the buildings are off the straight, and many more are in sad need of repair.

I always believe, when visiting a new place, in ascending a height near by in order to secure a bird's-eye view of the place and to pick up one's bearings. Such a place is at hand, a rocky hill 1000 feet high, distant from the city about one and a half miles, called Takht-i-Suliman, or, in plain English, the throne of Solomon, known to the Hindus as Shankara Charaya, or the holy mountain. On the top of this hill is a very ancient Hindu temple; it was built by Raja Sandiman, who ruled Kashmir during the period 2629-2564 B.C. It was repaired by Gopaditya (426-365 B.C.) and Lalitaditya (A.D. 697-734) and other later kings. Sikandar did not destroy it because Sultan Mahmud of Ghazni had offered his prayers in it.

From this perch of 1000 feet you obtain a splendid view of the valley, stretching in its breadth twenty miles to the south, right up to the Pir Punjal Mountains, that great wall of rock running up to peaks of 1500 and 1600 feet, the dividing wall between Kashmir and the Punjab.

In length you see about fifty miles up east and fifty miles down the river west. The winding Jhelum river catches your eye glittering in the bright sunlight, with its loops and turns, which is said to have given the idea of the Kashmir pattern on the famous shawls. Just below your feet, on the south, lies the European quarter, called the Munshi Bagh, where are the official houses and the church. Following the river downwards you see the European Club, then the Residency in its beautifully wooded grounds. Farther on you see the Post Office, Cox & Co.'s Bank, the Alliance Bank of Simla, and European agencies, and shops, till you come to the Sheikh Bagh, where are houses of the missionaries, the European cemetery and the former Residency where dwelt Sir John Lawrence and General John Nicholson when they were British Agents in Kashmir. Then the river takes its last bend before entering the city.

Now starting again looking west, at the foot of the hill is the famous Mission Hospital, then open ground which includes the golf course, polo and cricket grounds and the well-managed hotel of Nedou & Sons, the Roman Catholic chapel where the much-respected Father Boland resides, and farther on the State College in its extensive grounds. The various roads are well marked by their avenues of tall poplar-trees interspersed here and there with chinars, and then the city in the distance stretching right and left along the river, attractive on account of its mosque minarets and Hindu temples with their roofs, which are a cross between a spire and a dome, sparkling like silver in the sunlight, though the would-be

A CANAL IN THE DAL.

When unruffled this waterway mirrors perfectly the green and gold of the plane tree, the warm browns and pinks of the houses, the purple, yellow and cherry-coloured clothes of the women and children who play and gossip on its banks and steps.

silver is generally kerosene oil tins, or Huntley & Palmer's biscuit tins, flattened out.

On the north side, at your feet, lies the city lake called the Dal, ever beautiful at whatever time of the year you view it. Perhaps the springtime is the most beautiful, when you see the yellow mustard-fields interspersed with the pink blossom of the peach and apricot trees, and surrounded by the vivid greens of the reeds and rushes, willow and poplar trees, backed up by the blue mountains crested with snow, all these colours reflected in the clear waters of the lake. One always finds it most difficult to tear oneself away from that glorious view.

Looking across the lake, and rising as it were out of it, on the east side, is a rocky hill about 700 feet in height, called Hari Parbat. On the top stands a large Sikh fort, which frowns over the city, and is used for State prisoners like the Tower of London. From this fort we look daily for the correct time, as a gun fires at midday, at ten o'clock at night and 4 A.M. in the morning.

The ten o'clock gun is the curfew, and all good citizens are supposed to be in bed, and no one is allowed to cross the bridges in the city after gunfire. The morning gun awakens all good Mohammedans for their morning prayers.

The Hindus of Kashmir call Hari Parbat Sharika, and the Mohammedans Koh-i-maran. The following is the legend concerning this hill:—

In ancient times the people of Kashmir were very much troubled by the Daityas, or monsters who came up from the nether regions through a hole at this spot. So they prayed to their gods to save them from this nuisance, and in answer to their prayers the wife of Shiva, named Durga, came to their assistance. She transformed herself into a sharika—*i.e.* a maina—a very common bird in

Kashmir about the size of a blackbird. It has an unpleasant note not unlike the squeaking of a wheelbarrow, though it can be taught to whistle and talk.

She then descended to the nether regions and broke off a piece of Meru, the sacred mountain in that country, and carried it in her beak and dropped it on to the top of this vent-hole of Hades and so bottled up all the Daityas, and thus saved the people of Kashmir from further trouble.

This hill, therefore, is the Olympus of the Hindus of Kashmir and has been worshipped from time immemorial. Its eastern slopes are now occupied by the ziarats of Makhdum Sahib and Akhun Mala Shah. It is probable that Mohammedan shrines have here taken the place of Hindu religious buildings, just as on so many other old sacred sites in Kashmir.

Close to the foot of the southern extremity of the hill is a rock which from ancient times has been worshipped as an embodiment of Maha Ganisha (the elephant god). It is said that when Pravarasena laid the foundation of his new capital (Srinagar) the god, from regard for the pious king, turned his face from west to east so as to behold and bless the new city. The rock is now covered with so thick a layer of red paint that it is not possible to trace any resemblance to the head or face of the elephant god, still less to see whether it is turned west or east. The later Hindu chroniclers relate that the god, from disgust at the iconoclasm of Sikandar Butshikan, has finally turned his back on the city, and hence his face cannot be seen.

There is nothing in the traditional writings of the locality that would lead us to assume that the hill of Sharika was ever fortified in Hindu times. The present fort that crowns the summit of the hill was built by Ata

Mohammed Khan in 1810. From time to time there have been skirmishes between the rival princes round this fort. But battles were fought at the commencement of the Dogra regime during the time of Maharajah Ghulah Singh, and before that at the time when Ranjit Singh's generals finally routed the army of Jabar Khan and drove him out of the country.

The great stone wall which encloses the hill and the ground around its foot was built by Akbar in 1590, as an inscription still extant over the main gate proclaims.

The city from this point is a most quaint sight, especially in the springtime, for it gives one the impression of a vast green field cut up in small patches divided by dark irregular lines. The roofs are covered with green grass, and certain of them are scarlet with poppies or tulips, the streets and alleys making the crooked dividing lines. Sometimes the delusion is increased when one sees sheep and goats feeding on these airy pastures; I have even seen cows on their exalted pasturage. Then one notices that none of the houses have chimneys, the roofs have not such a steep slope as tiled or slated houses have, hence the delusion of their being fields is all the greater. Formerly the roofs were mostly thatched with rice stalks or reeds from the lake, but this fashion was the cause of such disastrous fires that the authorities will not permit any new house to have a thatched roof, so, as most of the thatched houses have been burnt out, all the roofs you now see are of mud for their top surface, and hence the grass and flowers.

The roofs are made thus: over the roof rafters are placed planks, and upon the planks are spread sheets of birch bark, which is most durable, and above the birch bark is spread wet earth three to six inches thick to keep the bark in its place. This birch bark is like paper; it comes off the trees in closely compressed layers much after the consistency of cardboard.

This birch bark has been used for ages in lieu of paper; the books of old were made of this, and even now many shopmen keep their accounts upon it, and always use it for wrapping up their wares which they sell to their customers.

The drawback to these mud roofs is that they are very heavy, and especially so when there is a heavy fall of snow followed by rain in the night. The sodden snow becomes so weighted that the roof falls in, with fatal results to the house and sleeping inhabitants; therefore every house possesses a trap-door on the roof, so that those in the house may be able to shovel the snow off into the streets, and as often as not on to the heads of those who walk in them. The house roofs are used for several purposes, amongst them as a drying-place for rice and fruits, and when in the autumn red chillies are in full view there is a fine show of colour. Then the Mohammedans use their roofs for prayer, as it is their custom to choose vantage points where they can be seen at prayer.

I was present at a big fire in the city when a mosque was in danger. The mullah, an old man with a long grey beard, climbed on to the roof of the mosque with his Koran, from which he commenced to read aloud, and earnestly hoped thereby to save his mosque. But it was of no avail, for he was obliged to take refuge on another roof, and then on to another, as the heat, smoke and fire drove him from one vantage point to another. It was a noble effort nevertheless, and grand to see the old man's pluck and faith in the midst of disaster. The heat of the fire seemed to create a great wind, so that his long grey beard was blown about like a flag, and his earnest old face lit up by the flames, and one could at times hear his voice above the roar of the flames rolling out in Arabic verse after verse from his sacred book. Arabic being the sacred language of the Mohammedans, the Koran must be read only in that language.

Having seen the city from above, we will now come right into it and view it from the river. We will take a boat and follow the river under the seven bridges.

Our boat is one of the many small boats called "shikaras" which ply for hire. It is about thirty feet long, something like a long narrow punt with long pointed ends, the bows sharper than the stern, both ends rising gradually out of the water. They are most extraordinarily easy boats to steer, as they draw very little water bow and stern, their deepest draught being near the centre of the boat, hence they can be made to spin round and round on their centre with ease. This easy handling of the craft is most useful in a crowded river. These boats are usually propelled by three or four men with paddles, the blade being the shape of a lotus leaf or a heart. The crew sit in the stern of the boat facing the way they are travelling; the passengers recline in the centre of the boat, with an awning of matting over their heads to protect them from the sun or rain.

The first bridge under which we pass is a modern structure of five arches, the piers built of solid masonry. This bridge some twenty-five years ago displaced one of the old cantilever bridges made of deodar or cedar logs, which was at one time covered with houses and shops, not unlike Old London Bridge. These bridges were introduced into Kashmir by Alexander the Great's officers, and most excellent bridges for wear they have proved themselves to be.

Just below this bridge on the left bank is the palace of his Highness the Maharajah—a great pile of buildings interesting in their way, but not exactly beautiful. Under the palace and on the opposite side of the river are his Highness' barges, chiefly built for the ladies of his zenana when they travel the river part of the journey from Jummu to Srinagar, and vice versa. The state barge is a handsome craft with much scarlet and gold paint, with seats for sixty paddlers. There are also smaller state boats called "parindas," or birds, with seats for thirty paddlers, which are used for short trips, and very smart they look with the scarlet top awning and the thirty paddlers in scarlet uniforms paddling as they do in perfect time to the cry of their captain. He stands up on the foot-board in glorious apparel of scarlet and gold, giving his orders to the crew as to time and stroke, for the strokes are many and varied, and some with great flourish of paddles raised on high, accompanied with much water display. Moored to the bank opposite the palace is an elegant steam launch presented to his Highness by Queen Victoria, also a modern fast motor launch from Thornycroft's. Below where these boats are mooredi s a handsome flight of stone steps leading to a memorial stone raised to the late Maharajah; below this again is the State Telegraph Office, which can be amusing as well as annoying at times.

On one occasion I went to the office to lodge a complaint on account of a telegram that I had sent to a friend which did not reach him for a day after he had received a letter that I had sent him at the same time. The official tried to comfort me by saying that if I found that the post travelled quicker than telegraph he would advise my making use of the post instead of the telegraph wires. I can remember the time when we could not even feel quite happy when making use of the post office when the Kashmiri stamps were in use. A friend of mine wishing me to send him used Kashmiri stamps, I directed and posted to myself thirty Kashmir post cards, out of which lot only three reached me to send to my friend, as other people besides my friend evidently wanted Kashmiri stamped post cards.

In those days if you wished your letters to reach your friends who lived in Kashmir it was wiser not to put stamps on them, for the postman in his efforts to annex the stamp sometimes made a mess of the envelope and therefore thought it wiser not to deliver it, but if it was not stamped the receiver had to pay double postage, which was profitable to the postal authorities. In those days I bought several sets of old issue stamps, thinking they would be valuable later on, but when I wished to give or sell them to collectors I was informed that they were reprints. So certain people connected with the Post Office must have amassed some wealth in printing off old issues from the ancient dies.

I fear Kashmiri stamps must have caused stamp collectors a good deal of heart-searchings from the method adopted in making those stamps. The stamp-maker would have sheets of paper, pots of paint and a brush with which to colour the paper. As the pot of paint became emptied he would fill up the pot with water, so that, supposing he was making red stamps, the first sheets would be a brilliant red, which would gradually become very faint until more paint was put into the pot to thicken it up. Thus it came to pass that stamp collectors are very chary about accepting Kashmir stamps. A friend of mine had collected a great many Kashmir stamps, and took them home to a stamp dealer, expecting to make a small fortune. The dealer looked at them carefully and then asked him to come to his inner room, the walls of which were papered with stamps which were forgeries. Pointing to the wall, he said: "If I take your Kashmir stamps, that is the only use I can make of them."

In those past years the business of making forged or reprint stamps was so great that a law was made to the effect that any Kashmiri found selling Kashmir stamps would be punished by imprisonment, and certain gentlemen who persisted in this fraud were put under lock and key, and so given time to think whether it was worth while carrying on this particular business. I think they must have come to the conclusion that it was not, for now it is not easy to find Kashmir stamp vendors.

Outside that State Telegraph Office and all down the river on both banks are lines of boats of all sizes moored, from the small shikaras propelled by one paddler, who may be a little boy or girl (for they commence their art at an early age), to the large barges in which are cargoes of rice and timber.

Families live in all the larger craft, and there is much to interest the traveller, whether he be a new-comer or a resident. It is always entertaining, for the boats are crowded with life of all sorts, from the lord and master of the family and captain of the boat to that irritating creature called a flea.

When the boats are moored you generally see the men of the boat sitting in the stern and smoking their hookahs, or playing with the small children, whilst their women-folk are at work, the old grandmother at her spinning-wheel, and the younger women preparing the food. This to the passer-by seems always to be in the preparing —*i.e.* pounding the rice on the bank with the heavy pestle. Others scare off the fowls and sparrows which are watching their opportunity to feed off the rice that is spread out on rush mats to dry in the sun. Others, again, are with their long-handled wooden spoons ladling the water out of the germ-infected river into the rice-pot that is on the clay stove in the boat. These women on the bank are now shouting loudly and gesticulating with their arms and cloths to frighten away a kite which has taken a fancy to some young chickens, and at that moment has made a swoop for them, whilst their mother is calling aloud to her offspring to take shelter under her wings. The kite, having been balked this time, flies back to its high branch of a tree near by to await a more favourable opportunity, and the women resume their preparations for the meal. They have not been long at peace when they are all called to action again, for a hungry pariah dog which has been sniffing with his nose in the air behind a stack of wood, and has discovered that there is something interesting in the boat, has stalked cleverly to the boat and is about to seize a piece of goat hanging on a wooden hook from the roof of the boat. All is uproar and rush again, but the meat has been saved, and the dog slinks off with his tail between his legs, disappointed, but not disheartened, for he has more patience and persistence than those who walk on two feet; he goes off and lies down in a secluded spot and pretends to be asleep, but he is not.

All is peace and quiet again, so much so that a little flash of beauty settles on one of the poles sticking out from the boat; it is a king of poachers, the blue and green kingfisher. His powerful little eye has seen the flash of silver in the shallow water close to the bank. In an instant he has disappeared head-first into the water and comes up conqueror to the pole with a wriggling little fish, which he gradually works round, end on, head-first into his beak, then a big swallow or two and the fish has gone to help his enemy to be strong to catch more of her family. I have always noticed that kingfishers are far more successful in securing their dinners than kites, and are certainly in better condition than the poor pariah dogs.

We must now switch our eyes off animal life and come back to our boatman's family. The lord and master of the family and captain of the boat, who has been quietly smoking and thinking thoughts, whilst the women are preparing his meal amid the usual daily excitement, is now aroused to anger as an old enemy of his in a passing boat reminds him of some unpleasant conversation they had had when last they met; past insults are raked up and curses on female relatives exchanged. Now a noisy battle of words has commenced, which soon resolves itself into a babel of voices, for the women of both boats have joined in with a will, and their shrill voices are heard well above those of the menfolk.

The preparations for the meal are forgotten as the crews of both boats are standing up and gesticulating with their arms and clenched fists. To the new-comer all this sounds terrible and looks as if a battle royal was imminent, with much shedding of blood; but there is no fear of this, for of all the many boatman fights that I have witnessed I have never seen one boatman hit another; it is merely a battle of words.

CHAPTER VII

MOHAMMEDANS AND HINDUS

WHILE the two boats are far apart the men are very bold, and say what they will do to one another if they could but come to grips. Then when one of the boats drifts on to the other, so close that they are touching one another, the warriors turn their backs upon each other and with much contempt say that they would not defile themselves by touching one another even with the end of their barge-pole; or when someone taunts them with cowardice, one will grip the other and cry out to his wife, saying: "Hold me! hold me! or I shall commit murder." Then the wives, screaming all the while, fall upon their respective husbands, who allow themselves to be torn apart. The boats now swing apart again, and both sides take a breather, only to start afresh.

Often this noisy battle lasts until both sides are utterly exhausted and their voices are but harsh whispers. When this is the case each party takes its basket hen-coops, which every boat possesses, and turn them upside down, which is a sign that there will be pax for the present, and this peace may last several hours, even to the next day. Then when one of the parties feels refreshed, supposing the enemy boat has not moved away, he will reverse the hen-coop and the fight will be renewed. These hangi fights used to be far more frequent than they are now, so that on a trip through the city you were entertained by several, coming in for the different phases of the play as you travelled along. No material damage is ever done in their fights except, if possible, to the character of the women, for there is no limit to the foul abuse and insinuations. I say "if possible," for the boat people as a class have no morals. They have got a bad name and they live up to it. The name "hangi" is itself a term of abuse—*i.e.* if you wish to describe a man as thoroughly bad you say he is only a hangi.

I will take this opportunity of warning my fellow-countrymen who are new to this country to be on their guard when hiring living-boats for trips, such as "doongas" and house-boats, for very many have proved to be veritable death-traps to the morals of young Englishmen, and in certain cases I have known them to end in speedy death. Never shall I forget the death-bed of one bright, cheery boy who implored me to tell anyone likely to be entrapped as he had been, so that through his suffering and death they might be saved from this terrible disease and death. He, like so many, was caught by one of the many scoundrels who are out to grab the money of young Englishmen, using women as their bait.

There is one special native firm which has made itself rich in this traffic. Against them I have warned many, and continue to do so, and have told the head of the firm that I will ever do so.

New-comers who have been harassed by this class of biped sometimes come to me for help and advice. I generally give them two instances of fact to guide their actions. I will pass them on to you now.

A colonel came to me in great distress, asking for advice. He had just come up the river from Baramulla to Srinagar, a journey of three days. He was paying off his boat when the boatman demanded Rs.500, the proper

Photo by] [*R. E. Shorter.*

Photo by] [*R. E. Shorter.*

(1) THE COMMON TASK OF WOMEN.
(2) WOMEN WATER CARRIERS.

Pounding Rice. The mortars are blocks of wood hollowed out : the pestles are heavy pieces of timber which makes this daily round in women's work very arduous.

It is the women's duty to convey water for domestic use. The constant practice of balancing the pots on their heads gives them an erect and graceful poise.

Photo by] [*R. E. Shorter.*

LEAVING SCHOOL.

Schoolboys going home by way of the river.

ENEMIES OF THE GODS.

Destroyed by His Highness's troops at the religious ceremony of Ram Leela.

fare being then Rs.3.8. On his asking the reason for the extortion, the boatman calmly told him that he had a dancing girl on board and that if he did not pay up the Rs.500 he would let it be known far and wide that the Colonel Sahib had been living with this woman for three days in his boat during the journey up the river.

The other case was that of a subaltern who found himself in a somewhat similar predicament, and he settled the matter without asking anyone's advice, for with one well-directed blow this loathsome biped disappeared out of the boat into the river, and the matter was settled without further ado. This particular biped happened to be the agent for the firm I have just mentioned. There are certain times in one's life when fists are both useful and necessary, and this is certainly the sort of occasion when we can with a clear conscience enjoy again those times we had in our schooldays when we punched a bully's head. It is of interest to note that that great soldier General John Nicholson of Delhi, in the early days, when he was British Agent in Kashmir, tried to put a stop to this filthy traffic.

I cannot leave the boatmen in such depths of infamy, for in every man, and in every class of men, there is some gold somewhere.

I respect the boatmen in their work as boatmen, for they have delighted me over and over again in their knowledge of boatcraft, for they are kings at it. I delight to see them in their boats forging up the river against a strong stream with pole or paddle, taking advantage of every swirl and eddy behind a projecting wall or pier of a bridge. They seem to know every crack and hole in the stone walls in which to insert their pole, and then put all their weight on to it just at the very moment when they can make full use of the shove,

Then, again, they can work really hard. They will tow your boat up-stream all day, and if really necessary will continue all night.

I was blessed with the possession of a man who was king of boatmen, Ismalia by name, bless him! That man would do anything for me. No man on the river or lake understood boatcraft better than he. In storm on the lake he never lost his head: whilst those around him would be screaming and jumping about in delirium, women tearing their hair and garments, Ismalia would be sticking to his job. He would jump into river or lake no matter what the temperature of the water might be, if he thought it necessary, or if ordered to do so. In times of danger he was at his best. In the big floods, at city fires, in epidemics, he was always on the spot.

In floods when practically all his brethren were making use of their golden opportunities for loot he was out saving life and property freely. I could write a book on Ismalia.

There was one thing that Ismalia feared, and that was the tongue of his spouse, and I do not blame him, for he had to live in the very small space of a boat with her always. I grieved over this many a time and oft, and tried myself to tame that tongue, but I regret to say I failed in the matter of bringing relief to my king of boatmen.

He might have relieved himself of that tongue if he had followed the example of another sorely tried "bhai" who possessed a spouse very similar, for she always did exactly the opposite to that which she was asked or advised to do. While crossing a rough bit of water the husband asked his wife not to sit on the edge of the boat, but to sit on the seat in the centre, otherwise she might be jerked overboard. She therefore, of course, sat on the edge of the boat, and before long she disappeared out of the boat and out of sight. When the boat reached the land the husband immediately walked along the bank to see if he could see any trace of his wife. The boatmen were astonished to see him walking up-stream instead of down. "Ah!" said he, "you don't know my wife; she always goes the opposite way."

Ismalia might have been rid of that tongue likewise, but he endured with patience and in silence, for that tongue also fought Ismalia's enemies many times and oft, to which fact I can bear witness. I said previously that the boatmen as a class are an utterly immoral lot, or words to that effect. Ismalia was an exception, for he was as white as they were black.

We always trusted our children with him, for we knew they would be absolutely safe under his care; no one could harm them if Ismalia were at hand. Let us hope that there are many other boatmen something like Ismalia whom I do not happen to have come across. Ismalia had a paralytic stroke and passed away from us into the fuller life, and I look forward to meeting again that king of boatmen. If the River Styx is still flowing and old Charon wants relief it would be the sort of job that Ismalia would love, and mighty cheering it would be to see his smiling face and red beard once more as he greeted one, paddle in hand.

I said above that the boatmen do not indulge in wordy fights so often as in the past, and that reminds me of quite the opposite practice of "saying their prayers," which also has become less frequent, for at midday one would see conspicuous places monopolised by men in the attitude of prayer, standing on the top of a wall, or on the roof of their boat, going through the genuflections according to Mohammedan ritual, which has to be performed three times a day, at sunrise, at midday and at sunset. The women, of course, do not pray in public, nor do they enter the mosques. In some of the richer houses the mullah will read Arabic prayers with them, which they seldom understand.

The faithful have to offer their nemaz (prayer) five times a day. Every Mussulman commences his "nemaz" by standing up with his face towards the Kaaba. He places his thumbs underneath his ears with fingers stretched out. This position is called "takbir." Then he lowers his hands and places his right hand upon the left on his stomach or chest, forming the word "Allah" with the fingers of his right hand. This position is "tahrim." Then he bends his body in the shape of a crescent, placing his hands on his knees. This is called "raku." Subsequently he touches the ground with his forehead. This is called "sajda." This process is repeated twice, and lastly he sits on his left leg. This is called "qada." After the completion of the nemaz he turns his head first towards the right and then towards the left, saluting the two guardian angels "Keraman" and "Katebin," the recorders of his deeds.

I imagine the reason of there being less praying among the boatmen is that as they are becoming richer they feel more independent, and have not so much to fear from the mullahs or from the religious opinion of their fellow-Mohammedans, for praying in public raises them in the esteem of their co-religionists. It requires courage for Mohammedans not to pray in public, just as it requires courage on the part of Christians to be seen praying in the street or public place.

This praying in public is no criterion of a religious life, for I have noticed that those who parade their praying most are the men least to be trusted.

Of course we find this the same with Christians; we naturally fight shy of the religious talking lot. In Kashmir anyway religion and life have nothing to do with one another; the better-living men do not parade their religion, and vice versa.

As one floats down the river one sees many bathing from the river steps. They are Brahmans; and there they stand knee-deep performing their ceremonial ablutions.

The Hindus generally rise very early. Before leaving their beds they lie on their stomachs and offer a short prayer. Those who are of a religious turn of mind sit square over a clean piece of cloth or a carpet of *kusha grass* or the skin of an antelope and tell their beads, reciting a sacred Vedic mantra like the Buddhist; or they practise concentration of mind or regulation of breath for some time. This is done in absolute privacy. Then they leave the bedroom and go to the river-side, and some of them perform necessary ablutions, while others sit for some time on the bank and perform daily worship (sendhia).

Having stripped himself, the Hindu sits on the steps of the bank. First he washes his left foot and then the right. This is because the body is believed by the Hindus to be androgynous, and the left side is considered to have feminine characteristics. As woman (shakti) is believed to be superior to man, the left foot is washed first. And every woman always sits on the left of her husband whenever they have to perform a religious ceremony. No ceremony is complete unless the woman takes part in it. Most Hindus worship God in the form of woman. Would that these Hindu men would put into practice some at least of their doctrines with regard to women, for then much of their unnecessary suffering would be lessened. Having washed his foot, he holds a handful of water and invokes through Vedic incantations all the spirits of the sacred rivers, such as Ganges, Jamna, Gaya, etc. With this water he washes his face, and then his Brahmanical thread and the tuft of hair on the top of his head with a separate mantra. After this he raises his hands with open palms towards the sun, invoking Varuna, the god of the air, to make him clean. Then he sprinkles water three times towards his left.

After this he places a piece of clay on the bank, divides it into three parts, sprinkles water over these portions with separate mantras, invoking the sun god to cleanse him. He picks up the first part and throws it towards all the four points of the compass; with the second part he besmears his body, and the third part he throws into the water. Then holding a handful of water he steps into the river and begins to bathe. When standing in the river he sprinkles water three times, in the name of the ancestors, in the name of ancient sages of India, and last of all in the name of the gods. Then he comes out of the water and puts on clothes, and again sits on the bank to regulate his breath and perform the remaining part of the ceremony. First he inhales a long breath through the left nostril, retains it for a few seconds and then exhales it very, very slowly through the right nostril. It is said that mental calm follows this breathing practice which lasts for some time. This is done three or four times. The ceremony is concluded with special movements of the hands, telling of beads and sprinkling of water in a peculiar way too tedious to be described here. That part of the worship which particularly attracts one's attention is the squirting of the water from their mouths, reminding one of a well-worked fire-pump.

All the way down the river you see washings of all sorts. Hindu women are continually washing their brass pots.

Hindus may not cook their food in anything else but brass utensils; they eat off brass dishes and drink out of brass cups. It is amusing to see Hindus trying to drink hot tea out of their brass cups, for the metal is always much hotter to the lips than the tea. They try to get at their hot drink without burning their lips. If they used earthenware or china, they could only use them once, and then they would throw them away as defiled and not able to be cleaned. They consider brass can be cleaned as other material cannot be cleaned. Hence one sees the Hindu women scrubbing away at their brass pots with sand and mud, but chiefly one notices at the *outside*, I suppose because it shows most and is easier to clean than the inside, especially if the neck is small. By the side of the brass scrubber you will see the priest with his brass and stone gods, which he has brought down to wash, or to perform some religious ceremony.

The priest first invokes the particular god through his mantras. Having done that, he begins to bathe the god which he believes to be in that idol. He mixes a little milk with water and begins to pour it on the top of it; meanwhile he recites a certain portion of Vedas called "Rudra mantra." This takes him about twenty minutes or more, according to the leisure of the priest. Then he wipes the idol with a towel and covers it with flowers and rice. He does not necessarily use a clean towel.

Here, again, squats a Hindu woman cleaning a fish with a knife, scraping off its scales and its inside (a Mohammedan, of course, having been the sinner who caught and killed the fish), and just below her will be a man cleaning his teeth with a piece of willow twig (the favourite tooth-brush), scooping up the water with his hand, with which he gargles. One often wonders how much of the inside of the fish or scales gets mixed up with the gargle. He also sniffs water up his nose, and altogether has quite a good wash-up.

Below the mouth-washer the dhobi is washing the clothes, which is an amusing sight if the clothes do not happen to be one's own, as he takes up the garments one after another and dashes them with all his might on to the stone steps, or on to a smooth rock which he has placed in position, on which to smash buttons or anything else breakable; then he squeezes out the garments by placing his feet on one end and twisting them round with both hands. He now spreads out the garments on the muddy bank of the river to be bleached by the sun. Whilst he is smashing more clothes on the rock he is obliged to keep his weather eye open in order to be in time to scare off pariah dogs and chickens, which seem to take a special delight in walking over anything which they should not; or sometimes it is a strolling cow or Brahmani bull which takes a fancy for a towel upon which to try her or his teeth; or it may be a crow has seen a pocket-handkerchief or a coloured sock which he thinks would not look amiss in his nest. Hence a dhobi's work is not altogether easy when he chooses the river bank for his washing ground.

English mem-sahibs often think ill of their dhobis; and sometimes they may have cause, for I have known a dhobi when he has lost a handkerchief cut a large one in two and so make up the number that was sent to the wash. I have often known a dhobi fail to return a pretty garment and give quite a picturesque excuse, when, if the truth were known, at that particular moment some gallant bridegroom would be wearing that very article as he parades round the town on his white and beautifully caparisoned horse, his handsome features being partly hidden by a silver and gold veil, and all set off by the final flourish of the peacock's feather on the top of his head. As a matter of fact, the dhobis are on the whole a great comfort, for they can turn out excellent work, and then when you come to the price as compared with English laundries it is marvellously cheap. Up to a year ago I paid three rupees only for one hundred garments washed—*i.e.* from a pocket-handkerchief to a bed sheet—which works out to rather more than one halfpenny per article; now it is more than a penny an article.

When one is in England paying the washing bill one just longs for one's fat dhobi. As a matter of fact, they are generally rather thin, but I have had the pleasure of having my clothes washed by two fat dhobis. One of them was a wise man in another matter than in clothes. My wife had taken him with the household to our hut in the forest, and he washed contentedly, we thought, in the lake. But he asked leave one day to return to the city to visit his family, promising to be back in three days' time; but he came not back, and in his stead he sent his lean old father, with a message to say that the neighbourhood of the hut in the forest was not healthy on account of the bears and panthers, especially the latter, and so he sent his old father to do the washing.

At every ghat or yaribal, which means a meeting-place of friends, and consists of a flight of stone steps, generally filthy and most abominably odoriferous, will be found a large stone with a smooth round hole in the centre. This is the public washing-tub in which amateur dhobis wash their clothes by trampling on and squeezing them with their feet as grapes are crushed in the wine vats. It is a pleasure to see people thus at work, for one can be certain that they will have clean feet, which is a rare sight in this land.

Among the many entertainments on the river banks is the sight of three or four women or girls sitting in a ring presenting their backs to each other. Each one seems to be scratching the head of the one in front, but, as a matter of fact, they have reverted to type, to their ancestors of the forests, and are relieving one another of irritating lodgers—in fact, according to Scout law, each doing a good turn.

It is extraordinary how dirty the Kashmiris are, considering the amount of water that is around them everywhere, and though washing opportunities are at hand they prefer to wear dirty garments. They have told me, when I have suggested washing, that it wears out clothes to wash them. Self-respecting women are obliged to wear dirty garments, for if they wore clean ones they might be taken for women of loose life.

I remember my pleasure, when I visited Burma, to be surrounded by clean people in bright colours, and to see women mixing freely with the men, and all happy and jolly together, without anyone thinking it evil or immodest. Kashmir was once like Burma, a Buddhist country. I wonder if the people were then clean and jolly like the Burmans.

I have spoken of the unpleasant smells on the river, but now and again one is cheered when one passes a party of sawyers at work on deodar logs, which is at once delightful and refreshing. Again, when one passes boats loaded with spices, or when meals are being prepared in the evening, one has quite a succession of interesting and pleasing whiffs. But nevertheless it is as well for a man to be armed with a pipe or a cigar, and a lady with smelling-bottle, when a trip is made on the river or in the streets of Srinagar.

Practically at every ghat you see water-carriers at work. Sometimes they are men called "bhishties," or heavenly men, and truly they are such in the hot weather. They carry a goat-skin and a wooden ladle, but generally this work is done by women, which is always pleasing to the eye, as the women carry themselves so elegantly when they carry the terra-cotta-coloured earthen jar on their shoulder or head. Water-carrying is supposed to be women's work, but real heavy work it is for women. To lift up a large earthenware jar full of water from the ground and hoist it up to the shoulder or to the top of the head is no light task. Times out of number have I seen men standing or sitting close by, but they never will give a helping hand, the reason being that it is not the custom, and that's the end of it.

We have been so taken up with the life and manner of the people on the river banks that we have not noticed the houses that overhang the river, which, though untidy-looking, are often most picturesque. Most of the houses are built with wooden frames filled in with brick. Built in this manner, they are the better able to withstand earthquake shocks than those built of solid masonry.

If you look at a house just completed by a Hindu you will notice an old and broken earthenware pot slung from one of the projecting beams. This is considered to be most important, as it keeps off the evil eye, for when the devil notices a nice new-built house he may take a fancy to it; but on closer inspection he sees the old broken pot attached to it, so realises that he has made a mistake in thinking it to be a new building, and hence will not covet it. This belief in the evil eye pervades all things, whether it be new-born babies or carpets. Mothers purposely keep the faces of their children unwashed, to ward off the evil eye. When they show you a baby you must always make some disparaging remark. The mother would be terribly upset if you said the child was beautiful or fat. As it is such a delicate matter, it is best not to commit oneself, but simply say: "What a child!"

If it is a carpet you will, if you look carefully, always find some flaw in it as to colour or pattern purposely made.

The houses as a rule need no flaws purposely made in their construction, as they are so often off the straight, and some have large props placed against the outside walls to prevent their toppling over, presenting often a very drunken appearance. When I first started building I noticed that the wall under construction was off the straight, so asked the mason to place a plumb-line against it; but he informed me that Kashmiris did not use them, as they could build without troubling about such instruments. Europeans might need them, but Kashmiris' eyesight was good, and that was sufficient. I finally demonstrated to him that his eyes had failed him in this particular instance, and impressed this fact on his mind's eye by making him pull the whole of the wall down and rebuild it. I believe that I really did convert him to believe in plumb-lines, although it did not then happen to be one of the customs of the Kashmir masons. There are only a few buildings which attract your attention after leaving the Maharajah's palace and the large modern villa close by belonging to Raja Sir Hari Singh, the heir-apparent and nephew to H.H. the Maharajah.

One house, a strongly built, pretentious-looking edifice of stone and brick, is that of a late Governor of thirty years ago, in those days notable, as it was the only house in the city that possessed glass windows. I can never pass it without thinking of my first call on the great personage who then owned it. He kept me waiting for half-an-hour, no doubt to impress upon me his importance and my nothingness. However, that half-hour was not lost time, for his servant entertained me by showing to me the wonders of the state-room. He drew my attention to a glass chandelier which hung from the ceiling in the centre of the room, and tried to make me understand the brilliant effect when the candles were lighted. Then he drew my attention to a valuable painting which the Governor had procured. It was no less than a German oleograph of the Thames at Pangbourne. The servant asked me to come to a certain spot in the room from where I could get the best view of this wonderful painting, he putting his hand to his forehead to shield the light from his eyes. I, of course, did the same, and was duly impressed. From there I was taken to the south wall, where hung a picture of Queen Victoria, Empress of India; this I was asked to look at from another spot, and then, lo and behold! instead of the Empress of India, stood a black and white English terrier. The servant looked at me to enjoy my wonder and surprise at such a marvel. We had hardly finished all the wonders of the room when the great man himself entered.

Lower down the river on the opposite side is the Maharajah's temple, where the Dharam Sabha, or religious council, meet to discuss religious subjects, and to excommunicate those of their co-religionists who have broken their caste by eating food with someone not of their caste, or some heinous sin of that description. The temple itself is the ordinary square stone building with a dome-like spire covered with sheets of tin; the inside is 10×10 feet, with a pedestal of stone in the centre on which stands the stone lingam known as the god Shiva. The worshippers bring their offerings of milk, sugar, rice and flowers, the priest being in attendance to take their money. This temple stands in a courtyard with a handsome stone stairway to the river, and above the stairway is a hall overlooking the river, where the Dharam Sabha hold their august meetings.

A little lower down the river on the same side and just above the third bridge, called Fateh Kadal, is the Church Mission School for girls, and a few yards lower down is the C.M.S. High School for boys. They are merchants' houses adapted to suit school needs. They overhang the river, and with their balconies and lattice windows are decidedly picturesque. Sometimes will be seen boys jumping out of the school windows and off the roof into the river, distances varying from twenty to fifty feet in height. It is the only building in the city besides the palace which possesses a flag. It has to do duty for a school bell. The flag is a red one emblazoned with the school crest and motto. The crest is crossed paddles and the motto is "In all things be men," which is ever a call to the citizens as well as to the boys to wake up and "play the game," of which more anon.

On the opposite side of the river is a large handsome building, formerly the house of a previous Governor, which remained uninhabited many years on account of its being haunted.

Some eighteen years ago Mrs Annie Besant, of Theosophist fame, took pity on the said building when she came to Kashmir on her crusade against the Mission School, and filled it with three hundred boys whom she spirited away from the Mission School with the help, not of Mahatmas, but with the aid of more corporeal beings in the shape of those Indian and Kashmiri officials who had become her followers for the time being, like the good old Vicar of Bray, until times did alter. Many interesting things happened in those days of war, and still more amusing articles appeared in the native Press in India, inspired by the good lady, about the Kashmir Mission School in general and Mr Biscoe in particular. One spicy bit of news which I am told appeared in forty native papers in India is, I think, worth printing for the forty-first time.

It ran thus:

"Mr Biscoe, a missionary in Kashmir, makes his Brahman boys drag dead dogs through the city."

Now this picturesque proceeding took our fancy, and we thought it ought to be immortalised, to show that one lie at least was really true. It so happened that I possessed an English spaniel, Taffy by name, though he did not happen to be a Welshman and very seldom a thief. He was withal a very loyal dog, for he was ready to die for the Queen. The rest was quite easy. I took Taffy to the stables, which are somewhat dilapidated, and therefore would look like a house in the city, and would make an excellent background. The boys were ready with the rope. Taffy went dead for Mrs Besant this time instead of the Queen; the rope was tied to Taffy's hind leg, which the boys grasped, and a photographer very kindly did the rest. So there were immortalised the words of Mrs Besant copied by forty papers in India, and who can say in what other countries this astounding news was not spread: "Mr Biscoe, a missionary in Kashmir, makes his Brahman boys drag dead dogs through the city." One of the many untruths spread about the country of the mission schools was absolutely true, for who could deny it! The deed had been photographed, and that, too, before the days of faked cinema films were thought of. I should like to say that I think Mrs Besant fully believed what was told her by her Kashmir and Indian friends, and had not then discovered their capacity for manufacturing lies. This fact, I think, is interesting as showing how some minds, and those clever ones, pick up untruths in their search for truth.

CHAPTER VIII

MOSQUES, TEMPLES AND SHOPS

WE are now at the third bridge, called Fateh Kadal, after Fateh Khan. On this bridge some sixty years ago was a pole and hook, on which used to swing the bodies of those who had been convicted of killing cows, as a warning to the citizens. This bridge, which is of four spans, used to be covered with shops, which have since been cleared away.

Just below the bridge, on the right bank of the river, stands a very picturesque mosque, that of Shah Hamdan, a large square building of deodar, with an elegant spire rising from the centre of the terraced roof. In the springtime this roof is red with tulips. There is a handsome carved verandah on the east side, where is the main entrance, and over it is an inscription written in Arabic: "This is the tomb of Shah Hamdan, who was a great saint of God; whosoever does not believe this, may his eyes be blinded, and may he go to hell."

This statement acts as a sort of pick-me-up as one enters the sacred building. The mosque ranks next to the Hazrat Bla mosque on the Dal in sacredness. It was put up to the memory of Mir Sayid Ali of Hamdan, who in the fourteenth century had great influence, and to him is ascribed the honour of being one of the chief oppressors of the Hindus.

This mosque stands on the site of a Hindu temple

which was demolished by the Mohammedans to make way for their mosque. There issues from the foundation of the former building a stream of water, which is a sacred place to the Hindus; they paint the stones around this spring vermilion, their sacred colour, and rarely can you pass that spot without seeing worshippers offering food, and praying towards that shrine.

On certain days of the year the sacred days of the Mohammedans and Hindus coincide, when one sees a great concourse of worshippers of both religions gathered together, the Mohammedans to worship Shah Hamdan, for the Kashmiri Mohammedans are great saint worshippers, and the Hindus to worship Kali, the goddess of murder, for that is her shrine, and it is called by them Kali Ghat. A little episode that happened there always comes to my mind when I pass the spot.

At one of these gatherings a few years ago three Mission School boys happened to arrive at the ghat in time to see three sepoys annoying a Hindu woman. They immediately interfered on the woman's behalf, to which action the sepoys objected, and ordered the boys off, but they stood their ground and awaited the attack. Fortunately for the woman all three boys were athletes and knew something of the noble art of self-defence, with the result that the three sepoys were obliged to retire bloody and discomfited.

On hearing at school next day of this scrap, I asked the boys if they could tell me which side the goddess Kali backed, as the fray took place at her shrine. Some boys said that she must have taken the part of the sepoys because she, being the goddess of murder, would prefer those who attacked, whilst other boys took the opposite view. Then a Solomon arose saying as Kali must be worshipped with blood she must have taken the side of

FATEH KADAL.

The houses shewn on this bridge were shops and have now been cleared away. Beyond the bridge can be seen the picturesque mosque of Shah Hamdan.

Photo by] [*R. E. Shorter.*

H.H. THE MAHARAJA'S SOLDIERS OF THE OLD ARMY.
FISHING ON THE JHELUM.

the boys, for they shed most blood, and to this theory all agreed with much satisfaction.

There is another mosque of interest a little lower down the river called Pather Masjid, which was built by the beautiful Queen of Jahangir, "Nur Jahan," but it is never used for worship as it was built by a woman, so is used as a store-house for grain.

It is said that the stones which formed a causeway from the river at Shurahyar opposite H.H. the Maharajah's palace to the Takht-i-Suliman, a distance of two miles, were used in the building of this mosque.

We have now reached the fourth bridge, called Zana Kadal, named after Zain-ul-Abidin.

Below the fourth bridge, on the right bank of the river, is a five-domed temple called Maha Shri, built by King Praversena, the second founder of Srinagar. It has been converted into a graveyard. The wife of Sikandar was buried inside this temple, while Zain-ul-Abidin lies buried outside it. Hence the whole locality is called Bud Shah, which was the title of Zain-ul-Abidin.

At this place we are at the centre of the city, where you find the rich merchants' houses, and where you can very quickly part with your rupees in exchange for shawls, carpets, furniture made of walnut wood richly carved, silver and copper ware, papier mâché, and articles of various designs. Shawls used to be the great industry, but those who made them were practically slaves; they were never allowed to leave Kashmir and were treated shamefully. It is said that every shawl cost the eyesight of one or more men, as the work was so fine, so it was really a great mercy when the shawl trade was practically brought to an end by the Franco-German War of 1870. Most of the shawls were exported to France, so that when the Germans demanded so great a war indemnity the French had no spare cash with which to purchase Kashmir shawls.

The stream carries our boat swiftly under the fifth bridge, called Ali Kadal. As the channel of the river is compressed, so the stream flows strong, and as the boat is swept under the bridge it is tossed about on the waves caused by swirls and eddies. It is here that the boatman's skill is watched with interest, especially when coming up-stream against the strong current. The boatmen have to creep up under the cover of the side walls, or under the shelter of the piers of the bridge, and then make a dash for the arch, hugging the pier so close that they can make use of the piles of the bridge to lever themselves upwards against the current.

Ali Kadal is named after Ali Khan, son of Zain-ul-Abidin.

About a quarter of a mile down-stream is the sixth bridge, Nawa Kadal, named after Nur Din Khan in A.D. 1666.

Before we reach the seventh bridge, Saffa Kadal, on the right bank is the elegant temple of Hanuman, the monkey god. This temple belongs to the Dhar family, and stands out well against the blue mountains in the distance, as its white walls and silver-like spire reflect the sunlight. At the back the mansions and gardens of the Dhar family cover many acres of ground. In the time of Ranjit Singh's conquest of Kashmir this family became chief advisers to the Sikhs.

The Saffa Kadal bridge is named after Saifulla Khan. The name of the builder and date of the building of the bridge is inscribed on the gateway of a mosque close by. This is an important bridge, as there is not another for twenty miles down-stream. It is across this bridge that the travellers from Srinagar to Central Asia start on their long journey.

Close to this bridge is a big square building called the Yarkandi Serai, the rest-house for Central Asian travellers, Yarkandis in their long, quilted, many-coloured garments, Tibetans, and men from Turkestan. These travellers arrive with their loads on ponies and yaks, with carpets, skins and china cups. How the china cups survive this long journey is always a marvel.

On the opposite side of the river to the Yarkandi Serai is a very beautiful maidan, called Id Gah, where the Central Asian travellers graze their yaks and ponies. On the farther end from the river is a very large handsome mosque, which holds 2000 worshippers. It is supposed to be haunted by ghosts and goblins, so that no one will enter it after dark.

A few years ago a Mohammedan from Ladakh who refused to believe in the story of this mosque being haunted was offered a reward of a hundred pieces of silver provided he fixed a peg inside the mosque at midnight. To this challenge he willingly agreed, and at midnight entered the mosque with a tent-peg and stone. He groped his way in the darkness among the great cedar-wood columns which support the huge roof and, having selected a spot, drove the peg firmly into the ground with the aid of his stone hammer. Having accomplished his task successfully, he turned towards the exit, when he found himself held firmly to the spot which he had pegged. Do what he might, he could not leave it. He struggled in terror, crying out for help; but who could hear? for the mosque stands in a large maidan far from any habitation. In the morning an early worshipper saw a heap of something on the floor, and on near approach discovered the lifeless Ladakhi. He was horrified, and went off in search of help. He soon returned with some friends, and they tried to raise the body from the ground, but they found it held fast to the spot by a peg. On closer inspection they discovered that the peg had been driven through the strong cloth of the Ladakhi voluminous garment, so the brave Ladakhi who disbelieved in goblins after all died in fear of them, and the one hundred pieces of silver did not change hands.

Some of the entertaining and amusing sights of the river are the boatmen's wedding parties, which are very frequent at certain times of the year. The party borrow a big doonga and pack it with their wedding guests. They will have twenty paddlers or so, who sit at the bow and stern, and as they paddle they raise themselves up and down in such good time as to make the ends of the boat swing up and down, giving an exhibition the while of fancy strokes, sending the water in spray behind them. It makes a most ludicrous effect, and is intended to be so. There will probably be a *nautch* girl or two, or men dressed up as *nautch* girls, dancing in the fore part of the boat, and musicians. There will be a punting-pole stuck up, with a piece of coloured cloth on the top for a flag, and if they wish to attract an extra amount of notice a man with a shot-gun will straddle the pent roof and let off his gun when the spirit moves him. A small boat precedes the marriage party, about thirty yards or so ahead, with one or two drummers who seem to put their whole soul into the drums. This business is to attract attention. They certainly succeed in doing so. The bridegroom sits in the centre of the boat on cushions, his face covered with a veil of tinsel and peacocks' feathers hanging from the top of his head. This boat with its show is propelled up and down the river through the city with much shouting and "tamasha."

The bride is not invited to this show.

CHAPTER IX

STREETS AND BAZAARS

WE will leave our boat at the bottom of the city and return on foot through the streets in order to see the life of the people in the bazaars. All the streets, with the exception of the main street, are very narrow, and generally very filthy. There are no sidewalks, so that pedestrians, equestrians, laden animals, laden men, cattle, fowls and pariah dogs are all jumbled up together. Consequently our progress will be much impeded. However, it will give us more time to take in and digest what we see. In the winter-time it is of course more difficult going in the streets on account of the pools of liquid filth. Then one has to be careful not to bump into pedestrians, for most of them are carrying "kangris" under their garments; also everyone carries a blanket over his shoulder, which is everlastingly slipping off, and as often has to be thrown on again; hence one is always liable to have a dirty blanket flapped in one's face.

One is continually entertained with amusing or annoying episodes, according as they happen to oneself or to someone else. For instance, citizens of this town are in the habit of throwing their slops out of the upper windows into the streets, and it is here that the amusement or annoyance arises, according as the slops fall on oneself or on somebody else.

The Municipality have lately passed a law against this custom of ages, but Eastern customs die hard. On the last occasion when the episode happened to be more annoying than amusing, I sought to uphold the Municipal law by calling at the offending house in order to obtain information regarding the perpetrators of the crime. But every obstacle was put in my way. The neighbours did their best to shield the breaker of the Municipal law. They first said that they did not know the name of the owner of the house, then that he had died some weeks ago. Others said that he was out; others, again, said that only women lived there, etc., etc. However, a friend of mine, an official, happened to be passing, so with his help the owner was found to be alive; also he was a man and not a woman, and he was not out, but very much at home, for he was made to appear. He happened to be a big man with a red beard. Mohammedans often dye their beards red to be like their prophet Mohammed. He came to me carrying a child of one and a half years old in his arms, saying: "The Sahib must not be angry, for was not the one who threw a little water out of the window but a very little child." I answered that a miracle must have happened, for the little child that I saw throwing the water out of the window possessed a red beard, and the colour of the beard was uncommonly like the beard of the man who was carrying the child. At this remark the crowd of citizens laughed loudly, whereupon my little child with the red beard, seeing that the game was up, put his hands together in the attitude of prayer and asked me to have mercy upon him, and not report him to the Municipal officers, promising to give up the custom of his forefathers in this respect.

The reason why so much slop-water comes from the upper storeys of the houses is that the top room is generally used as the kitchen, and does not possess sinks or drains.

Photo by] [*R. E. Shorter.*

SAFFA KADAL OR SEVENTH BRIDGE.

An important bridge as there is not another for twenty miles down-stream. Across this bridge travellers from Srinagar to Central Asia start on their long journey.

When one bicycles through the city one has to be very much awake, as the citizens lose their heads so easily. They often dance in front of one's cycle for quite a considerable time before they decide on which side they will go. After a time one learns how to behave under certain circumstances and with various types of individuals. I have so far learnt the following:—

When a child is on the road I look quickly to see if it has a guardian. If a little sister is with the child I do not put on the brake, for the little girl will most certainly protect the child, either by taking him with her to one side, or by standing quite still wherever she happens to be and clasping the child tightly in her arms to protect it. If a boy is the protector I have to prepare my brake for emergencies, for I cannot be certain if he will or will not think of the child's safety before his own, but probably he will do the former. If the mother or some woman is with the child I put on the brake, for invariably the woman will run to the side of the street herself and then call to the child to come to her, or tell the child to go to the opposite side. So, as one cannot possibly tell what the order will be, one has to slow down in order to be ready for any emergency. If the child happens to have a man for its protector, I put on the brake hard, and possibly dismount, for the man will not merely rush for safety, but most probably will lose his head, and do a certain amount of dancing in front of the cycle, and in order to save himself will give the child a shove to get a take-off on his mad rush to save himself. But if two men are walking together, at the sound of the bell they will both clasp, or shove against, each other, and finally the man on the right will rush to the left and the man on the left will rush to the right, thereby providing quite an amusing entertainment.

When all is over and they find themselves safe, they will join in the laughter with the on-lookers. This is my experience after many years of cycling through the city, and I have found this knowledge useful in saving my own skin as well as that of the citizens of Srinagar.

Of course one is bound at times to come to grief oneself. On a very greasy day in a narrow street by the river, where an old fishwife sits daily before her baskets of fish, my cycle side-slipped, and before I could wink I found myself stuck fast in one of the half-empty, slimy baskets on the top of the fish. The basket fitted my sitting posture like a glove, so there I had to remain with legs in the air until rescued by kindly hands. I fancy that the old fish-lady was too convulsed with laughter to be able to come to the rescue, and ever since that day the old lady, who always sits at the same spot on the top of that odoriferous stairway, always meets me with a grin as I pass. She and I always have the same thoughts when our eyes meet. We both grin at each other as we pass the time of day.

Animals and birds play quite an amusing part in the streets. I see a baker walking along with stately gait carrying a basket of fresh-baked cakes on his head (*à la* Pharaoh's baker); all of a sudden the basket is on the ground and the round cakes rolling in all directions in the muddy street, whilst the baker is looking about in the street angrily for the culprit, who happens this time to be a kite which is just soaring above him sampling one of his fresh-baked cakes. I was riding just behind the baker when the kite played so successfully its practical joke. I suffered in the same way on another occasion. I was standing up eating my lunch on a mountain road, and was holding a sandwich in my hand and was in the act of putting it into my mouth when I felt a sharp smack on my right cheek, and my sandwich was gone. I looked round sharply to see who had hit me and pinched my sandwich, but could see no one, when a few seconds later I saw gliding down the valley a kite devouring my sandwich. The kites have often astonished me by their smartness and audacity.

One familiar sight in the bazaars is the Brahmani sacred bull, swaggering down town with his rakish black india-rubber sort of hump swaying from side to side as he walks. He seems to have the run of all the greengrocer shops by the way; he shoves his nose on the counters and marches off munching the vegetables he has pinched in passing. Everybody makes way for him. That he expects respect from all can be seen by the look in his insolent eye. The cow tribe in Kashmir is sacred, and formerly anyone who killed a cow suffered capital punishment. Often they were boiled in oil and then hung from a hook which was fixed on to a pole in a public place. An old colonel told me that when he was in Kashmir as a subaltern he remembered seeing the pole fixed on the Fateh Kadal bridge, on which a boiled corpse hung as food for the birds of prey. That man had been convicted of killing a cow and thus suffered for his heinous crime. Until seven years ago the penalty for cow-killing was a life sentence, which now has come down to seven years only.

If one keeps one's eyes open as one walks through the bazaars one will see the great respect shown by the Hindus to the cow tribe, for as one passes, and generally they are plastered in mud, one will see a Hindu touch the holy animal with the shawl that he carries over his shoulder and then kiss the shawl at the spot where it touched the cow, so that in some way the holiness of the cow may enter him. Yet, notwithstanding this reverence for the cow, you will in the winter season see the cows starving to death—that is, those which are not giving milk, or are ill. They are turned out into the snow-covered streets to fight with the pariah dogs for the filth under the snow. Then when they fall exhausted they are attacked by the birds of prey, which gouge out their eyes, and when they are dead the pariah dogs share the carcase. This may happen at the very door of a Hindu, but I have never known them interfere to save them. This attitude of mind is most difficult for a Westerner to understand. I gave it up years ago, and started at a practical solution with my school staff and boys, who were chiefly Hindus, with what result you will see later on.

Among the chief inhabitants of Srinagar are the dogs, which in their time have accomplished much useful work, and are of use still, and will be so as long as the insanitary conditions of the city and habits of the people continue. When one remembers that very few houses, possibly one per cent., possess any sanitary conveniences, as the inhabitants prefer to make use of the streets as their forefathers have done before them, there will be little hope of improvement, and the pariah dogs will be needed. The Municipality have at last made a law, which met with strong opposition from certain city fathers, that no new house may be built unless provision be made for a closet.

When one has spoken to the people about their insanitary habits and the danger to public health, the one and same answer is given—viz. that their forefathers have always managed to live and enjoy their city, so why should they seek to change the ancient customs and conditions of life. Pariah dogs have always done their duty well, so why deprive them of their livelihood.

These poor dogs have a wretched existence, as they

belong to no one, and are continually stoned and kicked, and sometimes have scalding water thrown over them when they come too near to the shops and houses on their hunt for food. They are more often than not diseased and covered with mange and in the winter especially are a most pitiable sight to behold. They would be really strong, fine dogs if properly fed and cared for, but, as I said before, they belong to no one, they are pariahs. In the summer they often go mad. In the winter when they are starving they become savage, then they attack women and children. As one cycles through the city one is often attacked by them, but they have not much pluck unless they are in a large pack. They have their own particular quarters, in fact they divide themselves into parishes, and woe betide that dog who finds himself alone in someone else's parish.

I have often made use of this parish system when attacked by them and anxious to rid myself of their attentions. I encourage them to follow me out of their own parish into the adjacent one, when immediately they are set upon by those of the parish I have entered; not only am I immediately delivered from my persecutors, but am also saved from the dogs of the parish I have entered, as they are all busily engaged punishing the intruders and forget me and my cycle.

One has to be very careful of one's own dogs, for a fox terrier does not stand a chance when attacked by two or more pariahs. Many English dogs have been torn to pieces by them; they are dealt with as the hounds dispose of a fox.

One hopes that before many years have passed the citizens of Srinagar will have learnt self-respect, so that they will not need thousands of pariah dogs to keep their city clean.

CHAPTER X

TRADES, LEPERS AND BEGGARS

THE shops in Srinagar, as in all Eastern towns, protrude themselves on to the streets, so that when one is walking after dark one has to be careful not to trip up over the short ladder leading from the street up to the shop platform or seat.

When cycling or riding on horseback in a crowded thoroughfare one is apt to knock baskets of wares off the shop fronts into the streets.

On one occasion on a frosty morning whilst trotting down a narrow street my pony side-slipped—I was shot into a shop by the side of the shopman on the platform above, whilst the pony fell on his side under the platform, to the astonishment of the shopman and amusement of the neighbours. I was able to join in the laughter, as neither the pony nor myself suffered any damage.

When one stops in the street before a shop to make a purchase, for most of the business is done from the street, and not inside the shop, an interested crowd always collects, eager to take part in the bargaining. Quite often a man will join in apparently as one's friend and adviser, telling the shopman in a loud voice to play the game and not to cheat one, while at the same time he is talking secretly with his eyes or fingers to the shopman to acquaint him how far it is safe to try on his game.

Talking with the eyes was not new to me, for I had seen something of the eye language practised by thieves when I worked in Whitechapel in East London, and often came in contact with this class of sharpers. So when I found these kind helpers around me I felt as if I was again amongst old pals.

A great number of the shops are kept by Hindus, such as grocers', drapers', tailors', and snuff and drug shops also, where manufactured brass cups, bowls and Hindu gods are sold, but all the shops where articles of brass, copper, iron or wood are being made, and butchers' shops, are kept by Mohammedans.

There are very few eating shops and liquor shops, but the latter, I am sorry to say, are increasing, for those who go to drink do so in order to get drunk. If when passing these pubs. after dark you lift up the dirty curtain behind the counter you will generally see one or more prostrate forms on the benches or floor.

I can remember the time when no one dared to be seen carrying a liquor bottle in the street, as public opinion was against it, and the smartness with which they would hide it under their blankets when they caught sight of anyone used to remind me of a drunken coster-woman, one of my parishioners in East London, who had just come out of a pub. with a black bottle, and on seeing me covered it with her shawl. On my asking her what she had just tucked up under her arm, "Just bought a little of peppermint, for I do suffer that bad from stomick-ache," said she. Stomach-aches of the coster lady's kind seem to be on the increase in Srinagar, though one rarely sees a drunken man in the streets, as public opinion is still against the use of alcohol and a drunkard is generally despised.

A year or two ago an Indian gentleman generally known as a babu asked me to help him to start a temperance society, and did me the honour of asking me to become president of the same. I told him that

I did not think that there was any need for a temperance society at present, as there was so little intemperance in the country, thanks to the prophet Mohammed, who had forbidden the use of alcohol to his followers, and also on account of his Highness the Maharajah's disapproval of pubs. and drinking generally.

I also considered it to be unwise to call people's attention to the subject, as it might lead them from thinking to action in the wrong direction. My babu friend did not agree with my philosophy, for a few days afterwards he came to tell me that he had started a temperance society, and asked me to help him with a subscription, and soon I heard that weekly meetings were in full swing, for babus as a rule love much talking.

After a month or six weeks from the commencement of the society my babu friend came to me in great grief to seek my help, for, sad to say, the treasurer of the society had not only disappeared with all the money, but had taken off all the furniture which had been bought to furnish their meeting-place. Would I use my influence to secure the capture of the runaway and also the stolen property? This was not all the bad news, for at the meeting before the last one of the speakers had impressed upon the audience that it was folly to talk against drunkenness until they knew and understood it by practical experience, for one must always study a subject thoroughly before attempting to teach it, and, further, one can always help one's brother more efficiently if one has been through the same experience.

"So I propose," said he, "that at the next meeting every member shall bring a bottle of brandy—for is not that German brandy only one rupee per bottle?—and then, brothers, we will get drunk royally, so that we may understand thoroughly the sad experiences of our drunken brothers, but we must not drink too much that we all kick the bucket."

Well, this epoch-making speech carried the meeting, and at the next meeting the members came not empty-handed, so with the help of brandy from Germany they passed through all the stages of their poor drunken brothers. So satisfactory the experiment proved to be that they came to the conclusion that intemperance was more entertaining than temperance, and thus it came to pass the first Srinagar temperance society ceased to exist.

The fact that there are so few pubs. in the city keeps it quiet, and one seldom sees a brawl in the bazaars from this cause. The Kashmiris can give the Westerner points in this respect.

The vagaries of the poor lunatics wandering about the streets generally attract a crowd. The men often walk about naked. Sometimes a kind-hearted person will give them a garment to cover their nakedness, which they will as often as not dispose of at once, by tearing it into shreds, or setting fire to it and sitting down in front of it to warm their hands; this I have seen done on a very cold day in winter. It is especially sad to see the women lunatics wandering about, often with a baby, which they do not know how to take care of; and some men are so debased and vile as to take advantage of their madness by making them mothers, but in no way helping to keep them off the streets. I hope some day the authorities will understand that they have a duty towards these poor, helpless creatures.

Fortunately there is an asylum for lepers built by the State and handed over to the care of the C.M.S. Medical Mission, so that these afflicted people are well cared for. When one is accosted by lepers in the bazaars—they will often push up their fingerless hands in your face to draw forth your pity and alms—one can always direct them to the asylum all ready for them.

Srinagar, like all Eastern cities, swarms with beggars; most of them are professional beggars; some actually ride on horseback, which reminds me of the old English song:

> Hark! hark! how the dogs do bark,
> The beggars are coming to town,
> Some in rags and some on nags
> And some in velvet gown.

They exist in their scores, because the people *will* give to them, thinking that they gain merit by doing so. Many of the beggars are frauds. There is one man who has for years pretended to be a cripple; he crawls about naked except for a loin-cloth, and especially on rainy or snowy days he creeps along with body bent and crying and shivering as he moves with difficulty; he by this trick collects a goodly supply of coin. I met this poor cripple one morning on coming quickly round a corner in the street; he was running at top speed and roaring with laughter as he ran. He was not at that moment ready to help his fellow-countrymen to heap up merit. It does not seem to matter whether a man is known to be a fraud or not, he receives alms all the same.

One can apparently gain merit from bestowing coin on a fraud as easily as one can from giving to a case really needing one's help. Let us forget the beggars and look again at the shops.

There is one particular shop which attracts one's attention, and at first sight often gives one a start.

You see sitting in a shop a Mohammedan with a sharp knife cutting a bald head from which blood is often flowing. Is this a public murder or what! On closer inspection you see that it is only the barber at work.

It is the custom among the Mohammedans to have their heads shaved as bald as the coot; or if it is a Hindu's head, he prefers to have a clean pathway about four inches wide cut down the centre of his scalp from forehead to neck, except the place where his top-knot sprouts; that is left long enough for him to tie in a knot or two. Now many, if not most, Kashmiris suffer from diseased scalps. A sort of white fungus spreads over the scalp (it is called "scalled head"), so when the razorman sets to work he, like Shylock of old, is unable to do his job withput shedding blood. It is not the custom of Kashmiri barbers to sterilise their razors, so the infected blade passes on the disease of the last man to the next client, and so on.

The barber is also the dentist. He keeps an iron hook, which he shoves between the tooth and the gum, and then hauls. I believe the hook always brings up something if it does not break; let us hope that it is the aching tooth. They are also very clever at fixing a broken tooth to the stump or to the next tooth by wiring them together; in the same way they mend broken crockery. An old man on my school staff had his two front teeth wired to their stumps. I found it often difficult to concentrate my attention on his words, so interesting was the oscillating of his front teeth.

Still further, the barber is the match-maker. He arranges the marriages between families. The family which employs him allows him to see the girl that is to be wedded; he then visits the parents of the hoped-for bridegroom, and sings to them the lady's charms, which are always many. If he has been sufficiently paid by the family who sent him, he can allow his imagination and falsehoods to run riot, for the lady whose beauty and virtues he extols will not be seen by the bridegroom until after the marriage, when the bridegroom takes his bride to his private apartment and lifts the veil to see the lady with whom he is to spend his life. Many bridegrooms have to suffer as Jacob did of old when he discovered that the one under the veil was not his beloved Rachel. I have often been told of the disappointment suffered by bridegrooms to find their wife has only one eye, or the face disfigured with small-pox, for small-pox plays havoc with faces and eyes. Practically everyone in Srinagar has small-pox some time during his life, and generally when they are children. I believe it is a fact that half the children born in Srinagar die of this fell disease.

Well, back to the shops. The ones which generally catch one's eye are those where men are working at embroidery work; it may be silk, cotton or wool, the colouring and patterns often displaying great taste. Then there are the saddlers', where you see gay-coloured saddle-pads of reds, yellows and blues; the embroidery there is often bold and startling. The saddles are generally of cloth, for the Kashmiri prefers a soft seat to a pigskin one. A Mohammedan would not ride on pigskin, and to a Hindu all leather is anathema.

When one's eyes become tired of the streets and shops one can look up and notice the lattice windows, called "pinjra," of various designs.

In many of the bazaars the houses project so far over the streets that they almost touch at the roof. This is convenient for those who wish to escape from fire, or the thief who is hotly pursued and finds the streets unsafe. Occasionally when the houses take on such a list that they look like kissing one another beams are placed between the two to prevent the one from toppling over on to the other and embracing it.

If you raise your eyes a little higher you will probably see the everlasting snows.

How often has this sight of the mountains cheered one up! When on a sloshy day one is passing mud-bespattered pedestrians who seem to be suffering from the dirt and gloom round them, then one raises one's eyes to the everlasting snows and one goes on one's way rejoicing.

Srinagar, like most cities, has its quarters for certain classes and trades. The coppersmiths are as easily known by the continual din as the Brahmans' quarters by their conservatism to the custom of their forefathers in the matter of filth and superabundant stench. In the copper bazaar one can sometimes pick up some really elegant and quaintly shaped jugs and basins of ancient make, as well as excellent imitations of the same, which are sold to the unwary as the real article. The merchants continually do themselves well when passing off their dragon-shaped jugs of curious design as from Lassa.

There is a special jug which takes the fancy of most visitors, and that is a jug of copper, shaped like a duck, called "batish," or female duck, which is used for blowing up the fire, as it does in a most workmanlike manner. It is filled with water and placed on the fire, and when the water boils the steam issues from its long beak, which being directed towards the spot that needs its attention, the pressure of steam soon does its work, unless, as sometimes happens, it works too vigorously, when it blows the hot charcoal ashes clean out of the grate. When the duck has blown itself dry there is no other way for the water to find its way to the duck's interior again except through its beak, which aperture is too small to allow of water being poured in, so the duck has to be heated and then its beak held in a glass of water, which it will itself drink up until its body and the air within it cools.

Near the coppersmiths' quarters is a very large mosque called the Jumma Musjid, which is well worth a visit.

This famous mosque, the greatest in Srinagar, was originally built by Sikandar the Iconoclast in 1404 with the materials of a large stone temple erected by King Tarapeeda. It was destroyed by fire three times. The present structure was raised by Aurangzeb in 1674. This site is considered sacred by the Buddhists also, and even now the Buddhists from Ladakh and other places come to visit this place.

It is on this side of the city that you see many travellers coming in, for the main road from Central Asia enters here. Some of the travellers have never seen this great city before, and they look somewhat frightened and awe-inspired, for they have heard many tales of their friends falling among thieves, and finding themselves in the police lock-up instead of those who have robbed them, and, moreover, having lost all the money that they had brought with which to make their necessary purchases.

A villager is known at once by his dress and speech. They generally carry their shoes on their heads until they reach the bazaars, as they have learnt from experience that it wears out shoes to walk in them.

The women often carry much else on their heads, such as their cooking vessels and many household gods, as they walk behind their lords and masters; this habit teaches them to carry themselves gracefully as they walk.

It is a sight to see the milkmen coming to the city in the early mornings. They come in from their villages many miles distant at a jog-trot, carrying three earthenware pots full of milk, one on the top of the other, poised

Photo by] [R. E. Shorter.

on their shoulders. Even the thought of this great weight makes one's own back ache to look at them.

One might imagine that after a journey of four or five miles of trotting the milk would be turned to butter when delivered to the purchaser, but it is not so, as these men run bare-footed, and run without jerking, so easy is their movement. I expect the great weight on their shoulders makes them run easy-like. I have seen these milkmen after their long run when just outside the city stopped by the police and sepoys and forced to give up their milk on pretence that they have been sent by some big official, so unless there happens to be some God-fearing man near to defend them it is of no use their refusing. The ordinary man in the street is generally too frightened to interfere, so those uniformed robbers play their own game with impunity. I have had the good luck to come upon them at the right moment more than once.

On one occasion I saw four sepoys set upon a milkman, and they were foolish enough to tell me that they were doing so under orders from the British Resident. Their stakes were a bit too high, and they lived to repent taking the Resident's name in vain.

One is bound to get mixed up in comic operas in this land. Sometimes they are almost serious, bordering on the tragic, but most of them are of a humorous nature, or can be turned into such. Here is an instance:

Two villagers had just arrived in the great city and were properly awe-inspired. I happened to light upon them just as a gentleman in blue had discovered that these innocents might be useful to him, and was ordering them in a loud voice, with gestures to match, to remove a heavy chest from a shop. The two visitors to Srinagar were telling him that they had come to town on business and wished to get on with it, but the man in blue thought his business more important. These villagers naturally feared that this was a trick to get them in the lock-up, for they did not know what valuables might not be in that chest. So I asked them if they wished to work for this blue gentleman. They did not answer at once; they looked at me hard, and then at the gentleman in blue in a scared way. I suppose they were trying to ascertain who was likely to come out top, but as I was mounted and had a hunting-crop in my hand, they gave me the casting vote, and answered that they did not wish to carry the chest. So I ordered them not to carry it, but to go on with their own business and I would settle this little business for them; so they went on their way rejoicing. But not so the man in blue, for I ordered him to do his own job, by carrying the chest himself, and I saw him do it. It was a decidedly heavy chest, I admit, and as he bent under it it reminded me of the Turkish coolies I had seen in Constantinople staggering under their huge loads. I used to feel sorry for them, but I cannot say that I had any feelings of sorrow in my heart for this gentleman in blue.

Srinagar is a most interesting town from a human point of view, for one never knows what will turn up next, especially if one comes round a corner sharp. I hardly ever pass through the city without one or more humorous or interesting event happening.

CHAPTER XI

FASHIONS IN DRESS

IF one walks through the streets one has naturally more opportunities for picking up knowledge concerning the people than when one is riding. The people of the East as a rule walk slower than Westerners, so one catches up the people in front. It is interesting to learn the class of person one is overtaking. One can obtain the information to a great extent from the way in which the turban is tied, for the various trades have different ways of binding on their turbans, as well as those of different religions and castes. The Brahman, for instance, ties his tight like a head bandage; the butcher also binds his turban tight, but the cloth is a much broader strip, and more of it, therefore it is a much bigger pagri than that of the Brahman. Then many tie their pagris loosely, such as the carpenter or boatman, but there, again, they are not of the same shape. There are some who put the ends of their pagris sticking upwards at the back of their heads like a cockade, whilst others like to have a long tail down their backs. The turban or pagri, whichever you like to call it, is a very sensible head-gear. It keeps the head cool in the summer as well as warm in the winter; it acts as a helmet and a protection to the head from blows of any kind. It also sets off the face and is most becoming. Even an ugly face looks quite presentable when the head is adorned with a pagri. Its uses are unending. I mention a few, as I have seen them. A pony kicks off his rider and bolts at once; the would-be rider, when he has picked himself up, makes a rope and lasso of the pagri and catches the runaway, for a pagri may be sixteen yards long. A man wishes to climb a tree, the bole of which may be too smooth and of too wide girth to swarm. The pagri becomes a rope and is thrown, with the help of a stone, over a branch, and at once there is a way up the tree. It may be the rope at the well is broken; no matter, one or more pagris are at hand. A thief has to be kept secure until the police arrive; well, there is the pagri. It is used as a purse, a letter rack, a towel, a pocket-handkerchief. Your cook will probably strain your coffee with the tail of his pagri, and make use of it in any of his culinary arts. I have seen an official with several servants in attendance—this great man wished to blow his nose, and although he was himself wearing a pagri with a long tail behind, he notwithstanding called up one of his servants and blew his nose in the tail of his servant's pagri, a rather smart way, I thought, of making use of other people's property to save one's own.

Of late I have seen my pupils use their pagris in all sorts of ways in social service for the sick and distressed, tearing them up for bandages for wounds, for tying one unable to walk to the back of one strong boy who can, for towing boats to help boatmen, for catching runaway animals, and so forth. I guess the pagri is "some hat," as the Americans would say.

It is not the pagri only which enables one to distinguish classes and castes, etc., for the dresses also differ. Mohammedan men and women dress quite differently from Hindu men and women. It is true that they have a national dress called the "pheron," but its cut varies. The pheron is an ugly garment at its best. It is said that when the Afghans conquered Kashmir they forced the men to wear the same dress as the women, to be in keeping with their character. The Brahmans' pheron differs from that of the Brahman women and from that of the Mohammedan men and women in that it has long sleeves, which are almost twice as long as a man's arm. I have not yet discovered the reason for this length, but they do make use of it when drinking hot tea out of their brass cups, or when taking pots off a fire, as we use a kettle-holder, or when they are obliged to hold anything unclean, such as leather—for instance, the reins of a pony. Also they use it as a weapon. When they are angry they flourish this long sleeve about and beat their adversary with it, and a very amusing performance it always is.

This voluminous garment is most suitable for users of the kangri, because when they squat down and place the fire pot between their legs it forms a most excellent tent, in fact a primitive Turkish bath. I have seen it used on more than one occasion as a hiding-place. When a cheeky boy is running away from his wrathful pursuer, and happens to be lucky in reaching his mother, he is safe out of sight by the time his pursuer arrives at the house. The mother, who is squatting on the floor, of course, swears solemnly that she has not seen the boy, and suggests his seeking him elsewhere; but I have known one occasion when the mother was given away on account of a foot not being properly covered, one's reason suggesting that even Kashmiri women have not three feet. I myself have discovered a much-wanted man by this process of reasoning when he, though full-grown, had taken cover under a lady's pheron.

The Kashmiri Brahman in his own home, and often in the street, does not wear any unmentionables or socks, but ends up at the bottom with a pair of wooden clogs which are kept on to the feet either by a straw strap which goes over his toes, or by the aid of a wooden knob at the toe of the clog, which he grasps between his big toe and the toe next it. Leather is abhorrent to Brahmans; they prefer wooden clogs, unless their business may require their moving at a greater pace than one and a half miles per hour, and so compel them to use the leather shoe. No Brahman's toilet is complete unless he has his caste marks, which consist of a dab of red or yellow paint, or both, and often a third colour, grey, dabbed on from the middle of his forehead and down the bridge of his nose, also on the lobe of each ear, and on his throat near the apple. These three colours remind him of the trinity of gods, Shiva, Brahma and Vishnu. Then a medal hangs from his neck by a string made of gold, silver, or copper, on which is inscribed his fate, and is supposed to preserve him from (1) the evil influences of the planets, (2) evil spirits, (3) the evil eye. The engraving on the medal may represent the image of one of the gods or goddesses, one of the planets, or some magical figure.

Every Brahman wears a thread, which is thrown over the left shoulder and under the right armpit; it is made of three strands of cotton thread, until the marriage day, when three more cotton strands are added. This thread is never removed from the body, except three times a year: on the Brahman's birthday, on the Shiv Ratri and on the Hindu New Year, when the priest puts on a new one. It must be washed every day, and during the process a "mantra" must be recited in praise of the goddess Goitree. Should the thread break, it cannot be tied or knotted, for the previous knot is holy and must be burnt, but the thread may be thrown away. A new thread must be obtained from a priest. The thread must be in length twenty-six times the breadth of the hand for an unmarried man, and double the length for a married man.

There is one particular fashion in dress which often catches one's eye, and that is when the coat or trousers are made out of a than of white cotton cloth. On every than the trade mark is printed in blue. Sometimes it is the face of a man or animal and the number of yards in the than. Now the Kashmiri takes a fancy for this trade mark, so the tailor arranges that it shall appear on some part of the white suit. Sometimes you will see a dog's head on the seat of the trousers, or the maker's name in blue capitals on the tail of his coat, or as it can be seen to-day on the person of a certain very fat Government servant "36 YARDS" standing out in bold relief on that part of the garment which protects his bulky form, which makes one inquisitive to ascertain the exact girth of this individual. Anyway, it adds much to his importance.

The ladies, and especially of the Hindu persuasion, prefer their garments to be of very bright colours, bright oranges and pinks being their special colours; and they certainly brighten up their surroundings.

CHAPTER XII

BRAHMANS AND SADHUS

WHEN a Brahman takes up work as a clerk in the State service, which is the ambition of most of them, he dresses very much like the babu of India—he dons tight-fitting trousers. If he is able to dress in the height of fashion the legs of his trousers will be a foot or more longer than his legs, and have to dispose of themselves in many folds and creases at his ankles. Moreover the trousers must fit round the legs like a glove; so tight must they be that the only way to get them to pass the heel is by means of a highly glazed piece of paper, a shoe-horn being too thick and clumsy for the operation. Instead of a pheron he wears a coat and waistcoat, which are generally of black alpaca; below the waistcoat he puts on a cotton shirt, which is worn outside and not inside the trousers, as is the fashion in the West. This custom is important, for by wearing the shirt outside he always has a towel and pocket-handkerchief at hand. Athough he adopts a Western shirt, he very seldom runs to a collar and tie; if he has taken to a collar he generally forgets to send it to the wash. He usually wears the Eastern shoe with socks, but nowadays patent-leather shoes have come into fashion, but he usually forgets to lace them. Although this kit strikes one as a great mix-up of the East and

West, yet it is infinitely preferable to the unsightly and unmanly garb of the pheron. Where the Eastern has the better of the Western in dress is his head-gear, which, as I said before, is as becoming as it is serviceable.

When the Brahman clerk goes to his house in the evening he casts off his day dress and goes back to the dress of his forefathers, for in that kit alone can he really feel at home.

The manner of the Brahman putting on and taking off his garments is a true picture of his inside. When he is in his home he is an out-and-out Easterner in manner, customs and beliefs, but when he is in his office you might think by his talk that he had taken on Western ideas and beliefs, but it is not so, they mean nothing more to him than does his babu dress.

I have often marvelled at their powers of acting, for they are great, and in their power to keep it up.

Many a time and oft have I seen my fellow-countrymen taken in by their consummate acting and patience in order to gain their ends, and have likewise been duped myself. They are great readers of character, and find out your strong or weak points very quickly. They are past masters in the art of flattery. I have seen many Europeans fall before it, and through flattering become the personal confidants of their masters, to the detriment of any honest men in their department. In all my time in Kashmir nothing has distressed me more than to see my fellow-countrymen done down by these clever flatterers, for over and over again have I seen in consequence of it the honest men go under and the scoundrels flourishing. I can say further that I have seen honest men utterly beggared, and I know of several scoundrels now rejoicing in their riches who ought to be in gaol.

Brahmans & Sadhus

Many years ago at a ruridecanal meeting in London we were discussing how best to deal with that class of sharper who trades on religion in order to procure charity out of the tender-hearted, and giving our experiences how we ourselves had been taken in by them. When a certain padre stood up and told the house that as for himself he had always proved to be a match for them and had never been taken in, this statement was received with a roar of laughter, as this particular man was known to be an easy prey to the cadger, simply because he thought himself infallible. I fear we only hurt the feelings of this padre and were unable to shake the faith that was in him. It is a misfortune for anyone in England to believe himself to be a cadger-proof, but it is absolutely disastrous for those in authority in India to consider themselves proof against flatterers and intriguers, for it leads to so much unnecessary suffering and injustice.

I will give an instance of a simple case when I was not taken in.

A Brahman holy man, generally known as a Sadhu, visited me one morning, saying that he was interested in Christianity, and that he had heard what a wonderfully godly man I was, etc., etc., and would I give him a Holy Bible so that he might study it himself, and also asked me to appoint a time when he might come and study it with me. He was a curious object to look at: he was tall and thin, with long, tapering fingers, and long nails; the hair on his face, which was red, stuck out at a right angle, which gave the impression that one was looking at the sun in all its glory with red rays shooting forth, or it might be a halo around this saint's head. I did not rise to the Sadhu's pious request, as I felt that he had something much nearer his heart than the Bible. He seeing that I was not in a suitable religious mood asked leave to

Photo by] [*Vishu Nath.*

A BRAHMAN WOMAN.

Kashmir women do not have a working dress. This one has been squatting on a filthy bank cleaning her greasy pots with mud whilst wearing all her gold and silver and precious stones. She has no trinket box at home nor any place to store anything, so besides wearing all her clothes and valuables she has both pockets full, and tucked into her sash a handkerchief, knife, comb and snuff-box, and in the fold of her sleeve snuff and sugar in screws of paper, a needle and cotton and various other things.

go. He came again some days after, and finding me in a mood that he thought more in tune with the thoughts in his own heart, after a short preface of flattery he came wonderfully quickly to the point, which was this: Would I grant his son a scholarship if he sent him to the Mission School? I asked him why he thought that I should give his son a scholarship.

"Because," said he, "I am a holy man, and worship God all day long under a chenar-tree, and therefore cannot support my family."

"But," I said, "surely if you are a holy man and worship God your first duty would be to take care of your wife and family."

"No," said he; "for I have renounced them all, and spend my days sitting under a chenar-tree thinking of God."

I answered that I could be no party to such a life, for a husband's and father's first duty must be to his wife and family. But he failed to see my point of view and pressed for the scholarship. So, to cut the story short, we came to a practical agreement. I promised to give his son a scholarship if he on his part would give up wasting his whole day sitting under a tree and would instead get to work and earn a livelihood for himself and family.

He would not close with this offer, so we parted. About a year after this interview a tall, thin gentleman with a clean-shaven face, dressed in the ordinary babu's dress, with his shirt outside his trousers, and I think he had patent-leather shoes with laces untied, came up to me with a broad grin and held out his hand for me to shake. I racked my brain to think who my visitor could possibly be; that he knew me was evident from his broad grin; but it was not until I had grasped that tapering, muscleless hand that I tumbled to it. It was my scholarship-wanting friend, the holy Sadhu, but the red halo had departed. He was but a common or garden clerk in State service who stood before me. He had fulfilled his part of the bargain: he had given up a Sadhu's life for pen-driving and was receiving a monthly salary whereby he could support his family. So the bargain was clenched. His son came to school as a scholar and proved himself to be an exceptionally intelligent youth; from school he passed on to the college, and now is in the police and supports his mother, as my friend the Sadhu has passed to the greater life, into the Beyond.

Talking of Sadhus, every summer about the month of July the Sadhus swarm in from India, and pass through Srinagar on their way to the sacred cave of Amar Nath, the Lord of Life, which is situated in a mountain about six marches from Srinagar at a height of 13,000 feet. They arrive in their hundreds, a noisy lot of yellow-and-orange-robed or naked fellows, smeared with ashes. In the city one sees them marching in parties of ten or more, blowing their conch shells and waving bright red iron tridents, and holding out their brass bowls for alms. Crowding into the country as they do, they sometimes bring cholera with them and start an epidemic causing thousands of deaths. On one occasion when they had brought in cholera Dr Neve spoke to one on this subject, and he answered: "All men have to die some time or other. I die, you die, we all die, so what does it matter?" I have watched them often in cholera epidemics, when everyone is scared, and is in need of cheering and comforting. These naked, holy fellows march in parties of a dozen or so, in single file, shouting, stamping their feet in time as they go from house to house, collecting alms, telling the women that they will die if they do not pay up properly. Their appearance is enough to frighten the women, for they have long matted hair, and their faces and bodies are smeared with ashes, and very often they are drunk with bang or opium. The Hindus give them great reverence, for they are afraid of their curses. It is not only the ignorant people, but the educated Hindus also, who give the Sadhus great reverence. Much money is spent by rajas and others on them. An Indian gentleman speaking at a meeting for the C.O.S. said that £13,000,000 is spent on them annually.

I was returning one night from a Hindu reform club meeting with an educated Hindu who had been delivering himself of his ideas on temperance, and he asked me if I knew a certain holy man named Ram Chand. He was somewhat shocked at my ignorance when I said that I had never heard of his holiness, "For," said he, "this man is a very holy man, and I always go to him for advice." I asked him in what ways Ram Chand showed his holiness; did he help the poor or relieve widows in their distress? "Oh no," he said, "he does not *do* anything, for he is a very holy man." Again I asked: "How do you know that he is such a holy man?" "Why," said he, "he can hold his breath for three minutes." My companion then looked at me hard to see how I took this astounding news, this marvellous proof of holiness. I fear I am very mundane, so I could not work up any enthusiasm over it. Now it might have been different if he had told me that his holy man could swim under water for three minutes and make some use of his power of not breathing by saving the life of drowning persons, but I suppose if he did that no one would go to him for advice, and no rupees would come his way.

I fear the Sadhus that I have seen have not impressed me with the idea of holiness; no, not even when I have seen them lying on their beds of spikes, or those who have kept their fists closed and allowed their finger-nails to grow through their hands, or any of their many self-inflicted tortures. There is no doubt that there are some really holy men amongst them, but they are crowded out by the baser sort. I should like to mention one who showed himself to be an honest man and a sportsman.

A certain yellow-robed and much-travelled Sadhu visited Kashmir with his cheelas. He had travelled in Europe and America, and was highly educated. At the time of his visit a certain section of the Brahman community were very anxious to obtain his aid in establishing a Brahman school, so they asked him to attend a public meeting at their big temple so that he might add his weight to the scheme. During the proceedings the President made some false statements concerning the Mission School, which the Sadhu accepted as true, and therefore spoke against the Mission School.

Our headmaster having heard this went to see him, and invited him to the Mission School in order that he might see for himself. He accepted the invitation and brought with him one of his cheelas who had been a student in the Mission School. He became greatly interested in all he saw and heard, with the result that he called a meeting of the Brahmans in the temple and delivered a lecture on the methods of the teaching given in the Mission School, backing it up by giving his experiences of the schools in the West. He then advised all parents to send their boys to the Mission School instead of establishing a Brahman school, and finally called upon the President to withdraw his words uttered at the last public meeting and to apologise.

I give the case of a Sadhu acting in a gallant manner. It was told to me first-hand by an old lady. It happened at the commencement of the Indian Mutiny in May 1857. She was then a girl of seventeen, and was with a party of eight others who had managed to escape out of Delhi and were trying to reach Meerut. They had been in hiding all day and were commencing their march about sundown, and in keeping away from the main roads they came upon a Sadhu in the jungle. This man, seeing their distress, for they had been on the tramp for seven days, took pity on them and refreshed them with what food he had. They had not been with him long when a party of the mutineers' cavalry discovered them, rode up and commanded the Sadhu to give up his visitors, which he refused to do, so the mutineers said that they would take them without his leave. The Sadhu had put his visitors in his hut and sanctuary, and dared the soldiers to enter under the penalty of dire punishment which would follow his curses. The mutineers feared to disobey the Sadhu, so the party of British fugitives were saved. The old lady told me that in gratitude to that gallant Sadhu she always had a warm corner in her heart for this class of holy men, and never refused alms to those who asked help from her.

Most of the Sadhus that we see in Kashmir are those who come from India in the summer-time, whereas the Kashmiri Sadhus generally sit under a tree, or some spot considered to be holy, and are visited by their devotees, to whom they give ghostly advice. Schoolboys visit them before going in for public examinations to seek their aid in passing. To some they promise success for so much money paid in advance; to others they promise success if they will walk round some sacred spot a certain number of times or visit the goddess of learning at her shrine, which is some ten miles from Srinagar. You can see quite a number of students turning their feet that way. As a matter of fact, it is really good advice, as the examinees read their books continually all day and through a great part of the night. In order to keep themselves awake they tie their top-knots to a nail in the wall, so that their nodding heads may be kept in order. So the advice to go on a twenty-mile walk is really excellent, though the Sadhus are not aware of their wisdom in that respect.

One boy was absolutely worn out before the examination, as the Sadhu had ordered him to walk round the Hari Parbat hill three times during the night. The journey in the day-time would not be of any benefit to him; it must be every night for seven nights in succession. He was in consequence ploughed and very miserable, for, as he said, he had paid the Sadhu many rupees, which the Sadhu would not return.

The faith that these people have in their holy men is astonishing, considering the number of times they are fooled and swindled by them. We will now leave the holy men sitting under trees and thinking of God and return for a last look at the people in the bazaars. Hitherto I have spoken chiefly of the men, because it is chiefly men that you meet in the bazaars. The upper-class women never leave their houses except after dark, with the exception of the few who for certain urgent reasons are obliged to leave their houses, when they will wear a "burka." It is a white cotton cape which reaches from the top of the head to the feet. There is a sort of trellis window, about four inches square, made of coloured cord, through which they see the world. Women whose business in the street prevents their covering themselves up in this way will, when you pass, cover their faces with the shawl that every woman has on her head, and will generally turn their faces to the wall.

They have been taught always to get out of the way to make room for men. It is of continual interest to me to read the character of the men in this matter. Few men will make way for a woman, but will always make room for the swaggering Brahmani bull and the cow, and more often than not for the pariah dog, for the former have horns and the latter sharp teeth. The man with the proud look and high stomach carries all before him, until he meets a man who has a higher stomach than his own or the Brahmani bull.

A friend of mine, a subaltern of small stature, was crossing one of the bridges, keeping the centre of the road. An Afghan who was of great stature was also crossing the bridge in the opposite direction; he also had chosen the centre of the road. Neither of them would give way to the other, so their bodies met. Before the subaltern could wink he found himself under the great arm of the Afghan, who continued his triumphant march down the centre of the bridge, carrying the subaltern's legs to the fore and head to the stern, until he reached the end of the bridge, and then deposited him right side up in the street. What did the subaltern do next? is the natural question. Well, he did the only thing to be done under the circumstance, considering their relative sizes and strength: he took it in good part, as if he had quite enjoyed his ride.

Srinagar is an interesting city from a human point of view. I enjoy the people and their humour, as I hate the filth and stench of their streets.

There is hope for improvement, as of late there have come into the municipality some keen and intelligent citizens who want to get a move on, and are backing up the President in his arduous duties in fighting prejudice, custom and dishonesty; but at present it is like driving a coach and four with brakes on all four wheels and only one of the four horses wishing to pull. This is better than it used to be, for then the driver himself did not wish the coach to move. So we live in hope.

CHAPTER XIII

HINDU CUSTOMS

A FEW weeks before delivery the woman with child is sent to the husband's house with a few pots full of curd, which is distributed among the husband's relatives. The woman is given new clothes by her father on this occasion.

On the sixth day after delivery the patient has a warm bath, the water being mixed with certain drugs having medicinal quality, and her mother's relatives pay her visits.

During the first eleven days the visitors are not allowed to eat or drink in the house, with the exception of the very near relatives, as the house is considered infectious and unclean. On the eleventh day the patient puts on new clothes, made for her by her husband. The new-born babe is given its name and a ceremony is performed. The priest brings his horoscope and receives a good tip if it is a male child. The horoscope is a scroll of paper showing the planets that are favourable or unfavourable to the baby.

The oldest woman of the household procures a few pieces of birch bark. She rolls them up and then assembles the family members together. The pieces are then burnt, and the burning pieces are revolved several times round the head of each member in turn, while the old lady keeps on reciting the verse: "This is a good omen, may it recur."

For the shaving of the head of the child no definite

time is fixed. The relatives are invited to a feast. The family priest also receives his dues. New clothes are made for the mother, the child and the nearest relatives. Even the barber receives his share.

The Thread Ceremony.—Some days, not exceeding two weeks, before the day fixed for the ceremony the whole house is cleaned and white-washed. It is called Gher-Navii. After this ceremony the women go round to invite their relatives and receive money as a good omen. They hold regular nightly concerts, sometimes lasting for the whole night.

Henna Ceremony.—This takes place two days before the thread ceremony. On this day the hands of the boy and his women relatives are dyed red. The aunt receives a tip for performing the office.

One day before the chief ceremony of the Holy Thread the male relatives, neighbours and friends are invited; each man pays the host an eight-anna piece or a rupee as a good omen. On this occasion, generally, a lamb is sacrificed to the gods.

On this day women sing day and night without stopping. Generally they divide themselves into parties and sing by turns. They are given sumptuous feasts. The whole arrangement is in the hands of women. The aunt plays the most important part during the day. An altar is erected—the priests chant vedas, and incense is burnt regularly. At nightfall the boy is taken to the river bank to perform certain ceremonies. While he is away, his mother, aunt and other female relatives dance in a circle in the compound, for each revolution the female spectators have to pay one pice or more according to their financial condition. In this way the twice-born receives his second birth. This ceremony is usually performed before the eleventh year of the boy's age.

Marriages are arranged by middlemen, who are first-class liars. The house is white-washed, as in the case of the thread ceremony. This also is divided into three chief days—henna ceremony and devagun and the wedding ceremony. Women do the work, as in the former ceremony. The chief day is called lugan (marriage). The wedding procession goes to the bride's house. Again an altar is erected, and incense is kept burning. The priests chant vedas. The husband and the wife are made to swear to hold each other as one body and one soul. Through mantras their bodies and souls are united. They are never to separate, neither in this world nor in the next. The woman is called urdangi (half body—left side of the man). After the marriage is over the wedding-party is given a feast, vegetable food only being served; then they leave the house with the bride. When they reach the bridegroom's house the doors are closed against them by the bridegroom's sister, and are not opened until she is promised some present in cash or kind. In the evening both the bride and the bridegroom are summoned by the bride's father. The bridegroom is given some rupees, and then the married couple are sent back on the same night. The bride spends a few days, not exceeding a week, in her husband's house, and then returns to her father and spends some time there also. Every time the father wishes to see his daughter he has to pay some cash.

If both the bride and the bridegroom are of adult age they live as husband and wife, if not, the bride wears a gold-embroidered cap and sleeps in a separate room till they attain majority. On that occasion another ceremony is performed, without the priest. This is called "zuge," or marriage proper. On this occasion also the bride's father has to invite his son-in-law to his house and spend a good deal of money on feasts.

Till the death of the husband's parents the couple are not allowed to speak in public with each other, or at least till they have children.

The wife has to obey implicitly the behests of her mother-in-law or her sister-in-law, if the latter happens to be older than her husband. She has to rise early, and in case of poverty clean the house, fetch water, cook food and do sundry other things. Wives are, generally speaking, affectionate and devoted to their hnsbands.

Children are generally subservient to the will of their elders. But Western education has not left the child-world without the touch of its magic wand. They too want to be freer; and as most of their parents are ignorant it has been rendered difficult for them to control their children.

The ceremonies performed at the time of death of a Hindu are as follows:—The body is washed with warm water and wrapped in a piece of new cloth. A little ceremony is performed outside the house. The son or the brother or the nearest relative has to attend this ceremony. When it is over the body is placed on a plank and carried to the cremating ground. The men that accompany it continue chanting: "Sheo, Sheo Shamboo," etc. ("O God of Peace, forgive our sins"). After the body is removed the priest covers a small piece of ground inside the house with flour and places a basket over it with a lamp kept burning inside. He pretends to discover what body the soul has been changed into by reading the impression made on the flour. The body is then burnt in a peculiar way. The men come back, wash themselves in the river, burn a little fire on the river bank, turn round it seven times and then go to their houses. On the third day the son of the deceased visits the ashes of his father and brings a few bones, called "flowers," which are kept in the house till they are thrown into the Ganges, or a lake at Gangabal which is supposed to possess the same merit as the Ganges (Ganga = Ganges).

When the body of a deceased Hindu is carried to the cremating ground it is laid down in a corner, while certain elaborate ceremonies are performed, which may be very briefly stated here.

First three separate sites are selected, on which lamps called kulushas are placed. At this place eight Barous are invoked and propitiated through different mantras. These Barous are the attendants of the god Rudra, the master of death. Chit Shakti, the all-permeating vital force of the universe, forms the ninth Barou. Apart from this, two fires are burnt; the one is called "Vedic" and the other "Shavic Agni Sadhan." In these fires libations are offered to all gods and the Nirvana (absolute calm) of the deceased worked out.

Then a separate site is chosen at some distance from these fires. It is white-washed, and on it the plan of an altar is drawn. This place is enclosed with coloured threads fastened to pegs fixed in the four corners of the place. Within this enclosed area lamps are kept burning, and through the efficiency of the mantras the departed souls of the ancestors are invoked. Then a funeral pyre is constructed; the body is placed on it with its head towards the south, because it is believed that Petra-Loka, the abode of ancestors, lies in that direction.

The eldest son or the nearest relative sets fire to the pile of wood. It is believed that till then the ghost of the deceased hovers round his mortal remains and mourns for those whom he has left behind. To rouse dispassion in him, the son to whom he was greatly attached in this world is asked to set fire to his deceased father's body.

When the body is reduced to ashes the mourners leave the place and return home.

If the deceased be an old person, professional mourners, like those in Persia, are employed. The mourners are generally women. Early in the morning, while the male relatives (especially the eldest son) are engaged in performing religious ceremonies, all the female relatives assemble in a room and, headed by the professional mourner, sing funereal songs. This is continued for the first ten days, and is called "Van."

For the next ten days, if the deceased be an old person, ceremonies are performed on the river bank, water is sprinkled and balls of rice offered. In the evening the priest reads a portion of a book containing a description of purgatory, heaven and hell and the state of the departed souls in the next world before their reincarnation. On the tenth day the sons have to shave their beards.

On the eleventh day, through the efficacy of the mantras, the soul of the deceased is translated to the world of ancestors—until then it is supposed to wander about.

On the twelvth day a special ceremony is performed to satisfy the cravings of the spirit thus departed for its earthly attachments.

On the thirteenth day mourners shave themselves and put on new, or at least clean, clothes. During the mourning days—*i.e.* the first twelve days—no one who is not a near relative can eat or drink in the house of the mourner, for it is thought to be infectious (honch).

After this, fortnightly, then monthly, and, after the first year, yearly ceremonies are performed. On these occasions the presence of the son, the performer of the sharada, is essential, water is sprinkled in a peculiar way in the name of the deceased, and balls of rice offered, and a small fire is kindled in the middle of the house.

There are two distinct theories held about transmigration:

1. It is believed that the soul is given another body, human, animal or vegetable, the moment it leaves the previous body. This is controlled by the *law of Karma*—*i.e.* according as the actions of the deceased during life have been good or evil.

2. The soul is translated to the world of spirits for purification. There it is given an astral body and allowed to stay for some time, and then it is allowed to soar to higher and finer spheres, according to its moral worth.

Peculiar Customs.—If anyone leaves his house first thing in the morning and an old, ugly woman, or a one-eyed person, or a dog or donkey happen to come from the opposite direction, the unfortunate person will have either to retrace his steps or pass the time in great anxiety, fearing some misfortune. Educated men pay no attention to this nonsense, or pretend that they do not.

Pund or Sneeze.—Superstitious persons will never begin to do anything if someone sneezes. Rogues sometimes sneeze on purpose, in order to annoy others. They quietly put a straw into their noses and sneeze.

Crows, owls and kites are ominous birds, while bulbuls, swallows and hoopoes are considered fortunate. The bulbul is considered to be the messenger bird; its chirp is supposed to foretell some guest.

When a person falls seriously ill the patient's relatives take a vow to offer a sacrifice, and a fat lamb is brought before the priest, who lays the sins of the patient on it. It is then either killed or set free in some forest. The latter is very rare, though preferred to the former. This sacrifice is called "Raja Kat."

Small-pox is believed to be inflicted by a goddess called Shetala. When it occurs in its horrible form the mother takes a vow to present a she-goat or a she-ass to propitiate the goddess, but this belief is dying out among the educated classes, who now accept vaccination. The poor goddess is thus defeated and cast off.

The Hindus keep fast on the day that an eclipse is to take place. During the time of an eclipse they perform sharadas, and give away rice and money in charity. The women with child are not allowed to go out or do any work. It is supposed that if they do any work during that time the child in the womb will bear those marks on its body. The men generally spend that time in worship if they are free. No food that is cooked before the eclipse is used afterwards, because it is believed that unwholesome atoms emanate from the discs of the sun and the moon at the time of an eclipse.

Two different theories are held regarding the eclipse:

1. That Rahu, or Kitu, two celestial giants (stars), endeavour to eat up the sun or the moon that is eclipsed.

2. It is a mere shadow (Chahya mater).

The second belief is held by the Sanskrit-knowing persons; the first by those who believe in tradition or folklore only.

In the centre of the Tehsil of Nagam (old Nagrama) there lies an alluvial plateau known as Damudhar Udar, where an ancient popular tradition surviving to the present day has preserved the legend of King Damudhar. The King built a town on the Udar. In order to bring water to it he had a great dam, called Guddasten, constructed by supernatural agency. One day when the King was going to bathe he was met by some hungry Brahmans who asked him for food. The King refused

Photo by] [*Vishu Nath.*

Photo by] [*R. E. Shorter.*

A Brahman Marriage.

The bridegroom, aged 14, stands in the centre, priests are sitting in front. Pictures of various gods and goddesses lie on the ground.

Women at the Mill and Spinning Wheel.

Photo by] ONE OF THE THREE GLACIERS AT SONA MARG. [*R. E. Shorter.*

Sona Marg, "The meadow of gold" once the hill station of Srinagar is 10,000 feet above sea level, surrounded by peaks, of 18,000 feet.

to comply with their request until he had taken his bath. The Brahmans, therefore, cursed him so that he became a snake. Ever since the unfortunate King is seen by the people in the form of a snake rushing about in search of water far and wide. He is not to be delivered from the curse until he hears the whole Ramayana recited to him in a single day. As this cannot be done, it renders his release hopeless. It is said that several Brahmans have attempted to help the King in this way, but their exertions have always failed. The main features of this legend are well known throughout Kashmir. The inhabitants of the neighbouring villages point to a spot on the Udar, known as Satras Teng, as the site of Damudhar's palace.

Mohammedan Customs.—Marriages are generally arranged by a middleman, who appoints a day for nishani (engagement). On this day henna and some gold and silver ornaments are sent to the bride through the middleman. The bride's father gives a feast to the bridegroom's father and his party. On this day nikah, or the marriage contract, is drawn up and the mahra is fixed. The deed cannot be drawn up without the consent of both the bride and the bridegroom. They are therefore generally represented by some of their near relatives. The bridegroom's father has to pay the Qazi (ecclesiastical scribe), the mosque, the police, and various other people. On the following day the bride's father sends loaves and dressed meat to the bridegroom's father as a recompense for the trouble in paying him a visit. Some time after this engagement the marriage takes place. It lasts for three days in case of the son, and for two days in case of the daughter. Henna bandi is the first day. Feasts are given by both the parties to their friends and relatives. Henna and ornaments are sent to the bride. On that occasion all the women that have been called to the feast stain their hands and feet with henna. Merry concerts are held by women day and night. Next comes the wedding (enivoal). A feast is given to the bridegroom and his party by the bride's father. The marriage procession starts in the evening towards the bride's house; the procession is accompanied by torch-bearers, the torches being of several kinds. The low-class people and the boatmen march in a procession through almost all the streets and the chief markets of the city during the day. They are accompanied by a Kashmiri band, the loud noise of which seems to proclaim that the son of a grandee is to be married.

In the house of the bride a special hall is put in order. It is tastefully carpeted and dotted about with cushions. For the bridegroom a masnand, or elevated seat, is arranged. The priest who is to tie the nuptial knot takes his seat in front of the bridegroom. The Qazi indites the marriage contract and settles the mahra (jointure) upon the girl. After this a sort of nuptial prayer is offered. This prayer contains praises of Allah and Mohammed. The Qazi subsequently addresses himself to the representatives of the bride and the bridegroom, and asks them whether they have accepted each other as husband and wife. On this occasion the bridegroom is presented with a gift of clothes by the bride's father. Then handfuls of sugar are either distributed or thrown on the floor, to be picked up by the men present.

On this point the Mohammedan community in Kashmir are divided. Some say that this sugar ought to be divided, while others hold that it ought to be scattered. This divergence of opinion has lately caused a great schism among the Kashmiri Mohammedans.

The bride stays in the house of the bridegroom for seven days. During this time the bride's father has to send various dishes and suits of clothes to the bridegroom's father. On the third day of the marriage dry tea, sugar and cakes are sent to the bridegroom. These are distributed amongst the bridegroom's friends and relatives. Dressed meat and cakes are again sent to him on the fifth day. These are also similarly dealt with. On the seventh day a large quantity of dressed meat and specially prepared sweet cakes are sent to the bridegroom's father. Various garments are sent to him for the use of the bride. Besides this a number of fowls proportionate to the number of the sisters of the bridegroom is sent to his house. This is very important, and upon this depends chiefly the future happiness of the girl. In default of the performance of this function, the poor girl is given a bad time, and is looked down upon as a shrew and called by various ugly names. The bridegroom also receives a bakshish, generally in the shape of a fine shawl.

When a person is near the point of death his relatives and all those who are present begin to recite the Kalima, and if possible the dying man too is made to recite the same. Immediately after the person's death his eyes and mouth are closed. His relatives fetch a big plank from the nearest mosque and place the body on it, with the face turned towards the sky. The body is then washed with warm water. A hole is dug inside the house, so that the water with which the body is washed may not run in all directions, but collect in the same hole. The body is washed by a *professional* washer called Ghusal. Meanwhile the shroud is made ready. It consists of three things—the *Lafafa*, the *Azar* and the *Kamiz*. The first two are merely two sheets of cloth, while the third is a long shirt with a rent in the middle. The body is wrapped in these things. Then scents are sprinkled over the body, and it is placed in a coffin brought from the mosque. Another piece of cloth is spread over the coffin, and it is surmounted with a curtain taken from some ziarat. The bier is then carried on the shoulders, and those who accompany it keep on reciting the Kalima. The bier is then laid in front of some ziarat, with the head of the deceased turned towards the north, and the people perform ablutions and offer a prayer which consists of four parts. The first part contains a reference to the holiness of God; the Glorification and praise of His attributes; the second part contains the benediction on the Prophet; the third part is an appeal for the forgiveness of the sins of the deceased; and the fourth is a salutation to all present. This prayer is concluded by the Tabkir (Alluha-Akbar). The corpse is then taken to the graveyard and placed close to the grave. The topmost sheet is then removed, which is given to the sexton. The corpse is lowered into the grave with its head turned towards the Kaaba. The grave is then filled up and the coffin returned to the mosque.

Up to the first Friday after the burial the relatives and friends of the deceased go to the graveyard early in the morning every day and recite a few verses of the Quran. They then wend their way to the house of the departed person and are served with light refreshments, in the shape of tea and cakes. The priest plays an important part in this business, and receives a handsome remuneration. The sexton gets a meal a day, and gets some oil on the following Friday. All the relatives and friends again visit the tomb of the deceased, while to the son or the daughter are presented gifts of muslin and cash by their relatives.

The Mohammedans believe that after the dead body has been deposited in the grave two angels, called Nakir and Munkar, come to him and ask him the following questions:—

1. Who is your God?
2. Who is your Prophet?
3. What is your Creed?

If he replies to these questions satisfactorily, and says—

1. Allah is my God.
2. Mohammed is my Prophet.
3. Islam is my Creed.

—he is shown divine mercy and is translated to heaven; but if his answers are unsatisfactory the wrath of God descends upon him and he experiences the torture of hell and eternal perdition.

The Mohammedans also believe that there is on the top of hell a path called Surat. It is narrower than the breadth of a hair and sharper than the edge of a sword. Everyone will have to cross it. The virtuous will cross it with great ease, but the sinners will be hurled into the fires of hell.

When a man wishes to get rid of his enemy he goes to certain Brahman priests, practitioners of the "black art," who expect to be paid heavily for their work.

They make a figure of clay or wax which represents the victim. This figure they pierce with a sword or nails in that part of the body where the client wishes his enemy to receive the mortal wound. This art is done in private with incantations, and afterwards the figure is burned.

The Rev. T. R. Wade in his diary speaks of this ceremony having been performed by certain people in Kashmir who wished to rid themselves of himself, the Rev. Robert Clark and of the British Resident. Three fires were made for the Resident, two for Mr Clark and one for himself. Notwithstanding, all three survived for many years, and both Mr Wade and Mr Clark lived to a good old age. Evidently something went wrong with the incantations.

On the other hand, I happen to know of a rich and powerful man in the country who wished to bring about the death of a more powerful and richer man by this means, and certainly this more powerful man did die with a pain in his stomach not long after, so I expect the Brahman priests congratulated themselves on their success, or, at any rate, in having raked in a good haul of rupees.

I also happen to know of a somewhat similar instance.

A certain great man wished that his son might possess a certain great inheritance, but someone else's son stood in his way, so he approached certain priests for help. They told him that he must bring a certain goddess to his country and place her in his temple, whom he must worship assiduously, large gifts of money, of course, forming the bulk of the worship; but this worship would not be of any avail unless he procured the shirt, clippings of hair and of toe and finger nails of the young man who stood in the way and placed them on the goddess.

If he fulfilled all those conditions this young man would most certainly die in the month of November, three months hence.

This great man fulfilled all the conditions. The goddess was brought to his temple and worshipped correctly. She wore the shirt, hair, and finger and toe nails' clippings, and much money no doubt changed hands.

The fatal month arrived, and the angel of death also arrived, but he carried off the worshipper and not the would-be victim, who still lives, I am glad to say. I wonder how the priests explained the mistake made by the Angel of Death on this occasion.

Hindu Customs

The people of Kashmir are very superstitious, and give themselves much searching of heart and trouble in consequence.

At this moment as I write the citizens of Srinagar are in terrible distress owing, as they say, to the visit of a frightful creature which no one has seen. It is supposed to have been seen by many people, though no one will own to having actually seen it, but everyone tells everybody else that it has attacked women and children, tearing their faces and their breasts. It visits the houses at night. Some say it comes out of the river, and others that it is like a great cat. Consequently everyone shuts tight their shutters on these hot, oppressive nights, and beats tins and tom-toms to frighten the terrible monster away. Hence there is not much chance of sleep for those who believe in the monster or who make the noise, nor for those who do not, and have to endure the continual din.

Some years ago a terrible beast was supposed to inhabit the river one summer. The schools were closed for the summer vacation, and when we returned to Srinagar we found that no one had bathed in the river for a month from fear of this beast, so I asked the boys if they would like to kill it. They answered in the affirmative, so I called upon them to meet me at the Amira Kadal bridge (the first bridge) at three o'clock to swim right through the city, a distance of three miles, to the seventh bridge, Saffa Kadal, so that this terrible beast might burst itself with swallowing so many boys, and thus they would save their city.

At three P.M. punctually 130 boys leaped into the river. The bridges and banks and roofs of the houses were crowded with people to see what would happen.

Of course nothing did happen, and next day the

city was washing itself once more, for the bogey was slain. Some of the people say that this one is the son of the last one, and look to the schoolboys to settle this one when the holidays are over and they return to Srinagar.

CHAPTER XIV

BOAT-BUILDING

THE Kashmiris have their own special way of building boats, and very clever they are at their art. I have always been interested in boats and boat-building, but I had never come across boats built as in Kashmir. I have been told that the Kashmiri boatmen date their knowledge from the days of Noah, and when one looks at their big rice boats, which are uncommonly like the Noah's Ark of one's childhood, one always expects to see Noah coming out of the door of the cabin in the stern, especially when it happens to be at the time of the floods, when all the Kashmir valley is under water.

When I first came to Kashmir the saw was practically unknown, so all the work had to be done with axes and adzes. The boatmen would go off to the deodar forests and select a large tree, say 100 feet high and from 3 to 4 feet in diameter.

When felled they would split it in half lengthways, and out of these two halves would make two planks only, by axing off all the wood on the outside until these planks were of the requisite thickness, say three or four inches thick, according to the style and size of the boat that they were intending to build. This wicked waste of valuable cedar wood was most lamentable, but having no saws, this was their only way of securing their planks.

They would then bore a hole at each end of their planks, into which they would insert short ropes, made of hazel-nut branches, for hauling purposes. These planks might have to be hauled for several miles to the river.

The planks used to be left in the river or lake for two or three years to season. These two long planks were to form the sides of the boat, and as they would be about seventy feet long, they would be almost sufficient for the purpose. Another three or four trees might be needed for flooring and finishing off the boat.

It was, of course, a great score for the owners of the boat to possess hewn planks rather than sawn timber, for they would last nearly twice as long. In fact, the hulls of boats built of hewn timber are said to be good for forty years, and they are never painted or tarred.

In these days, with wood at the price it is, boats are being made of sawn timber, and therefore will last only half the time of the old boats made of hewn planks.

The builder, having hauled his planks up the river, selects a flat piece of ground on which to build, and from which he can launch his boat without danger of strain to the hull. These boats are made without keel, without bow or stern post, without ribs. In fact they are built like a box or coffin; some stays which do service for ribs are put in as a sort of afterthought.

Barges called bahhachas and kutchus are built on a different plan from doongas, the ordinary dwelling-boats, and shikaras, which are small pleasure boats, or fishing boats. The floor of the barges is made in three pieces, while the flooring of doongas and shikaras is in onc piece only.

Let us take the barge (bahaz). A flat piece of ground

having been selected, four or five logs are placed in a row to form a foundation for the planks which are to be joined together. The planks are now laid on to these beams, one plank being joined to the other by iron staples and nails.

The staples are from three to four inches wide, to allow of a good grip. These are hammered in almost red-hot, and immediately water is poured on them to prevent them burning the wood; when they cool and contract they possess a great clinching power. These staples are placed twelve inches or so apart along the seam. Then in the space between the staples holes are bored to receive a strong curved iron nail. This is inserted about one inch and a half from the side of one plank, and when driven home slanting into the plank protrudes about the same distance into the other plank. This nail is also driven home red-hot and cold water immediately poured on to it. This nail, being curved, has, like the staple, a powerful grip.

While the centre flooring is being put together other men are working at the two smaller pieces of flooring which are to be fixed on at both ends of the centre piece to make the bow and stern. When all the flooring is ready, then the great planks for the sides, called kinaras, are brought. They have already been cut to shape—*i.e.* from three to four feet wide—until they approach the bow and stern, when they are cut from the under side until they are one foot in width in the stern and half-a-foot in the bows.

These kinaras are now placed in position at each side of the platform, and clamped to the flooring in the same way as the planks have been joined together, with staple and bent nail. The flooring of the bow and the stern has to be raised to meet the kinaras, thus making a gradual sheer from the deepest part of the hull to the shallowest in the bow and stern.

Now in order to make this great box (for that is what it really is) rigid four or more stays are placed in position, two in the centre of the boat about three feet apart, and one at the place where the bow and stern pieces join the centre flooring. These stays consist of two strong beams, one placed along the flooring of the boat from side to side, the other parallel with it, attached to the top edge of the sides; then these two stays are joined up to each other by three uprights, two being at the sides of the boat and the third in the centre.

Now caulkers are put on to work, and they caulk all the seams with tow, and very clever they are at their job. The boat is now ready for launching. Beams are put in position from the logs on which the boat was built, to the water, and then the boat is hauled down sideways into the river.

When she is afloat the cabin is built on to the stern part, and a thatched roof is added to about three-quarters of the length of the boat, the forepart being left open to permit of the punters doing their work. And there is a craft which has a life of forty years.

When it becomes rotten, and too bad for patching, it is pulled to pieces and a smaller boat made of the good planks, and when that boat in its turn becomes unseaworthy it also is pulled to pieces, and a still smaller boat made of the remains, until finally it becomes firewood, and probably helps to heat the nails for the making of a brand-new craft.

I have during my time in Kashmir superintended the building of some fifty boats of different sorts, from a shikara to a house-boat, and from a coracle to a twelve-oared man-of-war cutter.

Boat-Building

On arrival in Kashmir in 1891 I found that the European community had a boat club. Colonel Sartorius, V.C., who was secretary, was leaving Kashmir, so I was asked to take his place and build some more rowing-boats. Although I knew very little about building boats, I thought I might at any rate learn, so with the help of some friends who did know how to build boats I superintended the work of carpenters who built them. I remember that I turned out a pair-oared skiff at the great price of five pounds, and that the paint for it cost more than the cedar wood of which it was made.

I also remember that I had some rather peculiar difficulties in getting the work done. On a certain day no carpenters turned up to work, nor for the next few days either. Later on I ascertained that the police were out seizing carpenters to go to the Gilgit road to work on a bridge under construction. No carpenter would go willingly, as the Gilgit road had its terrors, for so many Kashmiris who went never returned to their homes again. The police came to the house of my head man to seize him, but he managed to escape, and hid in one of the boats in the Dal Lake. Then the police seized his wife as a hostage, so he, being a gallant husband, went to the rescue of his wife, when he was caught; but after a few days he returned to my work with the help of the usual palm oil. Also he was a very old man, and could hardly have made the journey. However, I lost my second carpenter, for he was caught and driven off to the Gilgit road.

Notwithstanding this and various interruptions we got through with our work, and launched three pair-oared skiffs and a comfortable family boat generally known as a randan.

I was not satisfied with these boats, so when I went to

England on furlough I had a Thames pair-oared skiff built at Oxford, with a rather higher bow and stern than the Thames boats, as I did not want it to ship seas when on the Kashmir lakes.

I brought this boat out with me in the hope that many Europeans would have boats built like it, and we should have a fleet of smart English boats on our Kashmir waters; but I was to suffer disappointment, for instead of anyone asking for my boat as a model from which their carpenters could build, they said: "What a delightful boat you have got, do lend it to me." In that skiff I brought a section of an eight-oared boat, as it was one of my dreams to see eight-oared racing boats swinging along on the beautiful Kashmir waters.

During my holidays in the pine forests I searched for a tree with a stem clear of branches for thirty feet from the ground, for a racing eight is sixty feet long, and I wanted to get planks clear of knots, so if I could obtain clean planks thirty feet long I should do very well. It was a very long search, but at last I found such a tree, and a giant of the forest it was. I obtained permission from the forest officer to buy it. Trees season better standing than when felled and left lying on the ground, so I ringed it, and left it standing for two years, and then during my next holiday in the forest I collected woodcutters and sent them with the woodman who had sought with me for this tree of thirty feet of clean wood, with orders to cut off the thirty-foot log, and of the rest to cut it up in lengths of twelve feet for making into oars. I meant to have followed up the woodcutters, but was detained for some time.

Imagine my feelings when I arrived at the fallen tree to find that they had cut up the whole tree in lengths of twelve feet. The woodman must have had a lapse of memory, or something of the kind, for we had tramped through the forest on so many occasions together in search of this particular tree; then he had ringed this tree, and watched it drying for more than a year, and now when the time had come to secure our thirty-foot planks for our sixty-foot racing craft he cuts it up in lengths of twelve feet for oars, which could be obtained almost from any tree. The woodman was fortunately a man of few words and did not wish to argue when I explained to him that he must atone for his grievous sin by finding me a suitable tree as soon as possible. He stared at me in a sort of dazed manner, then lifted his pagri and scratched his head, and said: "Follow me, Sahib." I followed him down the valley, and there he pointed out a tree that had been blown down, and lo! to my astonishment I found a tree, truly about half the girth of the other, but on one side of which for thirty feet there were no branches, therefore clear of knots, which would answer my purpose. So this was cut and made ready for sawyers. These men had to be brought from Srinagar, twenty miles away. At last the planks were sawn and stowed away under our hut to season for two years.

My summer holiday of five weeks arrived again, and I intended to commence right away with the building of the eight in the forest, but a friend of mine was building a large motor-boat on the river and had borrowed my head carpenter, and when the time came for him to join me in the forest my friend begged me to let him keep him for another week, as he could not finish his boat without his help, and then when that week was up he implored me to spare him for yet another week. I was weak enough to grant his request, so that left me only three weeks in which to build the boat.

We had had fine weather up till then. The weather then changed, and it rained for the next three weeks, and as the boat had to be built in the open, the work was carried out under the greatest difficulties. However, the boat was built, and with the help of sixteen men it was carried through the forest with difficulty and down to the river at Srinagar, twenty miles distant. Before long my dream was realised of seeing a racing eight swinging along on Kashmir waters.

Every boat has a character of its own, which has to be appreciated and honoured if you want to get the best out of it.

This particular boat had a greater desire than all the racing eights I had ever been in, and that was not a few, of turning the whole crew overboard. This special trait in its character was sometimes annoying, though at the same time decidedly humorous.

We were out practising on the lake and had taken aboard a passenger lady doctor. She sat in the coxswain's seat and I stood up behind to coach the crew. I was teaching them how to stop the boat suddenly in case of a collision. To accomplish this without upsetting the boat with a rough crew is not easy. I was aware of this, so I commenced gently, first by holding up the boat when there was a little way on and then increasing the speed until we could hold her up hard when going at top speed. We had accomplished holding her up satisfactorily at all the preliminary stages, and now had come the time for the final test. I warned the crew that they must be smart, and at the signal bury their oars in the water absolutely together, otherwise we should upset. They answered to my challenge that they understood and were ready. So at the words of command, "Get ready! Are your ready! Row! Row hard!" we were off, swishing through the water. I then called out: "Easy all!" followed at once by "Hold her up!" when all the oars are turned a little more than the feather so that the blades go under the water. Then followed: "Hold her up *hard*!" when all the eight oars should turn square at once and the boat be brought to a standstill. But all the blades did not grip the water together; stroke side did do so, but bow side failed, with the natural result, over went the eight. The expression on the faces of the men was so amusing that I could not help roaring with laughter, and with my mouth wide open I disappeared into the lake with the rest. This was most unfortunate, as water went down my wind-pipe, so that I was of little use when I came up to the surface of the water in trying to support the lady doctor, and also in giving the necessary orders. Three of the crew had lost their heads and were trying to keep themselves afloat by hanging on to the riggers, with the natural result that the eight kept on turning round and round. Whenever we managed to get our lady passenger on to the upturned boat it would immediately be turned round. However, after a short time we managed to keep the boat steady, so that our passenger could sit comfortably on the keel until a rescue boat put off from the shore and took her away to drier quarters.

We then turned our boat right side up, baled the water out with our hands as we swam alongside, and finally one by one crawled into our places, and I was able to give the orders, "Get ready! Are you ready? Paddle!" and so we brought ourselves and ship safe to land. Later on we went at our practice for holding up our eight, and I think succeeded in obtaining the result we desired; but we refrained from taking passengers aboard when at that particular practice in the art of "Holding up hard."

When building Kashmiri boats for the schools I built boats to hold a crew of fifteen, but like the ordinary shikaras and with Kashmiri-shaped paddles. But I had to change both the shape of the boats and also the paddles, as the boatmen would steal not only paddles but also the school boats, and it was almost impossible to recover them. We lost more than fifty paddles in the year, so we now build boats on our own pattern. It is a mongrel, between a Canadian canoe, Venetian gondola and Burmese canoe. Our paddles are something of the style of Canadian paddles, but shorter and of thicker build. It is no use for the boatmen to take them, for they could not use them without being caught. So for the present our property is safe.

One of the chief features of the river is the increasing number of house-boats, inhabited chiefly by Europeans.

As no European is allowed to possess land or build houses in Kashmir, with the exception of a certain number of huts at Gulmarg, and in Srinagar houses for officials, a certain number on rent, house-boats become the houses of those who wish to stay in the country. These boats are of all shapes and sizes, from the doonga house-boat to the large barges such as one sees on the Thames, some of them being really beautifully furnished floating houses.

Mr Kennard was the first Englishman to build a house-boat, and although he built it more than thirty years ago it is still going strong. He was fortunate in securing the best hewn planks from well-chosen deodar-trees. Many of the house-boats which are not nearly so old as Mr Kennard's have broken backs, from the fact that they were built by amateurs, who did not understand that it was necessary for their hulls to be built with a good sheer or curve.

It is far more difficult to build adroitly a good house-boat hull that will last than it is to build the hull of a Kashmiri rice barge, although it may be larger, for the simple reason that whereas the Kashmir barges possess their cross-beams or struts to keep the hulls rigid, the house-boats have to dispense with them, as they would get in the way of their owners passing from one room to another.

Also people will have their upper structures built right on to the ends of their hulls both fore and aft, even where the ends rise out of the water, and this extra weight, with no upward pressure of water to meet it, naturally makes the ends sag.

This sagging gives to the boats a broken back and drunken appearance, which is unpleasant to look at, besides causing the boat to be unseaworthy.

My wife and I lived in a house-boat as our first home, and very pleasant it was. We anchored in mid-stream in order to get all the fresh air we could, and also to be free from annoyance, as I was pestered by cadgers of various sorts.

I found great peace from the fact of having thirty or forty yards of deep water between me and the mainland. I arranged to have an English rowing-boat moored to the bank so that anyone who wanted to see me could propel himself to my boat. I also knew that most of the cadgers could not row, or would not like to be seen rowing, which was in those days considered to be a most low-caste proceeding. To explain how efficacious was my plan, the following instance will suffice. I was told by my servant that a certain Brahman wanted to see me, so I told him to tell him that the boat was at the bank and he was permitted to make use of it. He was not pleased with this answer, and asked my boatmen to come over and fetch him, but they were deaf to his entreaties.

So my would-be visitor was obliged to do what the common boatmen do and propel himself. He unmoored the boat and shoved off, and then sat on the seat and tried to manipulate the sculls, but not being a waterman he did not get on very fast, and also, not realising that the current of the river is usually stronger in the centre than it is under the bank, he, instead of making use of the slacker water, pulled out to the centre, and never reached my house-boat, for the stream swept him past. He made a great effort to get near, but the stream was too much for him and he was carried down the river. I heard him calling, but his voice gradually became fainter and fainter, till he and the boat became a mere speck in the distance, and my troublesome visitor was gone. Later on my boatmen went down the river and brought the boat back and moored it to the bank, ready for the next would-be visitor.

I may say that the visitor who failed to reach me on that occasion later on learnt to row and to make boats, and for many years I have always been glad to see him at my home when he feels inclined to call, but he is a very busy man, and one for whom I have great respect, for he is an honest, hard worker.

There is one great advantage a house-boat possesses over a house on land, and that is, you can move its situation whenever you please. There are few more pleasant experiences than being towed up the river in your house-boat. The motion is most restful, as there is no jarring or shaking. You just hear the sound of the water as it laps against the bows of your boat as you forge up-stream. When travelling from one place to another there is no packing up to be done. You simply give the word, and your house moves to the spot your heart desireth. In the winter it is warmer than a house, for the rooms are smaller and therefore can be more easily and cheaply kept warm. In the summer a house-boat can be uncomfortably hot, but you can generally find a tree under which to moor it. But there is a danger to be guarded against, for the river is apt to rise unexpectedly by the sudden melting of snow, and when the river happens to rise at night, and everyone is asleep, your boat may be pressed up against a branch and be upset or sunk. So one must always look out for the danger when choosing a shady tree.

On one occasion during a flood my house-boat was on the point of capsizing, owing to its having become jammed under a stout mulberry-tree branch, and a catastrophe was only just averted by the promptness of Ismalia, my boatman, who dashed up on to the roof with a saw and severed the branch. Had it happened in the night it would have certainly meant a cold bath, and probably an end to one's earthly existence.

CHAPTER XV

EXPEDITIONS

IT is not so easy for a Westerner really to understand the Eastern unless they can live together for a while, for as a rule their acquaintance is very superficial. Most of us know them as servants, a few more as clerks who are seen only during office hours. Again, still fewer are met through social intercourse, at public entertainments or calls at one's house, but very few Europeans have the *entrée* into the houses of the people of India. To know people properly one ought to know them in their houses, where one can see them as they really are.

As it was impossible for me in the early days to get into the houses of my staff and pupils, except as a visitor for a short time to drink a cup of tea or to visit them when ill, I proposed to them an expedition together to a hut in the forest twenty miles distant. We were to go a party of twenty, and I had nearly completed all arrangements when I was told it was impossible, that their parents objected, or rather the Brahman priests did, saying that it was not safe from a religious point of view, for they might go to the forest as Brahmans but they would return Christians. I suppose the priests thought that I should persuade them to eat my food and so break their caste. The Brahman's ideas of Christianity and mine were on a rather different plane.

So the first expedition was a "wash-out." This set-back naturally made me all the more keen to get the better of the Brahman priests in this matter, for I knew that it would be so good for the health of the masters and boys, morally as well as physically, to get away from their filthy city to the lakes and mountains, and breathe fresh air into their lungs and wholesome thoughts into their souls.

I thought for some time, and at last I dreamed of a man-o'-war's cutter with twelve oars and sails. If only I could build and float such a boat we would get the better of the priests.

In due time the various materials were collected for making our boat. We found the deodar log out of which to cut our planks about forty miles below Srinagar and had it brought to the school. We sent to Calcutta for the copper roves and rivets. We had to obtain leave from the State officials to cut the mulberry wood for the ribs, for no one is allowed to cut a mulberry-tree. Then when all was collected carpenters were called and the boat was built in the school compound.

The staff and the boys had for weeks been watching this boat in building and had became almost as keen as I myself to see it afloat, and to become members of the crew. We had arranged to row down to Manisbal Lake and encamp there during the ten days' holiday at Easter.

The day came, but the boat was not quite finished; notwithstanding, we launched her that day at eight o'clock in the evening in the dark, so anxious had everyone become to start in our new boat. If I remember rightly, there were twenty in all in the boat, but we soon had to shift all passengers on land, for the boat naturally leaked like a sieve, as the planks had not had time to swell.

However, we were out to enjoy ourselves, and a festive time we had of it. We had a journey of sixteen miles before us before we could reach our dinner and beds. So the twelve oarsmen pulled away and the balers worked away hard to keep the water down. At midnight we reached our camp on the river bank, and right glad we were of our food.

Next day we dropped down the river another four miles and then into the beautiful lake of Manisbal. We were fortunate to come in for a breeze, so up went the sail. It was amusing to see the faces of the crew and passengers as the boat heeled over and cut through the waves, their first experience of sailing, a mixture of pleasure, excitement and fear combined. Presently the breeze freshened up and we were soon in a sharp squall. Now all sign of pleasure disappeared from the faces, and when we shipped water they began to cry out to their gods, "Rama," "Shiva," etc., and some threw out rice into the lake to appease the angry gods. Some began to weep, as they thought their last hour had come. So as we were nearing the shore I called out, "All who are cowards and wish to go ashore, hold up hands," hoping by the word "coward" that they would not like to hold up their hands, but I was mistaken. The angle of the boat and the spray coming on board were too much for their nerves. So I ran ashore and deposited all but three brave fellows, who continued to face the elements with me, and when the squall had blown itself out we landed, and the brave trio stepped ashore as heroes.

The boat had behaved well, and, moreover, by the evening had stopped leaking, so that several of the crew were able to sleep with me on the bottom of the boat. We anchored the boat out in the lake and were lulled to sleep by the lapping of the waves on our prow. This was the first time that they had slept on the deep, and in this way step by step they began to get over their fear of the winds and the waves, and all the hosts of demons and gods which inhabit them.

Next day we had planned to climb the mountain which rises straight out of the lake. There was much heart-searching over this, as they told me how the gods inhabited the mountains, and they looked upon it as almost irreverent to try to enter their abode. I do not know what they dreamt of that night, for they were evidently nervous about the morrow. We were up before light, had taken our food and started off at four-thirty A.M. A coolie came with us to carry our food. We arrived at the top at eight-thirty. As we were nearing the summit I noticed that they were not anxious to go on, as they felt so sure they were nearing the abode of the gods. At the top was a rocky peak. When we reached this I announced that we had come to the top and were therefore in the land of the gods and suggested our catching them, for if the gods lived on the tops of the mountains, and as we had reached the top, therefore the gods must be there. So I divided the party into two companies, one would go to the right and the other to the left, and in that way we should be sure to catch the gods.

Both parties started off in great excitement, and with a certain amount of fear, but what they expected to find I did not know.

As my party were approaching the back of the rock they heard footsteps, which set their hearts beating with fear and excitement, and as they came round the corner on tiptoe they fell into the arms of the other party, who were doing likewise. Great was the relief when they discovered that the sounds they heard were not made by the gods but by ordinary humans, and they exclaimed that after all the tops of the mountains were just like the bottoms of the same, and that their fears were unfounded. They all shook hands and seemed to be very delighted with the discovery. But sad to say it was not the same with our food coolie; his heart had failed him before he reached the top, and we did not see him again till our arrival in camp in the evening, on the lake-side. I fear we did not think of our coolie for good during that hungry day. This first trip to the mountain-top gave our party such an appetite for more mountain and other trips that the Brahman priests never got the better of us again in this line.

On another occasion we set off to see two lakes, Tarsa and Marsa, at the watershed of the Laddah and Hariwan rivers, and a delightful climb it was. On our third day it poured in torrents, so much so that we could not strike camp till midday. We then sent our camp on down to the foot of the mountain, which we intended to reach in the evening, whilst we made tracks for the lakes. These we did not reach until about five P.M., so that by the time we had retraced our steps along the heights towards our road to camp, and were still on the top of the hills, darkness came on, and we lost our way; also a terrific thunderstorm burst upon us; in fact we seemed to be in the centre of the storm. We were, of course, drenched to the skin. It was pitch dark, and the path terribly slippery from the torrents of rain, so our progress was perforce very slow as we groped our way downwards. Every ten minutes I called a halt to call over the names to see that we were all safe, and so we spent the night groping and slipping down the mountain paths.

In the early morning we reached a village, and woke up some of the inhabitants to get their help to find our camp. They were able to direct us, and at six-thirty to our relief we found it, and glad we were for some food and rest. But we could not rest long, as school commenced next day: therefore we wanted to reach Srinagar that night. We had before us sixteen miles of road, and twenty-five miles to row, as we had had our boats sent up to meet us. In order to speed up our march we decided to race to the river, which we reached about four P.M.

The boat in which I was rowing reached Srinagar at midnight, but the twelve-oared cutter stuck on sand-banks and did not arrive until nine A.M. next morning. Notwithstanding that the masters had been on the march for two days and two nights without a proper rest, they were at their places in school at ten-thirty A.M. I was so pleased with their pluck and hard work that I had mercy on them, and gave the school a whole holiday, and, to tell the truth, was not at all averse to a holiday myself, as I just wanted to sleep.

There is a river which joins the Jhelum at Srinagar, called the Dudh Ganga, which means the milk Ganges, but is called nearer its source Sangi Safed, meaning the white stone; it rises in the Pir Punjal. The Brahmans told me that it springs out of a white stone and therefore is of a miraculous origin. I proposed therefore that we should follow it to its source, to see if it really came out of a white stone, and not out of a glacier, which I considered more likely. So we made up a party to follow up the Sangi Safed. We were glad to leave the heat of the valley in the month of July and refresh ourselves in the land of snow and ice.

These trips give one great opportunities of getting to know the inside thoughts of those amongst whom one's daily work is cast in Srinagar. For round the camp fire at night, and in the tents after dark, the men open out and are their true selves, and we then really get to know one another. Then in our climbs, we have to face difficulties and sometimes dangers, and, in the common sharing of these, lasting friendships are formed.

One thing especially cheered me in these trips, and that was the way in which the teachers and boys put up with discomforts, such as hunger, cold and fatiguing marching. These discomforts and others they invariably bore bravely, and generally saw the humour in it all, and laughed heartily over their troubles.

The first night we were encamped in the forest, and the second on a marg near the snows, and on the third day we had found the source of the Sangi Safed. It issued forth from a small glacier which was more brown than white, from the debris which it brought down with it from the heights above.

The party were very pleased to have found for themselves the source of their white stone and milk Ganges river, but expressed the belief that their priests would not believe them, if they did tell them that they had seen the river issue forth from a glacier, and that there was nothing miraculous in it.

We were now near a notable peak, about 16,000 feet high, called Tati Kuti, which we decided to try to climb; from where we were it looked quite possible. After some climbing we found ourselves on the knife edge of a great spur. It absolutely was a knife edge, which fact we who straddled it will not forget, for we could not walk on it. Our legs each side hung down a precipice. We divided ourselves into two parties of seven each, and roped. For quite a distance our only mode of progression was to straddle the knife edge, and lift ourselves along with our hands, as the knife edge was decidedly painful. Progression was very slow, for when we could use our feet we had to use our hands also, as it was not a walking road by any means. It was about three o'clock that we found ourselves facing a precipice of several hundred feet. There was a great fault on this spur, and even if we had had time to continue our climb we should have found it impossible to go farther by that road; so we were obliged to return defeated, and suffer discomfort again on the knife edge.

Since that climb of ours this peak has been explored and climbed, but not by the way we attempted to climb it.

On our return to Srinagar the Brahman members of our party told their priests that the Sangi Safed issued forth from a glacier and not from a white stone, as they had traced the river to its source: but their answer was that they evidently had not traced it to its source, for if they had they would have found the white stone from which it issued. So there the argument rested, both sides being satisfied that they were right.

These school trips are profitable in many ways, for besides the main objects, which are for health and refreshment to body and soul, and the opportunities we have for understanding and appreciating one another better, there is always much to learn. It is seldom that you find a Kashmiri who appreciates the glorious beauties of his country. He likes the flowers, for crowds of people walk in the orchards around the city in the springtime so that they may enjoy the blossoms, but the mountains, with their foliage, their margs, their ever-changing colours and the lights and shades, they never seem to notice. I was standing one beautiful spring morning on the river bank, drinking in the glorious view before me of the green valley, the pine forests creeping up the hill-sides, and then the snow-covered tops of the mountains just glistening with dazzling whiteness, when a Kashmiri who was passing, seeing that I seemed to be staring at some object said: "What is the Sahib looking at?" I said: "These glorious mountains." He answered: "But, Sahib, haven't they always been there?"

No, that is not good enough! We want to open their eyes to see the glorious country they live in, to be proud of it, try to live up to it, and help others to do the same. Then again there is the animal world which, except to the few shikaris and villagers in the mountains, is a closed book. I have never known a Kashmiri boy collect birds' eggs. They do not know or care anything about them. I held up a jackdaw's egg one day in school before more than one hundred and fifty boys and asked them to tell me what it was. They exclaimed that it was an egg, and I elicited the fact that it was not a common barn-door fowl's egg, but none of them could get any further than that, with the exception of a Mohammedan boy, who said that he knew that it was a jackdaw's egg, for he had found eggs like them in a jackdaw's nest. All the boys turned round and stared at the prodigy of learning. So on our trip we try to learn all we can of animals and birds.

Eagles are always entertaining, and one is never tired of watching their graceful movements. One may be on a height, and, looking down several thousand feet, see an eagle gradually ascending. He never seems to move his wings, except just to set them like a sail to the breezes that meet him as he tops a spur or swings round an angle of a mountain. Every circle brings him higher and higher until, in an incredibly short time, he is circling above one as many hundreds or thousands of feet as he was, a few minutes before, below one. The use that an eagle makes of the wind in order to rise, without apparently any effort on his part, always brings to my mind how the Spirit of the Living God can be the power to raise us from things of the earth to things spiritual. We, like the eagle, have to possess the wish to rise, and set our wills at that angle which will enable God's spirit to lift us. The power is there always. The eagles seem to spend the whole day in sailing about, for rarely does one see an eagle make a nose dive after its prey as one sees the hawks do continually. But I did see a great dive on one occasion. I was out with a friend on the Pir Punjal range; my friend was just nearing the top, which is over 15,000 feet, and was walking on an edge, a precipice on his left and a steep snow slope on his right, and I was about five hundred feet below him, and was watching him plodding slowly along, and an eagle circling several hundred feet above him, when suddenly I saw the eagle close his wings and come down like an arrow from the blue, straight for my friend. I shouted my loudest, but I was too far off. My friend, in ignorance, climbed on, in fact I think the eagle would have reached him before my voice. But just as I expected to see my friend bowled over the eagle opened his wings and sailed off majestically: he had evidently mistaken his white sun hat moving over the snow for some animal. It was well for my friend that the eagle discovered his mistake before striking.

In our expeditions it was always our object to turn our days to full use, making forced marches and breaking former records, with the idea of hardening ourselves and creating fresh records for the rising generations of schoolboys to break. You see, the boys' fathers had never set examples for their sons in this line, so we thought it about time that they should have some ideals to live up to, and surpass, and create new ones.

On one occasion a party of fourteen made an expedition to the beautiful lake of Konsar Nag, which lies at the foot of a glacier, 10,000 feet below the twin Brahman peaks on the Pir Punjal. The lake is two miles by three-quarters of a mile broad; it is a lovely emerald-green, and very deep, and generally has icebergs floating on it in the summer. It was a beautiful trip, through forests and over grassy margs, where we found not only the usual carpet of flowers, but mushrooms galore, far more than the whole party of fourteen could carry away. On that one day we walked forty-five miles, and no one was the worse for the forced march.

On another occasion the whole school fleet took part in a thirty-mile race, from Srinagar to Pampur and back. The crews towed their boats most of the way up, and paddled and rowed back, a hundred or so boys taking part in it. That record was beaten by a race of three rowing boats for two days and one night from Srinagar to Islamabad and back, a distance both ways of ninety-six miles. Whether the super-energy did us any good or not I do not know; anyway, we have created records for future generations to beat.

I will now close this chapter on expeditions with one of our annual Wular trips.

At Easter we had our usual ten days' holidays, and according to custom called for volunteers to join the Wular Lake camp, which meant a healthy life under canvas at this beautiful and much-dreaded lake, which is about fourteen miles long by seven broad. We rowed the thirty miles down from Srinagar in our twelve-oared cutter, six-oared galley, and Thames skiff, a party of twenty-eight. We hoped that Æolus would be kind to us, as he had been on other occasions, and squeeze his wind-bags so that we might have full use for our sails, and try the nerves of our new hands. Well, Æolus did us very well on the whole, but I will recount only one of our trips. Some huge dredgers were being built at Baramulla, some eighteen miles down the river, and that gave us an object for a long day's trip. We were off shortly after sunrise, rowing seven miles across the lake, then down the Jhelum, about ten miles, and reached Baramulla at midday. The engineers on the dredging works were most kind in helping us to see everything of interest. The Roman Catholic padre at Baramulla most kindly entertained the crews to a meal, and at three o'clock, when we cast off, was present on the bank with all his schoolboys to give us three cheers; we returned the compliment by giving them a salute of oars.

Towing and rowing up-stream was a very different matter from our row down in the morning, for thousands of sleepers had been released up-stream on their long journey to the railways in the Punjab, and we had a great time trying to dodge them, which required most careful steering, and we were delayed a great deal in consequence. Then, to make matters worse, a heavy thunderstorm blew up against us. These untoward circumstances delayed us so much that it was quite dark when we reached the lake, and the seven miles of the dreaded Wular lay between us and our camp.

Some of the crew were for putting off the crossing until the morning, as they had never heard of any boat crossing the lake at night, and especially during a thunderstorm, and certainly no boat had ever sailed across under these circumstances. (Kashmiris do not use sails and hate the wind.)

However, at the order "Sails up!" every man fell to work, and in a few minutes the cutter was heeling over to a stiff breeze which came in gusts, and heading for what we believed was our camp in the thick darkness ahead.

We were congratulating ourselves at starting that there were a few stars to be seen, and an occasional outline of a mountain, but before long all our steering points were gone, and the only time we saw the mountains was when the lightning took pity on us. To make matters worse the wind kept shifting—in fact, before we reached home the wind had blown from every quarter. Consequently we had to be continually shifting the crew from one gunwale to the other. We had fortunately fixed cross-trees on to the foremast close to the deck, on which we could place one, two or three men according to the strength of the wind; but this caused us a little anxiety, for had the stay broken the men would have dropped overboard, and to pick them up in the darkness would have been somewhat difficult. So one's eyes were continually upon those forms, which could just be discerned, squatting like monkeys on the spar.

Fortunately we could see occasionally fires on the shore, more or less in the direction we believed our camp to be, and with the help of these fires and continual soundings we managed a fairly straight course.

All the crews were thoroughly enjoying the excitement of this night voyage, with the exception of the Sanskrit teacher, a Brahman who had not been on the lake before. He was praying out aloud the whole journey, and making various vows to certain of his special gods and goddesses, and calling upon them at intervals, especially when the boat pitched more than usual, or a big wave hit us. From his many prayers I gathered this much: he promised to the deities four special treats: (1) He would devote one whole day's fast to a certain goddess (I forget the lady's name, I regret to say). (2) Another goddess (I grieve to say that her name too has slipped my memory) was to have flat unleavened bread (chupattis). (3) He promised to Ganesh, the elephant god, some special sweet cakes. (4) He would present Hanuman, the monkey god, with rice balls mixed with sugar. (Our

Brahman friend evidently knew how to get round Mr Hanuman.)

The rest of the crew, although they also were Brahmans, were much amused, and were inclined to fool him; but I told them to let him pray to his heart's content, so long as he prayed in the spot where his ballast was needed, and he was disturbed only when his body was needed on the opposite thwart.

The religious man was evidently a man of perception, for he had purchased in the town some "sugar-candy"; as he knew that the gods would never refuse candy, he had brought this as a last resource, so that when his prayers and vows should fail the candy would be the *pièce de résistance.*

We had begun to pitch and to heel over a little more than usual, and evidently he thought that his end was nigh, so out came the candy, and the gods were smacking their lips, when their treat was snatched away from them by one of the crew who also liked candy.

To me all this was very interesting, as I looked back to the days when we made our first trip across this lake in the same boat fifteen years ago, but in daylight. Then all the crew held the same views as this frightened Sanskrit teacher; they were crying at intervals the whole journey to their gods, Shiva and Rama, and heaving out sugar and rice into the lake. Some called aloud "Shiva, Shiva!" whilst others went on muttering under their breath these sacred names, and a few bent their heads whilst the tears trickled down their cheeks as they wept silently and thought of their dear ones at home! . . . "Oh, my poor mother!" Well, we reached our camp at last, to the astonishment of those in camp and the villagers, as they did not expect us to attempt the night sail in a thunderstorm. Our Sanskrit teacher was more delighted than any, and was ready to fulfil his vows; but thinking it a pity that his vows should be wasted, we suggested to him that he might do some good with them, and instead of throwing all these promised delicacies into the water, from which element the monkey god and others were expected to take them, it would be more to the point if he gave them to some poor women in his district; and, somewhat to our surprise and pleasure, he fell in with this suggestion: so someone profited by that night's sail across the dreaded Wular Lake.

CHAPTER XVI

A TRIP TO LADAKH

IT was in the summer of the year 1896 that I had the opportunity of accompanying Dr Ernest Neve on a trip to Ladakh, or Lesser Tibet. From Srinagar to Leh, the capital of that country, is a distance of 224 miles, and takes usually twelve days to march—*i.e.* about seventeen miles a day, which is as much as loaded coolies or ponies can be expected to accomplish, as some of the marches are over high passes. I was, however, not able to get away with Dr Neve, as my school duties kept me, but the Commissioner of Ladakh, Captain Cheveneux Trench, kindly asked me to join his party. He, however, was starting four days before I could get away, so I had to make forced marches to catch up his party. I did the first four and a half marches in about thirty hours, by leaving Srinagar at midnight by shikara. Ismalia and his crew paddled all night across the Unchar Lake, and up the Sindh river to Gunderbal, which was the first stage. When I opened my eyes at six-thirty A.M. next morning I saw my first mount looking at me, and telling me, as it seemed, to hurry up. After breaking my fast I mounted and was off. The mare was a beautiful beast lent to me by Miss Newmam, one of our missionary staff. It was a glorious day, and the pony seemed to be aware of the fact also, for she bounded forward like a deer, according to her usual custom.

Our path led us up the Sindh Valley with the rushing, roaring river on our right. It was early summer, so the wild roses were in full bloom, and flowers in all directions, such as anemones, balsams, columbines, larkspur and ragwort, were one burst of green.

We were going so fast that we came upon snakes in the path before they had time to get into hiding. At about midday I came upon my own pony and the deer's sais waiting for me under the shade of a great walnut-tree. I soon changed mounts, the sais took back his own property, and I sped away up the path, which had now become rocky, as the valley gradually narrowed in. At about five o'clock I found my own sais and a third pony waiting for me, which took me up to Sona Marg, about eight miles distant, and to my camp, which some days before had been sent on ahead. Sona Marg is a lovely stretch of grass and flowers, at a height of 10,000 feet, surrounded by peaks of 18,000 feet, and three glaciers at the head of their respective valleys can be seen looking down upon one from the east. Sona Marg means "the meadow of gold," and at one time was the hill station of Srinagar. The natives tell you that there are many snakes there. They hold the belief that those valleys into which the mountain Hari Mouk cannot look have an abundance of snakes.

Next day being Sunday I rested, intending to start after midnight, so my tent was packed up ready for the start. I tried to sleep in the verandah of the post office, but the fleas thought otherwise and drove me out. The fleas on this Central Asian road seemed to be champion hoppers, for it was not only in the Sona Marg P.O. that we met. At twelve o'clock in bright moonlight we started. My servant was a fine lusty Mohammedan (who before my eyes on one occasion rescued two men at the same time from drowning); he tried to beguile the time by telling me stories of the ancient kings of Kashmir as we trudged on the nine miles, and by dawn found ourselves at Baltal, situated at the foot of the pass called Zogi La. It is not a high pass, being only 11,500 feet, but a steep road, and dangerous for ponies on account of the hard snow and ice slopes. The caravans lose many ponies on this pass. One of my ponies slipped down into the torrent, but was rescued, with its load—fortunately with little damage, thanks to the promptness and strength of my lusty servant.

At the top of the pass on the watershed there was deep snow for some miles. It was not unlike a frozen-rough sea, the snow having drifted into small hillocks like waves and breakers, and therefore not easy going. If there was so much snow in the summer, one can imagine somewhat of the dangers to the dak runners, or anyone else whose duty takes them along that road in the winter.

The following story was told me by one of the Moravian missionaries. He was on his way from Leh, which is the capital of Ladakh, to India on important business—viz. to meet his bride at Bombay—and was obliged to travel in the early spring, which is a most dangerous time for crossing the passes. He was nearing the Zogi La Pass when he was overtaken by a blizzard, and soon he found that he had lost his way as the fresh snow had covered the tracks of the mail runners. It was, of course, bitterly cold, and he could see no distance ahead on account of the blinding snow, driven against him by the strong cutting wind. After a vain hunt to find tracks, he was forced to give up the search, and as night was fast approaching he saw no possibility of surviving the night except through Divine help, so he prayed earnestly that his life might be spared.

He had only just finished praying when he saw

a figure which he thought must be a belated mail runner, so with thankfulness and joy he followed this figure, when suddenly it disappeared. He went to the place where he last saw the figure, and there he found a hole in the snow, into which he descended, and found himself in one of the stone shelters built for the safety of the mail runners. But what was his astonishment to find the shelter empty. No one was there! He then realised that his prayer had been answered in a most unexpected manner, and that his life had been spared for future service.

Even though I was crossing the pass in June I had miles of snow to traverse, and was glad when at last rocks and grass began to appear. I kept on the trudge till about three-thirty P.M. I was feeling very tired and sleepy, as I had been on the march since twelve o'clock the night before, so as I was well ahead of my luggage ponies I lay down by the side of the road for a rest, and knew no more until I found my servant looking at me, some hours later, and saw that the sun had set behind the mountains, and it was time to move on with the ponies and luggage, which had also arrived. The small stone huts which make up the village of Matayan were not far off, and I was glad to think of some food and sleep.

It had been raining hard a few hours previously, for when we entered the rest-house we found it deep in water, as the floor was below the level of the road. However, the legs of my camp bed were higher than the depth of water, so I kept dry; and in consequence of the water I was mercifully saved from an attack by the champion fleas of the Central Asian route. It would be great if all the rest-houses along the road could be turned into shallow tanks, then one might be able to use them with some comfort. Perhaps I am maligning them, for

I hear that there are now well-built rest-houses all along this road, so that my plan of tanks may be out of date. From Matayan down the rocky valley to Dras was a very hot march. The only trees that I remember were the tiny pencil cedars. The road below Matayan sweeps round the base of a magnificent mass of limestone, with splendid cliffs below, and giant steps above, culminating in picturesque castellated forms. The rushing, sparkling river was very inviting, and, as I was some miles ahead of my followers, I had plenty of time for a bathe. It was not all joy, on account of the rocky floor. I do not think I ever remember bathing off such a spiky beach.

I had not finished my ablutions when I discovered two pairs of dark eyes looking at me over a wall close by. Men they were, with long black hair. They looked so unprepossessing that I immediately came out of the water to get near my clothes and alpenstock, for I thought they were intending to annex them. What a plight I should have been in if they had been successful: miles from anywhere or any friend, in a scorching valley, with the fierce rays of the sun beating on my bare body, and no fig-trees at hand from which to make myself an apron. So I commenced putting on my clothes as quickly as my wet body would allow me, keeping my eyes on these black eyes and my right hand near my alpenstock. I sincerely hoped that I should not be obliged to fight until I had put on my boots, as the rocks were most painful. I might no doubt have saved myself from vain imaginations. These two fierce, wild men may have been watching me in order to take care of me, in that swift icy-cold river, with no ideas of robbery, for when in Ladakh I heard that the people are most honest, and one can always leave one's property about without fear of having it stolen.

Having bathed, the next thing I needed was food, for it was many hours since breakfast. I soon met two more long black-haired men who were carrying large round cakes of Indian corn. I bought one of them. I do not know how many days ago it had been baked, but it was extremely hard, stale and sour. However, I soaked it in a stream, and was then able to get it down, or at least some of it.

Later on I made friends with some villagers, and they, to show that they meant well, brought me as much milk as I could drink. I was then so thirsty that I did justice to their supply. I sat with these kindly folk until I saw my caravan approaching. When it arrived we continued our journey, and in course of time we arrived on a great open wind-swept plain, and soon saw a group of stone and mud houses, which calls itself Dras, the capital of the country of Dras.

Here I found a British officer encamped on his way back to India after ibex hunting. My camp was pitched upon the plain, and I had just finished my tea, for which I was most grateful, after that grilling march down that treeless valley, and was putting things straight when down came a great gale of wind. I had to hang on with all my might to one of my tent-poles to prevent the tent coming down, while my servant hammered hard at the tent-pegs. While this was going on I heard shouts, and saw the major's property fast disappearing out of his tent, sailing down the plain before the blast. So I ran to the rescue, and was just in time to save his tent from collapsing entirely, for one of his tent-poles had already fallen. The gale soon blew itself out, and all was peace and quiet once more, except for the visits of the prowling pariah dogs from the city of Dras.

Next day we were up betimes, and I marched on ahead

and arrived at the Commissioner's camp at Kargil in time for a late breakfast. His party consisted of Mr and Mrs Beech (Beech stood six feet six inches, a giant of a man); Mrs Darrah, whose husband, a great sportsman, was awaiting her in Leh; Jack Phelps and P. H. Church, who were on a long expedition to the district of the Pang Gong Lake, a salt lake 100 miles in length, and the Chang Chenmo, after "ovis ammon" and "ovis poli." I received a hearty welcome and a real good breakfast, which I much enjoyed after my forced march to catch up this party.

Kargil is the capital of a district called Purik, and is inhabited by Mohammedans of the Shiah sect. Colonel Ward mentions a curious custom in connection with the burial of their dead. An aperture is left in the earth over the grave, and a rectangular box of masonry is built over this, with a small door and window. Flour is dropped down on the body; this is done at intervals for a period of three moons. Afterwards the hole above the body is closed, as also the door and window.

That morning the Governor of the Province called on us. He was a Kashmiri Brahman, a little man, but from the size of his lower chest he evidently had done himself well. Captain Trench asked him to show him his statement of grain accounts, as there was a threatened shortage of food that autumn. He had received orders to keep large stores of grain in case of emergencies, the old fort on the hill having been requisitioned for such a purpose. The books were brought, and from them Captain Trench saw that his orders had been faithfully obeyed, and the fort was just bulging with grain, like the Governor's lower chest. Captain Trench was so pleased to hear of the great supplies that he told the Governor he would like to see how he had managed to store so much, and would visit the fort that very afternoon at three P.M.

At two-thirty the Governor with his suite arrived at our camp again, to invite the Commissioner Sahib and all his party to take tea with him at his house, but as it was such a hot day surely it would be more comfortable for the ladies if they and all the party came up later, say four-thirty P.M. Captain Trench accepted for the whole party, but said that he at any rate would visit the fort first and afterwards come on to tea. So we all climbed the hill towards the fort, and as we neared it the Governor again pressed Captain Trench to come straight to his house for tea and afterwards visit the fort, for was it not very hot?—and the evening-time would be cooler, etc. Captain Trench would not give in, and made straight for the fort, we all following him.

When we all entered through the large gateway into the quadrangle Captain Trench asked the Governor where the store-rooms were. The Governor pointed towards a certain door. Captain Trench asked the Governor to have the door opened, whereupon he called to a chaprasi to go and bring the keys. The chaprasi remained absent a long time, so the Governor again asked Captain Trench to come to his house for tea while the keys were being fetched. But no, Captain Trench was firm on the point, he would see the store first, and asked the Governor to hurry up his chaprasi. So another man was sent after the first. At last the servant arrived, breathless, with a huge bunch of large keys, and commenced trying to—or, to be truthful, pretending to—open the great lock. He went through the whole lot, but no key would fit it. So the Governor again broached the subject of tea, and apologised for the foolishness of his servant, explaining that the man with the right set of keys had left the office with the keys. So Captain Trench asked the Governor to send a man after him and fetch the keys. He said that he would, but this servant with the keys lived a long way off, and it would all take time, and again mentioned tea first.

Captain Trench's patience was beginning to give out, and he said: "Do not bother about the keys: we will soon burst that door open with that big beam," pointing to one leaning against the wall.

The Governor begged him not to do that, for he would send a man running to fetch the right keys. In an extraordinarily short time, considering the great distance this man was supposed to have covered, the man arrived, puffing and blowing, playing his part well, with another (?) great bunch of keys, though uncommonly like the first bunch which had proved useless.

The keys were applied, but the lock refused to be opened. Again the Governor expressed his sorrow for the delay, and was about to suggest tea once more, when the battering-ram again was mentioned, and Captain Trench made a move towards it. Then the Governor, seeing his game was up, gave a sign, and the key turned the lock and the door swung open. Captain Trench went in; the great store-room was entirely empty: not one single sack of grain was there.

Captain Trench came out and said to the Governor: "Why did you bring me to this empty store-room? I want to see your stores of grain, and not empty rooms. The Governor apologised to Captain T., and swore at his servants for having made fools of them all, and ordered them at once to open those store-rooms where the grain was. The servants' faces were a study, and their hands and knees literally shook, as they did not know which orders they were to obey—the ones given by the Governor before the arrival of Captain Trench or the ones now given. However, the Governor pointed to another door, and ordered it to be opened. Again there was going to be the same waste of time over the keys, when Captain T. cut it short by stepping towards the battering-ram and asking me to help him.

Then the door was opened, and we found this store-room also absolutely empty. At last the play was over —the chief actor, forgetting all his greatness, fell on his knees before Captain T., and with hands in the attitude of prayer pleaded for mercy. Captain Trench told him to go home, and he would see him at the Public Durbar next day. So our tea with the Governor was off, and we went back to camp with much to think about. Captain Trench had caught out this scoundrel properly, but how about providing grain for the people under his care with an empty store-house? Next day was a very great day. Officials of all sorts came pouring in from all sides on their ponies—some from villages 100 miles or more distant. There were Chaukidars, Chakdars, Lambardars, Zaildars, Tehsildars, Thanidars, and I do not know how many other dars and small rajas and wazirs, with their retainers, all in their best clothes. It was a great sight. All were on the tiptoe of excitement, for they had heard how the Sahib had caught out the Brahman Governor. A few were anxious and sad, for had they not worked with him and shared in some of the loot; but the great majority had known of this wholesale robbery, but had not dared to mention it, for was not the Governor a great man, of a noble family, and in high favour at Court.

Captain Trench soon made it plain what he thought of this great scoundrel. It was a treat watching the faces of the multitude as this villain received his deserts. I

Photo by] [*Vishu Nath*

FOUR LADIES OF LADAKH.

On the head of the figure to the right notice the magnificent "rough" turquoises. These are probably an heirloom. The white cuffs worn by the next are parts of a thick shell.

would not have missed that Court of Justice for anything. There we all were, in a circle, sitting in an orchard near the rushing river, and surrounded by the great mountains as silent witnesses at the great Court of Justice.

Captain Trench must have been very tired after it all, but he possessed à great heart, and was always brimming over with spirits and humour, so I don't think he had a sleepless night. He had done an unpleasant duty uncommonly well, and he had reason to be proud of it.

That night must have been a very unpleasant one for the Governor, but it was also an exciting one for our camp near the river, for we were wakened by a tremendous gale of wind. We were all soon out of bed trying to hold our tents up, and hang on to our property. I was myself soon sprawling on my bed with my tent on the top of me, and there remained until the wind had blown itself out. It was somewhat annoying to find myself defeated in this manner, but it had its amusing side also.

The following day we commenced our march towards Leh. Two of the marches were overlong and very hot, as there was no shade, and the reflection of light and refraction of heat from the wall of the rocks we passed made it rather trying. One was very thankful to have dark glasses. We started at four-thirty punctually every morning, and marched till ten A.M. to some shade, where we stayed till the evening, and then finished the march in the cool.

It was an interesting sight to watch the caravans from Central Asia and China passing, with the loads carried often on yaks, and some even on sheep's backs, the sort of sheep which grows a broad fat tail, which swings about most uncomfortably as the animal walks. The idea of loading sheep is a very practical one, for when the food which is carried by the sheep is eaten up, then there is no need of the carrier, so it is then eaten, the fat tail being considered a great delicacy. Some of these caravans are three years on the road before they reach their homes. Quite a number of these merchants have been to Mecca, and were returning, wearing the green turban which is the mark of a Mecca "pilgrim who has accomplished the 'haj.'"

The first monastery we come to is Mulbe. It is in a most commanding position, for it stands on the top of a rock about five hundred feet high.

A short distance before reaching this monastery is a large Buddha, carved on a rock, about thirty feet in height. On our return journey Dr Neve and I came in time to see a very pretty ceremony being performed before it.

There was a sort of maypole erected in front of the figure, decked with coloured paper or rags. Then a troop of thirty children appeared, dressed in bright garments, wearing crowns of flowers, and they were dancing round the pole and singing, reminding one of the maypole dance. Then came a monk, dressed in a white garment like a surplice, with a red fool's-cap on his head. In one hand he carried a Kashmiri fire-pot full of live charcoal and some narcotic mixture of hemp or opium. These fumes he kept inhaling, which made him become very excited. In his right hand he carried a curved sword, which he flourished about in a most dangerous manner. He commenced to dance round the pole, followed by the children. He shouted louder and louder, and twirled about his body faster and faster, while his sword was flashing and slashing about in all directions.

A man standing by me, whom I knew, who called himself a nobleman, told me in awed tones that this holy man was uttering the words of God. As a matter of fact, he was drunk with his opium fumes and could hardly keep on his feet, and I expect he soon flopped down on the ground, but we were unable to stay to see the show through to the end.

CHAPTER XVII

A TRIP TO LADAKH (*continued*)

SOME little time before we reached Mulbe we had heard noises like the bellowings of the bulls of Bashan, for they seemed to be more than ordinary bellowings. As we turned the corner we heard other sounds, such as the beating of drums and cymbals and squealing flageolets, and then came into view the monastery band. The monks were dressed up in their best red garments, with most curious and awe-inspiring headgear, consisting of huge red-cloth helmet-looking erections which gave the band a very smart and martial appearance. The trumpets which bellowed and brayed so loudly were of copper, about seven or eight feet in length, truly colossal.

Then came the abbot of the monastery with his following of monks, together with the great people of Mulbe, to welcome the Commissioner Sahib. They brought presents of food and large jugs of home-made cider, called "chang."

At Mulbe there is an inscription of King Ides abolishing living sacrifices. This was not, however, obeyed, and the people continued to sacrifice goats before the pre-Buddhist altars, tearing out the heart of the living animal. (See Dr E. F. Neve's book, *Beyond the Pir Punjal.*)

In the afternoon we were entertained by a game of polo, for every big village has its polo ground, which is generally kept in good order, the grass being kept green by irrigation.

The chief features in which the game differs from Western polo are the following :—

Firstly, there are two long stone walls, about three feet high, built along both sides of the ground, against which the ball is made to rebound; they are also used, by the way, for squeezing your adversary's pony, and if possible the leg of the rider, against the jagged stones, to his great discomfort. Secondly, all the players start at a gallop from one end. The leader then throws the ball into the air and strikes it with the full swing of his stick before it touches the ground, frequently driving it the whole length of the ground and through the goal-posts, which are marked by white stones. But the goal is not counted unless one of the attacking side dismounts and picks up the ball before any of the defenders can knock it out again. When the goal is won the band strikes up a joyful noise, accompanied by plenty of drums. The riders play in a most reckless manner. I have seen both ponies and players receiving terrific whacks, and blood flowing profusely; and sometimes the onlookers receive wounds from standing too near the wall. It is a very ancient and honoured game in these regions.

It is difficult to describe one's feelings as one enters this wonderful country of monasteries and lamas, for one seems to have arrived in quite another world, unimagined and undreamt of; one feels inclined to pinch oneself to see if one is really awake and not dreaming.

On the road one passes walls from 100 to 300 yards long, about eight feet high and eight feet broad, with a pent roof of flat stones of all sizes, on which are carved the same words, "Om mane padme hun," which means, "O God of the Jewel on the Lotus," or, as it has been interpreted to me: "May my soul, O God, be like the jewel of water which lies on the lips of the lotus leaf just as it is going to fall into the lake and be lost in the ocean of water [*i.e.* be lost in Nirvana]."

Monks roam over the country doing this pious carving work for those who will pay them. Merit not only comes to the men who place these stones on the wall, but to all those travellers who pass on the left side of the wall, and curses on those who pass on the wrong side. Hence there is no need of a policeman to tell all traffic to keep to the left; all travellers do it as if mechanically, and heap up to themselves merit.

Then on the road one continually passes "chortans," stone pagodas generally white-washed, and not only on the road, but dotted about in the fields and up the mountain-sides. They are of all sizes from three to forty feet high. They are hollow, and in them one will often find clay medallions vulgarly called potted lamas, for they are composed of the ashes of the monks, which have been stamped with the monastery stamps, not unlike prettily stamped pats of butter. Some of the stamps are very decorative, generally with the figure of Buddha in the centre of a circle, with writing around.

On the tops of the houses and on trees one sees bunches of flags made of coloured rags on which is inscribed this same prayer. When the flags flutter in the breeze this prayer ascends for the good of the individual who placed these rags to be moved by the wind.

As we pass through a village we see little paper windmills on the roofs which work a prayer wheel inside the house. This is a metal cylinder crammed full of paper on which is written hundreds of times this one prayer: "Om mane padme hun."

Along the walls of certain houses and always at the monasteries are found these cylinders of wood let into the wall at a convenient height from the ground to allow

Photo by] [*R. E. Shorter*,

THE BUDDHIST ABBOT AND HIS CHELAS OR PUPILS.

passers-by to pat them and make them revolve. In some villages they have huge prayer wheels worked by water, which pray automatically night and day, year in and year out for all the village. Lastly, you meet both men and women walking on the road carrying these wheels of metal, which they keep on the spin by the twist of the wrist, for a lead ball is attached to this cylinder by a metal chain, which adds considerable momentum. Some of these hand prayer wheels are beautifully ornamented with silverwork.

The people one meets are most picturesquely dressed. The men and the women wear a long woollen garment generally of red, but often of green or some other colour. The men have a leather girdle into which they stick a regular ironmonger's shop of goods, such as one or two knives, a brass opium pipe, a tinder-box, a metal purse, a long metal pen-box with metal inkpot attached, a whip of three thongs, the handle of which is always highly decorated with metal and paint, a cup for their tea and their porridge, and a bag of flour for their food on their journeys. The food is always most simple. They fill their cup with cold water, and then pour the flour into it and stir it with their first finger, and when it becomes a sort of watery paste they drink it. A most unappetising food it is, and gives them indigestion continually. Most of them also add an ikon to their belt collection. It is an image of Buddha of silver or gold in a casket of some metal, and a pocket Communion set of copper or silver with much ornamentation.

The Tibetan Buddhists have a religious service in which they use bread and cider. It is said that this religious service came from China through the Nestorian Christians, for there is a tradition that St Thomas introduced Christianity into China.

This pocket set is a most neat and clever arrangement, for the paten and stand are so made that they fit beautifully into the metal pot which is the chalice. Every Buddhist can be his own priest and give the Elements to himself.

Many wear a chatelaine attached to their leather belt, on which hang most of the things mentioned, and thus their belt is left free for other goods and chattels. Their shoes are generally felt top-boots, often of gaudy colours.

The head-dress is a cloth cap, not infrequently of the same colour as their dress, but I am not able to describe it as I have never seen anything like it; it is perhaps a little like a Balaclava cap or a helmet with flaps. It is most picturesque and odd-looking. The whole costume seems to suit the Mongol features excellently, especially with the long pigtail hanging down the back, which always covers the back of the cloak with black grease. The women dress much like the men, only their head-dress is different. They wear a "pirak"—that is, a piece of red cloth about six or eight inches wide, which starts from the forehead and continues down the back nearly to the waist. It is covered with rows of precious stones, chiefly rough pieces of turquoise, and silver ornaments. This system of carrying their wealth on their heads shows how honest these people are. Then on each side of the face, and sewn on to this strip of cloth, are two pieces of astrakhan, which are made to stick out at right angles to the face some six inches, like black wings. Altogether it is most becoming.

The women in this country are not "purdah," and are treated on equal terms with the men. It is most refreshing. They are not the least shy or bold. They are just their smiling jolly selves, like their menfolk.

I have mentioned a few pages previously that on entering Ladakh one seemed to be in a dream, for the country and people were so utterly unlike anything I had imagined or dreamt of; and it was not only the people and the buildings near at hand, but the hills all round seemed to be quite in keeping. It is the lamas' custom to build their monasteries on the top of the rocks, so that it is often hard to distinguish monastery from rock or rock from monastery. Then again, the air being rarer than one is accustomed to, every object seems to be nearer than it really is. The hills and precipices, which are absolutely bare of trees or grass, take on most beautiful colours, and the lights and shadows are far more marked than one has been accustomed to see.

CHAPTER XVIII

A TRIP TO LADAKH (*continued*)

LET us now visit a monastery. As usual, as we approached Lamauru, we were met by much noise and dust. The monastery band evidently was on the war-path, from the terrific braying and tom-tomming that greeted us, and the crowd of monastery dignitaries and village magnates kicked up much dust as they approached. We were taken round the monastery by the head ecclesiastic. We climbed the stone stairway to the monastery, which, as usual, was situated on the top of a cliff, built on to and into it in such a way that it was not easy to see where rock ended and the building commenced. Along the side of the stairway were rows of prayer wheels let into the wall, which we set spinning in the orthodox manner. At least I hope we did spin them the right and not the wrong way. I think we must have spun them round the right way, for our journey was prosperous. The chapel was full of interesting objects, and one did not know quite what to look at, for there seemed to be, and there was, such a crowd of interesting objects which I had never seen before. The building was like a hall, the roof supported by wooden pillars, with a gallery all round, from which hung a profusion of silk banners of Chinese design, chiefly dragons. On one side of the hall was a row of coloured figures, life-size, of Buddha and sainted lamas, which were arrayed in rich silks. Before each figure was a table or altar of very curious design, coloured with bright red, green, yellow and gold, carved with dragons and sacred symbols.

On the tables were metal cups and goblets, and on each table was a basin of holy water, an oil lamp burning, the chalice for the "chang" (cider) and paten for the bread, a "dorje" (a prettily carved brass or silver dumb-bell-looking article used by the priest during part of the service), also a little drum often made of a human skull sawn off at the top to allow for the skin to be stretched. There were also some goblets made of human skulls, and a human thigh-bone used as a trumpet.

Down the middle of the chapel are low benches in lines, end on to the row of figures, on which the monks kneel facing the altars as they read their sacred books. On the left side of the chapel are rows of copper beakers full of chang, from which the monks refresh themselves when they become sleepy over their much reading. Then on the left wall are shelves in which their books are kept. These are long strips of paper or parchment manuscripts.

There are five chapels kept each day. When any great person dies the monks are paid to read through a certain number of their holy books. They each take so many pages, and read through them aloud, all together, each one reading something different, so there must be a fair volume of sound. I do not know if volume of sound has any value and so adds to the merit of reading so many thousands of words.

These people have evidently thought out a truly mechanical way to salvation. When electric power reaches Ladakh and prayer wheels are worked by motors, merit will speed up a great deal and Nirvana will be within reach of all. The chapel needed much cleaning. There was an overwhelming smell of lamp oil, or burning fat; grease pervaded the atmosphere, in fact everything the monks touched, for they were filthily dirty, their red garments being more or less black with grease. Fortunately their heads were shorn. They seemed to be a happy lot of brothers, always ready to laugh and joke, in fact, just like the pictures of the monks of the West in days gone by.

There are nuns who live in separate buildings. Many of them are so like the monks that it is difficult to tell one from the other, at least to an unpractised eye, as the following incident will show.

A few days later I was in Leh with Dr Neve. He was in the hospital helping people to get well quickly. I stayed outside to try and cheer up the patients who were waiting their turn outside, as many of them seemed to be rather nervous and frightened. I noticed one person who seemed to look very depressed, who I thought was a monk and not living up to his usual jovial self, so I poked him in the ribs and told him to cheer up, when a voice called out to me from behind, but too late: "Take care what you are doing, for that lady is a nun." It was a Moravian missionary who spoke too late. Well, I did all that an English gentleman could do. I apologised most humbly, but the nun would not have any, and I failed to cheer her up.

Well, our triumphal march to the capital, Leh (a town with a population of 3000 in the winter, which grows to 6000 in the summer, when all the traders from east and west come in), was as entertaining as it was interesting. Monastery bands, town bands, feasts and polo matches succeeded one another, but the reception given to the Commissioner Sahib at Leh was the culmination of great doings. Seven miles from Leh, in the valley of the Indus, a large sandy plain, there met us a great cavalcade of

Photo by] [*Vishu Nath*

LAMAYURU MONASTERY.

The air being very clear and dry here 11,000 feet above sea level, the distance of any object from the traveller is difficult to gauge. This scene should be visualised in shades of pink and yellow with deep dark shadows, the only green being that of the willows.

Photo by] [*R. E. Shorter.*

FLOATING GARDENS ON THE DAL.

The foundation of a " garden " is waterweeds, grass and mud tangled together and anchored or pinned by a stake driven through it to the bottom of the lake. Melons, cucumbers and tomatoes are readily grown on the rich mud beds.

grand folk dressed in most weird costumes, uncommonly like a well-got-up pantomime.

There were men dressed in Chinese silks, with their smart blue and gold caps with tassels, Ladakhi officials of various grades, from the Joint-Commissioner, a fine-looking Mohammedan, to his fat babu who sat on his pony like a monkey, his stirrups being so short that his knees and fat stomach met. But the figure which took my fancy was the church dignitary; he resembled for all the world Cardinal Wolsey risen from the dead. He wore a scarlet cloak which fell over the pony's back and almost touched the ground, and he sported ye old cardinal's hat. I never saw him smile, which was in contrast to all the others, who seemed to be out for a holiday. Whether he was upset about not having his proper position in the cavalcade, or whether he had the stomach-ache is uncertain, or maybe his cardinal's hat was uncomfortable. It certainly was hardly the sort of hat I should have chosen to ride in. Perhaps his dignity did not allow him to show his feelings. Anyway, everybody except the cardinal seemed to be in good fettle after their morning's ride. We all fell into some sort of order and rode for the capital.

You can see Leh from some miles distant as it is built up the side of the rocks, with the palace and monastery towering above. Leh is 11,700 feet above sea-level, so one needs a little time in which to get acclimatised.

When we arrived through the fine gateway into the main street we found both sides lined with H.H. the Maharajah's troops and the crowds of citizens behind them. The monastery band was in full view on the roof of one of the buildings and made the usual joyful sound. This main street of shops has a fine avenue of poplar-trees, which gives most grateful shade in the hot summer weather.

As it is very broad, it is the polo ground. It seemed most strange to see the players dashing up and down the main street, often hitting the ball into the shops. Fortunately the shops in Leh do not possess glass windows, otherwise polo in that street would be an expensive amusement.

Captain Trench was finally escorted to the Residency, which was a two-storeyed stone building in quite a nice garden. There is not a great selection of trees in Leh, poplars and willows being all that I remember seeing in this part of Ladakh, but in lower Ladakh there are apricot, apple and pear trees.

The Commissioner's chief duty is to look after the traders' interests on this main caravan road from India to Central Asia, Yarkand, Turkestan and to China.

I went to the Moravian missionaries, who had kindly invited Dr E. F. Neve and myself to stay with them. They have been doing a great and useful work here for many years, by means of hospital, schools, and visiting the people in their homes. They had then a congregation of about thirty Christians.

The history of one of them with whom I was connected for some years is interesting. A certain monk in a monastery in Nubra was dying, and he sent for one of the missionaries whom he knew to visit him. Nubra Valley is some fifty miles from Leh over the other side of the Kardang Pass, 17,400 feet high.

The missionary went at once, and was in time to see him before he died. The monk told him that he heard the Gospel through the preaching of the missionaries, and believed in Christ as his Saviour, but had not been bold enough to confess openly on account of the persecution which would follow, but as he had failed to do the first thing he would do the second, and that was to give his son to the missionaries to be brought up a Christian. The monk passed away like the dew drop off the lotus leaf, let us hope, and his son was taken to the mission at Leh, and remained with them until the age of fourteen, when he was sent to the Mission School at Srinagar. The missionaries took the opportunity of some friendly Tibetans going down to Srinagar on business and delivered Joseph, for that was his Christian name, to their safe keeping. I remember the interest and pleasure it was to welcome this quiet and stolid Ladakhi to the school. He arrived in his Tibetan costume, looking most quaint, for I had seen few Tibetans up to that time. I am glad to say he was proud of his national dress and wore it all the time he was at school.

Joseph had a hard time of it among the Brahman boys, who laughed at his dress, which, as a matter of fact, was far more becoming than theirs, and also tormented him on the quiet because he was a Christian.

Joseph never allowed himself to be drawn by his tormentors, he never retaliated, nor did he show the least fear of them, but I did not see why his persecutors should have it all their own way. I believe in a boy managing his own affairs among the boys without help from outside if possible, so I set to work to teach him to box. He became an apt pupil, as he started fair, without any lee-way to make up in the matter of cowardice or weakness of any kind, so in a short time he became thoroughly respected, notwithstanding the difference in religion or dress, and before he left school was the most respected and, I might say, popular boy in the school. As he was preparing to return to his own country, I asked him what profession he would choose. Would he care to join the State service, as very few Ladakhis were educated and all posts were filled by Kashmiri Brahmans and Indians? It would be good for the country if some of these officials were natives of Ladakh. I pointed out that if he took that line he would have power and influence later on, which he could put to good use. His answer was: "I do not want power or riches. All I want is that I may have opportunities of preaching Christ to my people. I would prefer to be a missionary."

He returned to Leh, and in course of time became headmaster of the Mission School, which post he has held for many years, where he is training his own countrymen, and preaching Christ to them by life as well as by words. I am glad to say that his education has not given him any ideas of being a babu, and therefore too much of a gentleman to do manual labour, for in the vacations he is to be seen driving his yoke of oxen and carrying manure on his back in a basket very similar to those used in Switzerland for the same purpose. His education has not unmanned him, as it has done so many in Kashmir and India.

So the dying monk in the monastery at Nubra did well for his country, though it seems odd to those who do not know the way of monks that they should have sons to bequeath.

The mission at Leh has been blessed with some very fine missionaries. They have to be a very whole-hearted lot, for their pay is a mere pittance, and until lately they did not return home on furlough, but died at their post like Dr Marks and Dr Redslop, but I am glad to say that in these days there is a wiser and more humane policy, for surely it is wiser that a missionary's life should be lengthened by periods of rest than that he should live a short time and have to be replaced by a novice. It is

Photo by] HIGH STREET AT LEH. [*G. W. Millais*

A polo match is in progress, therefore the street has been cleared.

Photo by] [*Vishu Nath.*

A WINTER SCENE.

Down either bank of the river are boats lived in as to half their accommodation by whole families (of two or three generations), with cocks and hens and sometimes a goat or a cow, and used as to the rest for stores of unhusked rice or firewood.

more humane in that parents may be permitted to see their children now and again, whom they have sent to school in the Homeland. The missions in Srinagar and Leh are able to help one another in various ways. During the war Dr and Mrs Heber were able to come to the help of the Srinagar Mission Hospital at a time of need, and much were their services and presence appreciated.

Outside the town in the waste of sand is a little oasis; it is the Christian cemetery, in which lies, among other honoured remains, the body of Miss Irene Petrie, a most gifted missionary, who compressed into the short space of three years a most marvellous amount of living work among the women and children of Srinagar. She came up to Ladakh on her much-needed holiday, and passed away shortly after her arrival at Leh from typhoid fever, which she had contracted in Srinagar. Her sister, Mrs Ashley Carus-Wilson, has written her life, which is well worth reading, as it tells of a beautiful life spent in the highest service.

I had heard a good deal about the Kardang Pass of 17,400 feet, some miles from Leh, the one on which there is so much loss of life of luggage animals. The air is so rare that the pony and donkey men often slit up the noses of their animals to allow of easier breathing. The traders use yaks to a great extent on this pass, which they ride to save themselves from mountain sickness.

As the sun was so hot I chose the night for my trip, and started at eight P.M. on my pony, as a yak would be too slow, with a mounted Ladakhi guide. At twelve o'clock my guide disappeared; I did not see which way he went, and it was too dark to find any path, so I dismounted so that my eyes might be nearer the ground. The pony did not feel inclined to move, so I tied him to a rock and went off in search of some landmark, for I seemed to have reached the top of the ridge. However, I soon found I could not walk more than twenty paces at a time, and a most splitting headache came on. It felt as if my head blood vessels would burst, and I had *mal de montagne* properly. After wandering about aimlessly I became aware I was up against a precipice. When the moon rose it was now one A.M., and then I saw I was under the foot of a glacier, a great cliff of ice over seventy feet high, which seemed to bulge out at the top like the curve of a huge breaker. It was very impressive, and for the moment I forgot my headache.

I had meant to stay on the pass to see the sunrise, but my powers of endurance gave out. My one desire was to get down the mountain, where I could breathe in comfort, so I descended to the rock where I had left my pony, and I soon began to recover my equilibrium as I descended. When I returned to Leh I made inquiries after my guide, but I never discovered what happened to him and therefore never knew why he gave me the slip.

About twenty miles from Leh is a very large and important monastery called Hemis, and once in every twenty years they have an especially important religious play, so Dr Neve and I hired ponies and joined the happy throng of pilgrims.

It was an interesting and amusing sight to see people of all classes making their way on foot and horseback to this far-famed monastery. On several ponies were two riders, the man in front and his lady behind. As polyandry is the custom in Ladakh, the wife is therefore the lord and master, so one expected to see the lady riding in front and one or more husbands riding pillion, for we often saw three passengers riding one horse. We passed two ladies

Photo by] [*Vishu Nath.*

LAMA ACTORS IN THEIR RELIGIOUS PLAYS.

Note the resemblance to Chinese rather than to Indian decoration and design in these figures.

Photo by Commander] [*E. C. Tyndale-Biscoe, R.N.*

(1) The Frances Aberigh Mackay Memorial School for Girls.
(2) Men in the Making.

This illustrates the great change which has come over the youth of Kashmir who had hitherto been taught that strenuous action was " bad form."

riding on the same pony, an old lady and a pretty, rosy-cheeked damsel, and they smiled and nodded to us as we passed them. We thought they must be very up-to-date women, when all of a sudden we remembered that they had been our hostesses some days previously, for a certain Tibetan nobleman and his wife and daughter had entertained us at tea. But there was good reason for our not recognising them, for it is the custom for all respectable ladies to cover their faces with mud, so that these noble ladies with whom we drank tea were brown with mud, whilst these smiling ladies on horseback had beautiful rosy cheeks. Apparently when on a pilgrimage they need not wear this unbecoming veil of mud.

It took us two days to reach Hemis. The monastery is situated in a very narrow valley on the side of a mountain and not on the top as is usually the case, and to this fact, I am told, the monastery owes its escape from plunder when the country was invaded by Sikhs. This monastery is a very rich one and possesses stores of rich Chinese silks and jewels. The abbot showed us a great many of his treasures.

The play took place in a very fine courtyard, the monastery towering above one like a huge castle, a very impressive building. It contains three hundred monks, who wear yellow robes and are superior to the red-robed ones. The play lasts for the whole of one day and till noon on the second day, with no interlude, and is wearying to a degree. The idea of the play is to teach the people the power of the monks in future life. They act all the known, or rather unknown, horrors of hell and the only way of salvation through the holiness of the monks. Not a word is spoken; it is taught entirely by sight.

The acting is guided by the monastery band as to time, fervour, quietness, tempest, hell fire or death. The band is directed by the precentor, and he by a big book in front of him. There is a fire burning in the centre of the court. Then there enter monks, dressed up in hideous masks with faces of various animals, such as dogs, tigers, dragons, etc.; they carry large three-pronged forks, and throw a clay figure of a man into the flames. The devils commence dancing round, pretending to stick their forks into the figure, and seem to be enjoying the sport of tormenting their victims. This scene continues for what seems to be an interminable time, when in come a party of monks from the great door of the monastery, dressed in coloured silk garments, wearing huge masks, and commence to march round and round hell fire, making various passes with their arms towards the flames. They begin with painfully slow steps, which are so monotonous that they get on one's nerves, the band playing softly but in terribly slow time.

Then the music quickens slightly, and then a little quicker, then quicker, until these holy monks fairly spin like dancing dervishes. The band works itself crazy with the screeching of its pipes, crashing cymbals, bellowing giant trumpets and resounding drum. Then all of a sudden there is dead silence, and we are all thankful for the respite. Then the whole dance commences over again from the very beginning, with one step every three seconds, and again working up to the whizz-bang. By this time this lot of holy men are tired out with their exertions and they disappear through the same great door from which they came. Immediately come in a second lot with a different set of great masks, some of them wearing most benign faces. They with the help of the band try their charms in marching and dances, and so one party succeeds another all through that day and part of the next without any success, for the flames of hell still burn on and the devils have it all their own way until a party of super-holy monks arrive, who come with holy water, with which they conquer the flames, and then the devils one and all rush out of the arena amid a tempest of crashing and shrieking; but above it all is the sound of a mighty wind caused by all the monks whistling their loudest, and the whole band of devils, pitchforks and all, disappear into the monastery. I thought it would have been more impressive if they had all disappeared over the precipice or, if they could not manage that, down the rocks out of sight.

Well, we were mighty glad to see the last of these devils, and the blessed monks also, for our nerves were anyhow after all we had heard and seen, but all was not over, for the people were to see the priest perform a sort of high mass. In an open space rigged up as a chapel facing the courtyard which all could see was an altar with its usual complement of ornaments, lamps, holy water, chalice and paten.

The priest entered wearing a garment just like a surplice. He turned his back to the congregation and commenced his service at the altar.

Presently in came stealthily a clown with a coloured bladder in his hand with which he hit the priest over the head with a mighty whack and then darted behind a pillar and hid. Then again he crept up behind, stalking the priest, and dealt him another blow; but still the priest took no notice, so absorbed was he in his devotions. After another blow or two the priest looked round to see whence the blows had come, but of course he looked in the wrong direction, and the clown cocked a snook at him, a real gutter-snipe snook, from behind the pillar. It was all so like a Western pantomime that we could hardly believe we were watching a real Buddhist religious ceremony in a real monastery. The people all round were thoroughly enjoying the play and were laughing heartily.

I could not find out the reason for this last act, but I suppose it was to show that the monks when engaged in their religious duties were too deeply engrossed to be disturbed by assaults of the devils. Well, it was a great show, and one wondered how much of it was believed by the people who had come from such long distances to see their religion acted.

It seemed to me that they were too jolly and cheery a lot to believe much in devils; they evidently saw the humour of it all. The abbot of the monastery told us that the monks had been practising for a whole year at the play, and showed us the rod of correction which he used on those monks who failed in their parts. It was a thick black stick weighted with brass. I felt sorry for those monks who did not live up to the form of Friar Tuck, and had not a good cushion of fat to protect their bones when the brass stick descended. But perhaps they knew the schoolboy's copy-book trick.

The great monastery mastiffs interested us, but we were thankful that they were chained. We were told that the dogs used to be kept in lieu of graves for the monks, or, in other words, to eat up the dead members of the brotherhood.

Some of them are very savage brutes. A friend of mine who was attacked by one had a bad time, although he himself was an athlete; he was obliged to go to bed for a day or two after the attack. I myself had a narrow shave one day. I went into a monastery uninvited to have a look round. When coming through a very narrow passage I saw one of these dogs fast asleep, as I imagined, and foolishly thought I could pass him if I walked delicately. But no such thing. The sleeping dog was very much awake, and unfortunately was not chained and came for me at once. I fortunately had an alpenstock in my hand, which I immediately presented to his open mouth; but the passage we were in being narrow, I had no spare room for wielding my weapon. I of course stood perfectly still, and then commenced to back slowly. The beast followed me inch by inch as I retreated inch by inch, with the point of my stick ready to jab in his mouth. That mastiff saw me off those premises all right, and I was glad to have got clear without damage. It taught me to be careful when visiting my clerical brethren in their religious houses.

We had now to turn our faces towards Leh and then to Srinagar. At Hemis we bade farewell to Phelps and Church, who started off on their long trail for the Tibetan plateau in search of their big game, ovis ammon and ovis poli.

We reached Leh on the second day, where we bade our kind friends the Commissioner and missionaries good-bye and started on our way west.

At the stages we always preferred to pitch our tents and sleep in them rather than face the champion hoppers in the dak bungalows. At one of the stages a young officer asked us to dine with him, and Neve noticed that he had some plate belonging to himself. This curious phenomenon was not difficult to explain, as this officer had been a guest in Dr Neve's house and so had his servant, and the servant in the interests of his master had annexed the said articles, thinking it would be more worthy of his master than that which his master possessed. This is not an uncommon custom of servants who visit houses with masters who do not know of this custom, and do not overhaul their property before leaving a friend's house. Personally I possess a bearer who knows this trick, and he always asks me to ask my friends to allow their servants to count over the spoons and forks, etc., before leaving the house, to see, of course, that they have not left anything of their master's property behind.

Another custom I discovered of quite a different kind, which interested me.

I saw a coolie sprawling on the road with his mouth on the ground and apparently blowing smoke. On asking what it meant I was told that the man not having brought his hookah was not going to be done out of his smoke. He had made a small tunnel. At one end he had placed his tobacco and lighted it, and was sucking the smoke through the tunnel into his mouth. How one lives and learns!

After leaving Mulbe we turned off the caravan road in order to return via Suru under Nun Kun and down the Wardwan nullah.

We passed the monastery of Shergol. It is built into the rock. The windows seem to be in the face of a precipice. The entrance and exit is peculiar, for a basket is let down by a rope, in which the visitor sits and is pulled up—a most excellent arrangement for keeping out undesirables. Our first view of the Suru river was superb, and reminded me of pictures of heaven which I had seen in children's picture books. We were up on a ridge and looked down upon the river where it widened out and was full of islands covered with willow-trees, and giant peaks rising behind and above the nearer hills forming the valley.

When we reached the bridge we found that it was far too frail for our ponies. The river itself could not be forded, and was too swift and dangerous to permit of the ponies swimming. What was to be done? The question was soon answered by the pony-men taking the loads off the ponies and carrying them across, then tying a rope round a pony's neck, the pony being forced into the river whilst the rope was held by the man who walked across the bridge, thus keeping the pony's head up-stream, so that the strain was lessened. In this way all our ponies came across safely, but the man on the bridge had some difficulty in keeping his feet as the strain on the rope was fairly severe, especially in mid-stream.

The village of Suru lies under Nun Kun, a fine pile of rock, the summit being 23,500 feet above sea-level. It is one of the peaks that we can see from near Srinagar, and looks like a white pyramid. From where we stood, looking up from the Suru river, it was just magnificent, its great glaciers shining in the sunlight.

Just outside the village is a lonely grave, that of Captain Christian, who died of typhoid whilst on a shooting expedition. We spoke to the head of the village about safeguarding the grave.

On our march from Suru we came across a great number of marmots, living in communities like rabbits. They are of a reddish brown colour and of the size of a small fox. They place sentinels around their village, who sit on the top of a rock to enable them to get a good view of their enemies, and whistle louder and louder as they see one approaching and then dart into their burrows. They are most fascinating animals. They seem to like the wild garlic that grows profusely in these regions.

We entered the Wardwan Valley by the Do Nullah Pass, and had to walk for seven miles on a glacier; it was exciting work jumping the crevasses. We were careful to take off some inches on this side and land with plenty of ice to spare on the other side, in case of the ice being rotten. One of our coolies did fall into a crevasse, but he was saved by the load on his back getting hitched on to the ice. We were glad when all our party reached camp safely. We were careful to select a safe place for our tents, for we passed the spot where Lieutenant Genge, I.M.S., encamped, and during the night he with all his servants was swept away by an avalanche. The Wardwan is an exceptionally narrow valley, and hence the mountain-sides are very steep and precipitous, so that snow-slides and avalanches are very common, and one has to keep one's weather-eye open for them.

During our march Dr Neve managed to fit in a good deal of medical work. He would see the patients after our tea, and also, if necessary, in the morning before starting. Some patients followed us from camp to camp, when it was necessary for them to have continual treatment. Dr Neve during this tour performed forty-two operations for cataract. It was great to see the delight of the people who received sight. After the operation, which was accomplished in a marvellously short time, Dr Neve would hold up his fingers and ask the patient to count them. When the patient found that he was correct in his counting, and could really see, a smile began to pervade the face, which grew wider and wider as he realised that it was no dream or sorcery, but naked fact, that his sight was restored. Of course the eye was bandaged up directly, and the patient was given strict orders not to undo the bandage for two weeks. The removal of the cataract is a wonderfully neat and quick operation, and one envies those who have the power to give such joy in so few seconds; it is very little short of the miraculous. And then there is the greater joy of the missionary doctor who bestows the great gift freely and without payment, like the Good Physician who went about Galilee healing all manner of diseases. From the Wardwan we climbed the pass, and dropped down through pine forests into the Kashmir Valley, crossing beautiful grassy margs and sparkling streams, until we finally reached the river at Islamabad, and found our boat waiting for us. Oh, the joy of being able to travel without moving our legs! I do not know when I so much enjoyed a boat journey, the tramping over, and now gliding gently down-stream for forty-eight miles to Srinagar and home at the end of it.

CHAPTER XIX

KASHMIR MEDICAL MISSION

IN the European cemetery at the Sheikh Bagh, which is situated near the first of the city bridges, is a grave which I never pass without taking my hat off, for in it lies the mortal remains of Lieut. Robert Thorp, who gave his life for the Kashmiris in the year 1867.

The grave lies under the shadow of one of those beautiful chenar-trees, which are a continual comfort to those seeking shelter from the summer sun, and a joy to behold when the leaves take on their glorious autumn tints of pink-scarlet.

Robert Thorp came to Kashmir, like many other British officers, to shoot big game on the mountains; but his mind was soon directed to a more important matter—namely, the sorrows of the Kashmiris under maladministration. He found the peasants, who were Mohammedans, suffering terribly under the rule of Hindu officials, who sucked the very life-blood out of them. They paid their taxes in kind, the State claiming half the crops, and the State officials who collected the grain taking a quarter or more.

There was such an army of Hindu officials whose duty it was to collect the grain that, when all had been supplied, both lawfully and unlawfully, there was very little left for the zamindar and his family who had farmed the land.

Often it happened that the farmer and his family had to live on roots, or anything they could find on which to exist. Apopros of this system of collecting the grain the Kashmiris tell the following story:—

"Once upon a time there was a very great nobleman, who was a Pathan, who lived in the mountains to the north-west of Cashmere: his name was Mos Deen Khan. One day he went upon a journey to Srinagar, in Cashmere, in order to pay his respects to the king of that country, and it happened that on that occasion he rode a horse for which he had a very great regard. He was indeed so fond of this horse that he used to call himself 'the father of the animal!'

"When Mos Deen Khan reached Sat-o-kuddel, which is the seventh bridge over the Jhelum at Srinagar, he alighted from his steed that he might proceed to the royal palace on foot; and having given many instructions to the groom with regard to the well treatment of the horse, as well as special orders on no account to ride him, he sent him back to his abode in the mountains.

"But when Mos Deen Khan got half-way to the palace of the King he bethought himself that perhaps his servant might ill-treat his horse; he therefore sent another of his attendants with orders to overtake them, and ascertain whether the beloved animal was well cared for. The menial departed, and found the first servant riding the horse. He thought, 'It is better for me to ride at my ease than to quarrel with this servant, who may perhaps afterwards falsely accuse me to my master'; so he too mounted.

"Now when Mos Deen Khan got very near the palace of the King he again bethought himself that perhaps it would be better to send a still more trustworthy servant to be a check upon the conduct of the others with regard to his horse. But when the third servant overtook the party, and found his two predecessors riding, he also mounted; and the horse, which could have carried one, became so exhausted under the weight of three, that, on reaching his stable, he died."

The application of the story is obvious enough, and is a good illustration of the natural wit of the Kashmiris.

There was another matter which troubled them much, and that was the forced labour on the Gilgit road. Gilgit, an outpost to the north of Kashmir, 200 miles from Srinagar, was garrisoned by Kashmir troops. It is situated in a foodless region, so the troops had to be fed from the Kashmir Valley. No road had been made there, so all the supplies had to be carried by coolies. These men were collected from the villages with the aid of press-gangs. The sepoys always brought in more than were required so that those who had money could buy themselves off their hands.

At Bandipore they were collected and loaded up. The only rations allowed them was a seer of rice per day; this they had to carry, plus the straw for making their straw shoes, plus their load of food for the garrison. No provision was made for them as they crossed the snow passes, so that many died on the road, and often it happened that when they did reach Gilgit they were sold as slaves to the wild inhabitants of that inhospitable region. The grandfather of one of my servants, who was sent there, was exchanged for a Chinese dog, but later on he escaped.

Dr Arthur Neve, in his book, *Thirty Years in Kashmir*, writes:

"To the Englishman the word Gilgit should recall the many gallant deeds of the nineties—the capture of Hunza, the relief of Chitral, and the Pamir Commission. During the last half-century Kashmir is the only Indian native state that has increased in area. And the increase was not desired, but was forced upon the Imperial Government by the advancing power of the Russian Empire and the intrigues of its frontier officers."

The triangle of mountainous country which lies between Kashmir on the south, Russian Central Asia on the north, and Afghanistan on the west is one of the wildest in the world, and one of the least accessible. Great empires have existed on both sides of the mountains; armies have from time immemorial marched along the southern skirts to conquer India, and along the northern to subdue the fertile countries of Central Asia; at times there have been great migrations of tribes from the vast plains of Mongolia to invade the West; but the Hindu Kush valleys have stood out above the flood of migration or conquest, and their primitive tribes offer most interesting problems to students of language and race.

For many years after I came to the country the mere name of Gilgit struck terror into the Kashmiri. For him it had the most alarming meaning. It spoke of forced labour, frost-bite on the lofty passes, and valleys of death, where the camps were haunted by cholera and starvation. Early in April one year came word that the frontier tribes were on the warpath, and orders were issued for a levy of 5000 porters to accompany the two regiments sent to reinforce the garrisons.

I was at Islamabad, endeavouring to fight an epidemic of cholera by sanitation, and noticed coolies collecting from all the surrounding region, each with a blanket, spare grass-shoes, his carrying crutch and light frame of sticks and rope in which to carry the load upon his back. And I was present at the great concourse in a green meadow in front of the mosque when a sort of farewell service was held for those starting on this perilous journey. Loud was the sobbing of many, and fervid the demeanour of all, as, led by the mullah, they intoned their prayers and chanted some of their special Ramzan penitential psalms. Even braver men than the Kashmiris might well have been agitated at such a time, when taking farewell of their loved ones. Who would till their fields? What would happen during their long absence to their wives and children? To what perils would they themselves be exposed in the crowded bivouacs and snowy passes of that deadly Gilgit district?

Hence one can understand what a pitiable sight it must have been to see the families bidding farewell to their men-folk when they were needed for the fields, and whom more than likely they would never see again.

To Lord Roberts was left the honour of putting a stop to this unnecessary suffering. He was sent to Kashmir by the Indian Government, at the request of the present Maharajah, to reorganise the Kashmir army, and the Gilgit transport was one of the first matters he tackled.

Now the name Gilgit has lost its terrors, for there is a fine road for pack-animals, and men go there without fear, for on the passes huts are placed on piles from six feet to twenty feet high, so that there is always a refuge for travellers when crossing those high passes when deep in snow and blizzards are sweeping across them.

Then again the condition of the shawl weavers was pitiable, for they were practically slaves, and never allowed to leave the country, as I have mentioned elsewhere. No Kashmiri women were allowed to leave the country, for it was hoped that by this restriction it would prevent their husbands from trying to escape to India.

To give a concrete instance of this, the late Rev. W. I. Stores told me that when he was chaplain in Kashmir he was leaving the country by the Pir Punjal route, when at the pass his progress was blocked by a guard of sepoys, who told him to hand over his coolies, as they were not allowed to leave Kashmir, being shawl weavers who had offered themselves as coolies, hoping that under the shadow of a Britisher they might escape to India, and further ordered the cook's wife, who was with the party, to return. She had dressed herself in Punjabi women's clothes in the hope of escape.

Lieutenant Thorp during his stay in the country made it his business to collect information regarding the persecution of the Kashmiris, of which these stated were by no means the worst of their troubles. He brought the evil condition of the people to the notice of the Indian Government, and also wrote to the papers in England, to try to raise up interest on their behalf and so bring deliverance. However, trouble came upon him, and he was ordered out of the country, and because he refused to go he was bound to his bed and carried towards the pass by sepoys. He, however, managed to escape, and returned to Srinagar; but it was of no avail, for next morning he died of poison after his breakfast.

No doubt this gallant young officer thought, when he realised that his end was near, that all his efforts to help the slaves had been of no use; but if he thought so he was mistaken, and he probably knows now that his life was not laid down in vain.

Other British officers had seen the S.O.S. and answered the call—such as Sir Robert Montgomery, Lieutenant-Governor of the Punjab, Sir Herbert Edwards, Colonel Martin and Colonel Urmston (with whom rests the honour of having put a stop to the burning of Hindu widows in Kashmir). These men met together to consider how best they could help Kashmir, and they agreed that the Kashmiri needed spiritual as well as bodily help. So they subscribed Rs. 14,000, sent it to the C.M.S., and asked them to send to Kashmir a medical missionary, for he would gain the confidence of the people, and they trusted that the Maharajah and his officials would welcome a doctor to their country.

The Society selected Dr Elmslie, a Scot, who came to India as the first medical missionary. Dr Elmslie arrived at Srinagar in the spring of 1864. His life was hard and difficult, for he had no hospital, his operations being performed under the trees; also orders were issued that the people were not to visit the doctor, and sepoys were stationed around to keep them away, as the sick persisted in coming for relief. Several patients suffered imprisonment for disobeying the order of the authorities.

No Europeans in those days were permitted to stay in Kashmir in the winter, and no exception was made in the doctor's case.

Dr Elmslie worked for eight years, and died in 1872, on his way out of Kashmir. The Rev. T. R. Wade worked with him, and did excellent work in the early days of the Medical Mission. The Society then sent out Dr Theodore Maxwell, to whom, because he happened to be the nephew of General John Nicholson, the hero of Delhi, the Maharajah granted a site for the Mission Hospital, on a hill called Rustum Gari, which lies below and is a continuation of the Takht-i-Suliaman. It is a splendid position overlooking the Dal or City Lake.

Dr Maxwell remained until 1876, when ill health compelled him to retire, owing to continual worries. Meanwhile there was a young artillery officer, named Edmund Downes, who had resigned his commission in India in order that he might become a medical missionary, preparing for the work in Kashmir, so once again a soldier came to the relief of the down-trodden people of Kashmir.

During his time a terrible famine came upon the land, from two causes—viz. an exceptionally early winter, and grasping officials. The farmers were not allowed to garner their crops until the officials had measured them, and the officials would not measure them until they had been paid (unlawfully) by the farmers for allowing them to garner their crops. The farmers were holding out against this imposition as it was excessive, and the officials on their side would not modify their demands. Then came a heavy fall of snow which made harvesting impossible, and so thousands of Mohammedan families perished; but the Hindus were less hardly hit, as they were fed out of the Government storehouses.

It was at this time that the missionaries came to the fore—viz. Dr Downes and the Rev. T. R. Wade, who had been sent up to help. They wrote home for help, and with the money had food brought up from India on ponies. They started relief works. They dug a canal from the river to the Dal, so that boats could pass from one to the other. This canal has since been widened and now forms one of the principal waterways. They also started an orphanage for the orphan children and an asylum for destitute women, and in various ways did their best to alleviate the sufferings of the stricken. They had much to contend with, as certain officials objected to this work of mercy being done by Britishers. Fortunately the British Resident, who was a strong, humane man, backed them up, and saw them through many difficulties.

But the famine lost us Dr Downes, for his wife's health gave way, as she herself told me, on account of the terrible sufferings of the people day by day of which she was an unwilling beholder, since so little could be done in comparison with the hugeness of the task.

In those days Dr Arthur Neve arrived. He had hoped

to be sent to Equatorial Africa to help in the pioneer work around Lake Nyanza with his friend Bishop Hannington, but a doctor was badly needed in Kashmir, so Dr Neve went East, and was soon giving of his best to Kashmir.

When he arrived he found a line of mud huts on the side of the hill which answered the purpose of a hospital.

Arthur Neve was a man not only to see visions but to see that they were fulfilled. His vision was a fine up-to-date hospital with every necessary scientific appliance. This he lived to see an accomplished fact. For he and his brother, Dr Ernest F. Neve, who joined him four years later, gathered gradually from their fees and donations such sums yearly as not only were ample for the running of a big hospital, but for adding to their buildings, until it reached its present splendid dimensions. It is also interesting to note that whereas in the early days of 1860 the then Maharajah would not grant the doctor an inch of ground at first on which to put up even a hut in which to care for his sick subjects, the present Maharajah gives yearly a donation to the hospital, and free electric light, and has on several occasions visited the hospital when new buildings were being opened. In the early days the officials tried to obstruct the doctor and patients in every way; now they and their families gladly accept the medical help and skill which this hospital offers.

The hospital contains 150 beds.

In-patients per annum	1,719
Out-patients „	16,158
Operations „	4,143
Total attendances	38,954

The European hospital staff now consists of three doctors—E. F. Neve, Cecil Vosper, M. R. Roche—two

English nurses—Miss Nora Neve, the niece of Doctor Neve, who came out first in 1891, and Miss Lucy M'Cormick—and quite recently Miss H. Smith has joined the staff. These ladies have no easy task, for Eastern assistants have not the same sense of duty as Westerners, and hence it means an immense amount of supervision, as mistakes and carelessness may spell death.

Then in this hospital, like many others in India, members of the family of the sick person come into the wards to help nurse their relations; this may lighten work in one way, but makes it heavier in others.

During the summer months the work increases much, so that it has been the custom for the Society to send help. The following names will bring happy memories to the minds of those who have visited Kashmir in different years, and those of the country who have received so many kindnesses from them.

Thinking of them according to time: R. Venables Green, Esq.; Dr W. F. Adams, who has now a practice in Essex; Dr Sydney Gaster, now at Quetta Hospital; Dr Somterton Clark, in England from ill health; Dr H. T. Holland, who was in Kashmir and who was a tower of strength in the dark days of September last when Dr A. Neve passed from us; Dr A. J. Turner, in practice at home; Dr H. E. Rawlins, who was obliged to retire through ill health, now in practice in England; Dr H. V. Starr, who was cruelly murdered at the Mission Hospital, Peshawar, in April 1918; Dr Reeve Heber, who came at a time of heavy strain at the hospital, and who is now back at his hospital in Leh.

It is indeed a worthy list, and Kashmir is to be congratulated on having the help of such men.

It is impossible for me to convey to my readers the greatness and importance of the work that has been, and is being, carried on in this splendid institution, so I will pass on the account written by Dr Arthur Neve himself of a day's work in the hospital:

"For the last two days the roads leading into the city have been thronged with villagers, tramping in and singing as they tramp, drawn by the great shrine at Hazrat Bal, where the hair of Mohammed is displayed on certain festivals. These are the great days to which the people, especially perhaps the women and children, look keenly forward, for not only is there the display at the shrine, but the opportunity of showing off their best clothes and jewellery, and of seeing the shops of the city and making their frugal purchases. A bundle on the man's back contains a few days' rice and condiments, and the wife carries a fat cock as a present to the mullahs.

"But there is a second pilgrimage centre with a special attraction for the many who have sore eyes or various surgical complaints—namely, the Mission Hospital—and the waves of the rising tide begin to lap in at the gates. It is scarcely the busiest season, but already 135 beds are occupied, and all these in-patients have been personally seen before ten A.M. The hospital seems full of interesting cases, and we find that 107 different towns and villages are represented in the wards. Then comes the first preaching at eleven A.M. to a dense mass of people, and soon we and the nurses and some thirty helpers are dealing as rapidly and effectively as possible with the string of patients passing into the consulting-room. Some merely need a little medicine, others go into the minor operating-room and are prepared for operations; the women pass to the female dressing-room, while some are sent straight to the wards. By noon a hundred have been seen; but many very serious cases remain to be dealt with—a child who has fallen from an upper storey and broken his skull, a woman who has fallen and sustained several internal injuries as well as external wounds (she died, the child recovered), and a man with a fractured leg, as well as many requiring serious operations. But at noon we adjourn to the chapel for our usual prayer and service with the assistants, and then we separate to various wards to give some Bible teaching.

"By twelve-forty-five P.M. everything is once more in full swing; and in one room some private paying patients, including a high State official, are being attended to, while operations are being performed simultaneously in two other rooms. By two-thirty P.M. most of the out-patients have been treated and two more out-patient addresses given, and the European members of the staff take a hurried lunch, while the patients who have been dealt with are gradually dismissed. Then again we plunge into the operating; so far six major and forty minor operations have been done. A bad smash is brought in after ten days' journey, from a town where there is a doctor. 'Why did you come?' 'Oh, Sahib, the doctor wanted to cut off my boy's leg, and we heard that you save legs.' An antiseptic leg-bath was ordered, splints were applied after removing some bone, and the leg was kept on. (He was able to walk in two months.) And so the hours passed. By four P.M. over 350 patients had been seen; but it was getting on for seven o'clock before our last operations were finished, and even then I was called along to the wards to check some bleeding in a case which had been operated upon earlier in the day. Well, it had been a good day's work; we three doctors and two senior assistants had between us performed twenty or twenty-one major operations and fifty minor. Our work was done, but the nurses' work went on till nearly midnight."

The busiest season is in April, May and August. In the first month on one day there were 438 out-patients.

The teaching is an integral and essential part of the work in order that our motives may not be misunderstood, and that the full message of Christianity may appear—a message for the hearts of the sorrowful and oppressed, as well as for the bodies of the suffering. Dr Wilfrid Grenfell, C.M.G., the distinguished medical missionary of Labrador, says:

"I always kept pasted up in my surgery, where sometimes the continuous stream of patients calls for more sympathy than I have to give, and is likely to make one irritable and useless because unsympathetic, these old words:

"'He did kindly things so kindly,
It seemed his heart's delight
To make poor people happy
From morning unto night.'"

Work in a hospital must always be exacting and often very wearying to the flesh, but it, like all else, is relieved by humour at times. The Rev. T. R. Wade, writing in his diary some fifty odd years ago, speaks of the patients as being very superstitious; for they when leaving the hospital would go straight away to their priests to thank them for their recovery and to pay them, believing them to have been the cause of their recovery. Mr Wade would say to these superstitious folk: "You give us all the *kam* and *taklif* [*i.e.* the work and the trouble], whilst to your priests you give all the *dam* and *tarif* [*i.e.* the pay and the praise]."

These same words can be said with truth to-day to many of them, though of course much superstition and ignorance has been cut out and cleaned away.

One day I saw a man who was just leaving the hospital

holding out his hand to Dr Arthur Neve and making a request. Neve turned to me laughing, saying: "This man is asking me to go shares with him over the tumour that I have taken out of his back," for, said the patient, "you surely would not have taken all this trouble over me, and taken out the tumour, unless you were going to make money over the sale of it."

On another occasion at the hospital a fine strapping Mohammedan about forty years of age came up to me and then burst out crying. His tears literally poured out of his eyes down his cheeks, making the wooden floor wet, as he stood before me, for the Kashmiris possess truly colossal water-tanks.

I asked him what was up, and he sobbed out between his gulps: "I am an orphan! I am an orphan!" How could I comfort this poor orphan? Fortunately I remembered that I also was an orphan. So I took out my pocket-handkerchief, which I stuffed into my eyes, as my water-works were no match for his, and therefore I could only sob out, "So am I! So am I!" Nevertheless our sobs, if not our tears, intermingled. The result was magic. The water-cocks were turned off and our heaviness was turned into joy as we laughed together and forgot all about being poor orphans. He was, of course, only trying it on in the hope that I had a soft heart which melted at tears and would shell out rupees.

The Kashmiris are an amusing folk, and their water-works add quite a large part to their enjoyment in life, for they are great actors.

Beyond all this work in Srinagar there is left untold the thousands of patients that are relieved when the doctors go on tour, in the valley itself, and to the regions beyond, giving relief to those who would otherwise have to endure their pain and sufferings till death relieved them.

No wonder then that when Dr Arthur Neve passed away from us to the Greater Empire, into the fuller and real life, in September, 1919, there was such a following to the grave as had never been witnessed before, numbering two or three thousand. Not only did they weep, but showed their sorrow practically by meeting together next day to consider what suitable memorial to raise to their friend of nearly forty years.

Besides the work in the great hospital, the State has placed in their hands the care of their leper hospital, which contains over 100 inmates. The hospital stands on a promontory in the Dal Lake, in a most beautiful position. The lepers are encouraged to do a certain amount of gardening in order to keep them occupied, and so keep their minds off their miserable condition.

I will quote from Dr Ernest Neve's book, *Beyond the Pir Punjal*:

"In Kashmir there is no compulsory segregation of lepers. Those who come to the hospital do so voluntarily, and stay just as long as they like. For this reason it has been found difficult to develop industrial work amongst them. It is important that those who are well enough should have some occupation. They are therefore expected to keep their own rooms clean; and odd jobs—such as grass-cutting, white-washing, path-making and so on—are encouraged. There is also a little school for the children. Most of the lepers come from hill districts around the valley of Kashmir. Many of them belong to the herdsman class. Leprosy is not hereditary; it appears to be propagated by a limited contagion among those who live in crowded huts and under insanitary conditions. There are two chief types of the disease. In one of these there are pale, leprous patches, with loss of sensation. This form affects fingers and toes, which drop off, and it appears to correspond more closely with the leprosy mentioned in the Bible than the other form. The second form, the so-called tubercular leprosy, is far more disfiguring. The body is covered with lumps, and, as these are very numerous on the face, the patient's features are distorted, and sometimes look quite leonine. In many the eyes are attacked, and incurable blindness follows only too often.

Advanced cases are turned out of their homes and people refuse to eat with them, so their condition is very sad. The less marked cases often continue to live in their villages, and they are a source of danger to others. I remember once, when travelling in a mountainous part of Kashmir, going to a cottage and asking for some milk. A man brought me some in his bowl. I was just about to drink it when, glancing at the man, I saw that he was a leper. There are undoubted risks when lepers are mixed with the population, living, sleeping and eating with healthy people. It will at once be perceived that the larger the number of lepers in the hospital the better will it fulfil its intention; and the longer every leper can be retained in the institution the better for himself and the rest of the population. The treatment is chiefly palliative. But many of the lepers improve very much, and in some the disease appears to become, after a time, completely arrested. Food, clothing, bedding, in fact all that they need, is supplied to the lepers; and as funds admit we are gradually furnishing the whole hospital with first-rate iron bedsteads.

The spiritual work in the leper hospital has been uphill, and in some respects it affords a means of estimating the difficulty of the work in Kashmir, and the apparent slowness of progress. In the leper hospital the patients owe practically everything to Christian work. In their own villages most of them are outcasts, although the people give them alms. The contrast in the leper hospital must be very striking to them. Here they have abundant food and many comforts, with cosy little rooms and firewood in the winter. Their wounds are dressed daily, and a friendly interest is taken in them. When we go to this hospital, after visiting all the patients, we gather them together and read a portion of Scripture, following it with simple explanation or a short evangelistic address. Attendance at this service is voluntary. In the summer nearly all come: in the winter the number drops to thirty or forty. The patients listen with attention. They are not good at answering questions; many of them seem to be afraid lest that should be taken by the others as an indication of an intention of becoming Christians. From time to time, however, some have professed their faith, and have been baptized. These have all been subject to a measure of persecution from the other lepers, who promptly refuse to eat with them, and object to live in the same room, and not infrequently show much bitterness. And yet the very people who act in this way often say Amen quite fervently at the close of the prayer with which our service is ended. The fact is that they are ready to assent to a good deal of Christian teaching, but object to baptism, because they realise that a baptized person is no longer one of the great Mohammedan brotherhood, and is therefore from their standpoint a renegade.

The first to become a Christian in the present leper hospital was K.K. He is intelligent and independent, and certainly the best of the lepers. In the first instance he was influenced largely through reading a copy of the New Testament which was given to him.

There is still a tendency for the leper hospital work to

grow and increase. Before long I have no doubt that we shall be able to accommodate more than 100 lepers in the institution. It is interesting to know that all this work is, owing to the enlightenment and liberality of the Maharajah of Kashmir, carried on without any charge whatever upon the funds of the Church Missionary Society. If there were no Christians at all, the work would nevertheless be interesting and encouraging, for is it not a literal carrying-out of the command to "heal the sick . . . and say unto them, The Kingdom of God is come nigh unto you"? And if many of the lepers are somewhat unresponsive, and their gratitude is not always conspicuous, do we not know of ten lepers who were actually completely restored to health, and yet of whom only one stranger returned to give thanks? Who can say that some of these lepers, taking all their circumstances and the heavy handicap of disease into consideration, may not be really nearer the Kingdom than many Christians who, enjoying health and the innumerable privileges of a Christian environment, with all that this means, are nevertheless content to live lives of luxury and ease, unmindful of the White Man's Burden, and the great claim of Christian opportunity, which calls us all to work while it is yet day?

The people of Kashmir are fortunate in having much medical assistance, for besides the two well-equipped State hospitals in Srinagar, the one for the general public, and the hospital for women, there are dispensaries in all the important centres.

The present chief medical officer is Colonel Duni Chand, who decided on a medical career from reading the life of Dr Livingstone, so the State is to be congratulated in having an officer who works for the love of relieving pain and distress. Also the women of the city are fortunate in having had lady doctors in charge of the Zenana Hospital who have never spared themselves in their solicitude for their suffering sisters. Dr Janet Vaughan is the present lady in charge, and fortunate are the women of this city in having such a friend amongst them.

At Islamabad there is a well-run hospital, founded by Mrs Bishop—better known as the traveller and writer, Miss Isabella Bird—which is fortunate in having two devoted ladies in charge, Dr Minnie Gomery and Miss Newnham.

In Srinagar the women have been blessed in having amongst them Englishwomen who have for years given of their best to relieve them in their times of sickness and distress.

To mention one, Miss Newman, who has given nearly thirty years of devoted service, who both night and day has been at their beck and call, tending the sick women not only in their houses but also ready to crawl into the little cabins of the barges to minister to the sick and dying. Only those who know Kashmir bazaars and Kashmir boat life can truly appreciate what this means.

CHAPTER XX

EDUCATION

THE indigenous schools of Kashmir have always been in connection with the mosques, where the boys are taught to read Arabic so that they may be able to read the Koran, but not necessarily to understand it.

Likewise the Brahmans have their schools, where Sanskrit is taught so that the boys may be able to read the sacred Hindu books. To these two languages, Arabic and Sanskrit, Persian was added, and now a certain amount of arithmetic is taught. The scholars range from the age of five years to sixteen or eighteen. They are all taught together, in the same room in the winter and in the verandahs in the summer, but they may be divided into groups. Often there are not enough books to go round, so boys club together to look over one book. The books are as a rule ancient volumes belonging to the boys' parents, so as they have done service for years, these books are generally much the worse for wear, torn, and smeared all over with grease and black, and often the unmistakable signs of curry and rice are upon them. Every scholar brings with him a board, about twelve by seven inches, which is his slate, a wooden bottle filled with chalk and water, which is his ink and ink bottle, a pen made of a stalk of Indian corn, and lastly a piece of glass, generally the bottom part of a brandy bottle, with which to polish his wooden slate, so that it may have a smooth surface on which the pen can run easily. A great deal of time is spent during the school hours in cleaning the chalk writing from the boards and then polishing them. It is quite hard work, so provides exercise for them, which is the only exercise the boys ever get when at school, as athletics are not for gentlemen, and scholars are gentlemen! Long before you arrive at one of these schools you are aware of its existence by the shouting of many voices, which increases as you approach—that is to say, if you have been seen, for the master likes the world to know that he is at work, so urges the boys to be more vehement in their learning and acquisition of knowledge.

When you enter the room you will see thirty to fifty scholars squatting on the floor in small groups, swinging backwards and forwards as they commit the sentences to memory by shouting them out. As every boy is learning a different word or sentence you can imagine what the babel of sounds is like. So stirring is the sight and sound that you feel inclined to join in and shout out some nursery rhyme or something in keeping with the bedlam. You will see by the side of the teacher, who is also swinging and rolling out Arabic or Sanskrit, as the case may be, a bundle of nettles: this is in lieu of a cane. The legs of the boys being bare he is able to inflict punishment with ease. Also you will see by his side a die such as is used by the printers for stamping coloured patterns on cloth. This school die is for printing a pattern on the legs of his pupils to prevent them going into the water, for as none of them can swim they might get drowned. They go on the principle that only those who go on the water or in it can get drowned, therefore do not go near it and you will be safe. This mark is to show the parents that the schoolmaster has taken proper care of their sons, in keeping them from the river.

Education

Before entering the schoolroom your nose will have communicated to you the fact that there are plenty of dirty clothes near at hand, and on entering your eyes will corroborate this fact. The teacher has certainly been most successful in keeping his scholars from the water. If it happens to be the winter time, when all the windows are fast closed, and every boy plus the teacher has a kangri under his pheron, you will have no desire to spend unnecessary time over the inspection of the school.

If a visitors' book is presented to you to sign you will probably write in it that the subject of hygiene should be added to the curriculum of this particular school.

If it is the summer time when you pay the school a visit it is not at all unlikely that you will see the teacher comfortably tucked up in the corner of the room fast asleep, and the boys not making so much noise as usual, as they are hoping that his sleep may be a very long one, with no bad dreams to disturb his rest.

It was about forty years ago that the Mission School was started, where English was taught. Then the State followed suit with a school, and then two schools which, in the course of time, became Middle Schools, and later were raised to High Schools, and affiliated to the Punjab University. There are now in Srinagar two State High Schools, a Mohammedan High School and the C.M.S. High School.[1]

In these the boys read up to the matriculation examination standard for the Punjab University. After passing this they generally enter the Sir Pertab State College, in Srinagar, whilst a few go to one of the colleges in Lahore or to the Kashmir State College at Jammu.

All education in the state is free, so that the youths of

[1] At Baramulla there is the Roman Catholic High School and at Islamabad the C.M.S. High School.

Kashmir have every facility for acquiring knowledge suitable for examinations.

Examinations, next to rupees, are the god of the so-called educated class, for by means of passing examinations the scholars hope to get State service and become eligible for wives attached to some wealth.

The result of higher education being free is that the boys from all classes crowd into the schools, and every year over two hundred youths offer themselves for the matriculation examination, out of which over one hundred will pass, and out of them forty or fifty will go into college. The remainder immediately join the great crowd of unemployed who are for ever trying to get into State service, and so in Kashmir, as in India, we have a class of discontented unemployables. They have been brought out of their station in life, where they could have got work, but now they think themselves superior to anything that is in the line of manual labour, for they have reached the gentlemen cult and aspire to a clerkship, which, though the pay is small, gives the chance of pickings, not to mention the visions of loot later on, according to the custom of their forefathers.

A long-felt want has of late been supplied in the shape of a Technical School, raised to the memory of the late Raja Sir Amar Singh, K.C.S.I. It is a fine large building outside the city, where there is plenty of room for expansion. The State is to be congratulated in having secured the services of Mr F. H. Andrews as Principal, for what Mr Andrews does not know in his line of business is not worth knowing. He also tumbled at once to the weak spot of the Kashmiris in general and craftsmen in particular—viz. want of self-respect, which shows itself in shoddy work. For instance, you will buy a most beautifully carved table of walnut wood, a joy to behold if you do not inspect it too carefully. If you do, and turn it upside down, you will see the mortises have not been cut to fit, the vacant space having been filled with extra pieces of wood, or putty. Or later on you will probably find the table warping, as it has been made from unseasoned wood. I tell these carvers of my visit to the monasteries in Burma, which are richly carved outside as well as inside, and the figures are carved in positions where no human eyes can see them as carefully as they are carved in front, for if man cannot see them the gods can.

Mr Andrews has taken on a difficult business, which is nothing less than to teach the Kashmiris to become honest in their work, to be satisfied with nothing but that which is the best. I marvel at his patience and determination in winning through. He is, by the way, also arranging the wonderful treasures discovered by Sir Auriol Stein in the buried cities in the great Tibetan plateau.

The education of girls is of course very far behind that of the boys. It was somewhere in the nineties that one of the Mission ladies started a girls' school in the city; it was of course by no means popular, as it shocked the prejudices of all proper-thinking folk in Srinagar. The girls who were brave enough to attend were very timid, and their parents were somewhat on the shake, as public opinion was very much against them. The school continued until the first Prize Day. The lady superintendent had invited some of the European ladies of the station to come to the function, thinking it would be an encouragement to the girls and their parents. All the girls were assembled in the school when, on the appearance of the English lady visitors, someone in the street shouted out that the Europeans had come to kidnap the girls. Others took up the cry, and ran to the school windows and told the girls to escape by jumping from the windows, the men below catching them as they fell. Before the visitors could enter the school the scholars had literally flown: the girls of course lost their heads on account of the shoutings from the street. It was a terrible moment for the lady superintendent as she saw her girls disappear out of the windows, for she feared they would be damaged by the fall. It is said that one of the lady visitors was wearing a rather wonderful hat, which upset the equilibrium of the citizens who were standing outside the school. Be this as it may, this episode ended the existence of the first girls' school in Srinagar for some time.

Time is a great healer, so once more girls came to school again, and now there are, besides the three Mission schools for girls, a State School, a Mohammedan School and five Hindu schools for girls, three of which are now Middle Schools, and will soon be High Schools.

At Islamabad, Miss Coverdale, of C.M.S., has a school of one hundred girls, who are very devoted to her, which is no wonder considering the love and care that is shown towards and for them. The education of the girls is of the first importance, for they will be the mothers of the future generation.

It is the women who at present more than the men hinder progress. They are very conservative, because of their ignorance and superstition, and are far more under the power of the ignorant priests than are the men. Also, now that the boys are being educated and having their minds opened, it is most necessary that they should find wives like-minded, instead of, as at present, having to marry ignorant and undisciplined girls, who ever remain a drag on them, and whom they often term "but animals."

It is fortunate that the C.M.S. boys' school has

attached to it a girls' school where the sisters of the boys can receive similar education. Miss Fitze, who is the Principal, has by her devotion, patience and tact worked wonders amongst them, so that from a collection of dirty and undisciplined girls has arisen a school of clean, self-respecting little maidens, who enjoy life to the full, and will in due time become true helpmates of their brothers' class-mates in the boys' school. Then the boys who have cast off superstition and ignorance, and various other evils, will have wives after their own heart; and both together will train up their children to become useful members of the community.

Then, but not till then, can we expect to see a clean city, and the old stage coach get a move on. There is one matter which needs setting right, and it is this. Every year the State College turns out twenty or so graduates, and some of them continue their studies at Lahore, and take their LL.D., etc. Now unless these men are connected with the high officials in the State they are not given that employment for which the State has itself fitted them. All high positions in the State are given to non-Kashmiris—*i.e.* men from the Punjab, Bengal, etc. Now I do not consider this is playing the game.

India is in these days calling out loudly, "India for the Indians," that foreigners must give place to India's sons, etc. If this cry is right and true, why should the same Indian call out, "Kashmir for the Indians"? Why should not the sons of Kashmir have a place in their own country? They certainly have not, for foreigners take all their high posts. Let those who wish for fair play for themselves allow the same treatment to others.

CHAPTER XXI

A KASHMIR MISSION SCHOOL

IN writing of the Mission School I fear the pronoun "I" will obtrude itself *ad nauseam*, but I do not know how to avoid making use of it. Perhaps this nuisance may be somewhat mitigated if my readers will bear in mind the founder of the schools, the Rev. J. H. Knowles, B.D., and the ten years' spade-work that he had to undertake in digging the foundations; then the labours of my European fellow-workers, who have helped so much to strengthen the structure, and lastly the great body of Kashmiri teachers, who have worked most loyally and cheerfully in the work of building up the schools to their present position. In the early years my brother George put in several years of solid work, without remuneration, and set an example which has ever been an inspiration to the staff, so that whenever there has been a special bit of good work done they say, that is "Gog Sahib."

Then there are the following short-service men who have given two or more years' welcome help:—the Rev. C. L. E. Burges, M.A. of Trinity College, Cambridge, scholar and wrangler, whose chief work was to instruct the staff in the teaching of mathematics; A. B. Tyndale, M.A. of Magdalen College, Oxford, who started a technical school, and taught Brahman boys carpentry, thus breaking the Mohammedan carpenters' ring which prevented them teaching Brahmans their trade.

I may mention another difficulty which beset these budding Brahman carpenters. One of them, having arrived at man's estate, wished to take unto himself a wife, but no Brahman could be induced to give his daughter to a man who was engaged in such an ungentlemanly job as that of a carpenter. He put up with his lonely condition for some time, but finally the desire for a spouse proved greater than love for his adze and saw, so he gave up his unholy profession and took up the work of a chaprasi, which was considered to be an honourable profession, whereupon the Brahmans smiled upon him and he became a married man, bless him!

Miss Helen Burges taught the school staff the kindergarten system, which has proved so useful to us, but at the commencement created difficulties, for several parents removed their sons from the school on account of it, for, said they, "We send our children to school to learn and not to play."

The Rev. Cecil Barton, M.A. of Trinity Hall, Cambridge, was associated with the schools for several years, and his life and teaching have been a real help to many, and his memory is still green. Then came the Rev. F. E. Lucey, M.A. and scholar of Worcester College, Oxford, and stroke of his college boat, and F. C. Hall, Esq. The latter was able to stay only a year, as he was called to work elsewhere; the former has been my colleague for many years, and no one could have a more loyal fellow-worker; he supplies by his brains and other powers those things in which I am deficient.

Dr Kate Knowles, M.B., London, for several years identified herself with the schools in a most thorough manner, and did invaluable work amongst the women-folk belonging to the staff and students, and helped them and their neighbours to respect and care for their women-folk.

Charles Musgrave, M.A. of Christ Church, Oxford,

O. H. Robinson, B.A. of Queens' College, Cambridge, and S. T. Gray, B.A. of Jesus College, Cambridge, stroke of his college boat, followed one another as short-service men. Charles Musgrave went as chaplain to a Guards' division, and afterwards served in a Tank division. Oliver Robinson first joined up in the war as chaplain, but later joined the ranks, and gave his life in the great cause. Sydney Gray left us to do his bit, but he came through the ordeal safely.

Rev. Marcus Wigram took my place in the school during one of my furloughs, when the school benefited by his experience and kindly nature.

The last to join the staff was the Rev. J. S. Dugdale, M.A. of Rugby and Oxford, who threw himself heart and soul into the school. We look forward to welcoming him back in the near future.

Whatever we Westerners may have accomplished could not have been done without the willing co-operation of the Kashmir staff, numbering now seventy-five, who of course know the lives and characters of the students of the school in a way that we cannot.

Practically all the staff are old students, so we are like one large family bound together with many ties. We have been in travail together, we have fought together, we have comforted one another in defeats, and rejoiced together in our victories and in our joys. Hence we might choose for our motto with truth that of the old P. & O. Company, "Quis Separabit?"

As in the commencement of the hospital so was it with the school, many obstacles and difficulties had to be overcome. Parents were warned not to permit their sons to attend the school, and as these warnings were not attended to, one or more of the scholars were put into the lock-up for persisting.

THE GHAT AT THE C.M.S. GIRLS' SCHOOL.

Here are seen typical waterside houses. The mud roofs are green with grass, often spangled with flowers. The lattice windows have in one been pasted over with paper to keep out the cold. The houses seem to be on stilts; this is partly because floods used to be of frequent occurrence.

Photo by Commander] [*E. C. Tyndale-Biscoe, R.N.*

A SCHOOL REGATTA

and a foul. In times not long past none but those of low caste would handle an oar, and the introduction of rowing met with no small opposition, but now, so great has been the change effected by example and precept that all the students in the school are enthusiastic " wet-bobs."

A Kashmir Mission School

Times change. So that when the Rev. J. H. Knowles arrived, in 1881, he soon gathered together a goodly number of pupils, who were eager to learn English, as that language began to supersede Persian in certain State offices. When I arrived, in 1891, to assist Mr Knowles in the school there were 250 scholars attending school. Never shall I forget my feelings of surprise and amusement and, to speak the truth, disgust also: surprise, to see these bundles of human beings squatting on the floor, most of them with their mouths open, as different from that class called boys as I had ever imagined; amusement, on account of their ungainly costumes, for every one seemed to be wearing a very dirty nightgown, and their foreheads were plastered with red paint, and numbers of them wore huge golden earrings which would have torn the lobes of their ears off if they had not been supported with string over the tops of their heads; disgust at the offensive smell that pervaded that schoolroom, for practically every one of these bundles had a concealed fire-pot full of hot charcoal, which was emitting fumes of carbon mixed up with unwashen bodies and dirty clothes in which they had been sleeping at night as well as wearing them all day. It was wintry weather, for it was the month of December, the city lay deep in snow, and the streets consisted of pools of black filth; hence their long garments brought much of the city mud into the school. Then, as I inspected them more closely, I noticed that their finger-nails were abnormally long and all in the very deepest mourning. On inquiry I found the possession of long nails to be one of the signs of gentility, as it was an incontestable sign that they never disgraced themselves with doing manual labour of any kind, and therefore belonged to the "sufed posh"—*i.e.* white flower, or tip-top class, as they were by birth the highest caste. When

I had been in the school a few days, I told them I thought that black nails were hardly in keeping with white flowers, and insisted that clean nails should be the complement of the white-flower class.

On the occasion of my first Prize Day the Resident, Colonel David Barr, was present in the school hall to give away the prizes. He called me up to him, and I thought he wished to make some pleasing remark, when he whispered in my ear: "What a dirty lot of boys you have got, Biscoe. I will give a prize for the cleanest boy next year." The boys were all dressed in their best, and had brushed themselves up for the great occasion, so you can imagine my chagrin. I had forgotten that the Resident's nose had not been trained as mine had been.

After my introduction to the bundles on the floor I thought I would make a good start by asking the Principal of the school to grant the boys a half-holiday in honour of my arrival from the West to teach them something (which looked doubtful). Mr Knowles kindly accorded my request, and announced the half-holiday. I expected to see the bundles wake up into life and make some sort of joyful sound, but instead I only heard groans. I asked if that was the way Kashmiris cheered, for it sounded to me uncommonly like groans. I was told that my surmise was correct, it was groans, for the bundles were much displeased at my request, for had they not come to school to learn? What good were holidays? I began to understand that I had come to Kashmir to learn rather than to teach, so I set myself to study the character of the Kashmir schoolmasters and the bundles. It was not easy, for I had so much to unlearn, and also had to try to look at things from quite another point of view.

To start with, nearly all the 250 or so bundles were Brahmans—*i.e.* the tip-top caste of the Hindus. They were twice-born, so they told me. That again means many things—such as, the food they might eat and what they might not eat. To start with, they could not eat with any person who was not twice-born; they could not even eat with their Maharajah, should he be kind enough to invite them to do so, for he was of a lower caste, being of the Kashatri or soldier caste. They only eat food cooked by a Brahman, and the cook must not wear trousers when he prepares their food. Then the place where the food is cooked must first of all be spread with cow dung, for a cow is their holy animal. (By the way, I have discovered that fleas do not like cow dung, and so avoid rooms spread with it, hence their cooking places have one great asset, for I know by experience that fleas or other such-like insects do not object to the bodies and clothes of the twice-born.) Then they gave me lists of food that they may not eat, such as tame fowls and tame ducks, and their eggs, but they may eat wild fowl, and their eggs. They may not eat red apples or red tomatoes, but they may eat yellow ones.

I was surprised to find that they might eat flesh, as they are not allowed to take life, but they said that they might eat flesh so long as some non-Brahman killed it. But they get terribly mixed up in their yea-yeas and their nay-nays. I had two Brahman munshis at different times who were brothers. On the first occasion I was living in a house-boat on the lake, and to my surprise saw my Brahman munshi fishing, and as I came up to him he said: "Please, Sahib, kill it for me," bringing to me a fish he had caught. So I said: "Why do you not kill it yourself?" "Oh, Sahib, I cannot kill it: I'm a Brahman and may not take life." "Then how is it you fish?" I said. "Oh," said he, "there is no law against catching fish, the law is against taking life." So my munshi caught fish, I killed them for him, and he ate them.

Some months after this incident I was up one of the valleys, living in a tent, and the brother of the Brahman fisherman was my munshi. On my way to the river to fish I called to my munshi to bring along a rod for himself, as we were rather short of food, and therefore a second rod would be useful. "Sahib," said he, "I cannot do this, for I am a Brahman." I did not say anything more on the subject, and he came to see me fish, and sat near me. When I had hooked one I just swung it over to him at the end of my line and said: "Please knock it on the head for me, munshi." The munshi without a word took it in his hand and killed it, and continued to do this service for me every day when I went fishing, but nothing could induce him to catch a fish himself, for was he not a Brahman? These two Brahman brothers, it seemed to me, might very well enter into partnership in the fisherman's line, and do a good business.

It is very difficult to understand the Brahman's ethics. Often it happens in the summer-time, when one is taking a class, a mosquito or fly settles on one's hand. By force of habit I end its life with a slap. At once the class of Brahmans jump and cry out: "Oh, oh! you have taken life! you have taken life!" and suck their fingers hard, and then crack their knuckles, which is a sign of disgust and horror. They have of late given up this custom of showing horror at the death of a fly or mosquito, for they hate the retort, "Don't you eat mutton?" which generally follows their cries of horror. They will not kill insects. I have seen a boy pick a flea off himself and then quietly put it in a place of safety, down the neck of the boy next him, for if he had put it on the floor it might have been trodden upon, or perhaps have returned to his own person. This belief of theirs in the preservation of pests is very unfortunate, for our library books and pictures are continually destroyed by them. All houses are infested with fish insects; no one will kill them, they just shake them out on the floor, and in a few minutes they are back again at their destructive work. It is the same with rats and mice, which abound. The furthest they will go in the matter is to catch them in traps, and then carry them to the opposite side of the river and there release them; but as people on both sides of the river play the same game, rats do not decrease greatly.

In the days of my apprenticeship I learnt that I must not touch my pupils for fear of defiling them, for in a forgetful moment I would pat them on the back or head to cheer them up, at which they would squirm as if I were a leper, or one of the untouchables. As a matter of fact, it was necessary to be careful where you did touch them, as they nearly all were suffering from some head or skin disease. On one occasion, as I placed my hand on a boy's head, he wearing only a skull cap, without the usual pagri, I said, "What have you under your cap?" thinking I felt peas, at the same time picking off his cap, when, lo and behold! his head was thick with smallpox! I did not pat his head a second time. Most of these ideas of theirs as to food and holiness were of little consequence to school discipline until it came to the matter of their belief in the unholiness of leather, for that knocked out boxing gloves, football, and even rowing, for the leather on the oar they jibbed at, although I said they were not to touch the leather button, but simply grasp the oar and pull.

To get over these difficulties took months, but to surmount them was imperative, as I could see that it was athletics of all sorts and every kind which these bundles needed. One great obstacle was their idea of gentility. They held firmly to the belief that a gentleman did not work, and to hurry in any way was the mark of a low-caste being. It was quite true that every person in Srinagar in those days who considered himself a gentleman would never think of walking faster than two miles per hour, the pace of the ox. So any kind of game requiring energy was ruled out.

The reason why I made such a point of games was not merely to wake them up, and if possible to turn the bundles into boys and then into men, but it was to make them fit for social service, and to teach them the joy of service for others. The reason of this was threefold. (1) From what I knew of their past history. (2) From what I saw daily in the streets of Srinagar, the treatment of the weak, and of the low-caste, and the impurity that was rampant. (3) From my desire as a Christian to introduce them to Him who taught all men to love one another and show it by practice and not by talk.

Those Brahman bundles in the school were the sons or grandsons of those officials who had bullied and squeezed the Mohammedan peasants for years past, and their large houses in the city, with all their wealth, were a standing witness to their looting powers, for the salary they received from the State was quite insignificant.

Now their parents had sent them to school, so that they might get State employment and follow in the steps of their forefathers, and by aid of their English education they might even go one better than their progenitors. Now how was one to combat this? By teaching them to hate wrong and love right, to hate oppression and love to protect the weak, in fact to be the exact opposite to their fathers.

Now talking would not accomplish this, nor would reading books. They must be taught to love right by doing right, and to hate evil by fighting evil, and to suffer in doing so. Now bundles could not do this, therefore the bundles must be turned into boys by athletic exercises, and athletic boys turned into manly and true citizens by continued acts of kindness.

Now in such a city as Srinagar there was no lack of opportunities for knights-errant, for as I have already pointed out it is women who have to give way to men in the streets; it is women who have to fetch and carry water in their heavy earthen pots; it is women who are done down continually because they are only women, and even the poor madwomen are misused by the filthy bipeds after dark.

Who can see the treatment that the animals receive in the East without wrath? Overladen, starved, with sore backs of every description and yet carrying riders or loads on them. Cows and donkeys in the winter-time fight with the pariah dogs for the filth in the streets.

Then there is the immorality after dark, which no one would tackle, because one should not stir up dirt. Well, it is anyway the duty of a head of a school to protect his boys.

How could any of these things be tackled with bundles? The dry bones must be made to live and be made strong. Athletics will create the muscle and skill for self-defence, and social service give the desire for the defence of others.

Now all this was to lead to Him who taught us social

service, and who can give strength to carry it through, for the fight has to be one to the finish; and the fight while they are young and in the school is nothing compared to what it will be in the bigger life outside the school in a country like Kashmir. By nothing but by the power of God will they be able to carry on this warfare against the powers of evil. I soon discovered that one had to commence on an infinitely lower level in this school than I ever imagined.

To start with, lying was considered to be one of the arts to be practised. A champion liar was more honoured in this country than a champion boxer would be in an English Public School. I can remember my surprise and joy when a Brahman boy told me the truth, in the face of punishment. It was the first case of its kind after I had been in the school for five years. During the next year three boys spoke the truth when naturally they should have lied, and in the seventh year five boys rejoiced my heart by their veracity. After that year they continued to improve, so that now I rarely have a lie told me, in fact as rarely as I had the truth from their lips in the early days.

Of course I am always careful not to ask a boy a direct question when there is punishment at the back. I generally tell him to give me his answer, say half-an-hour hence, and this gives him time to pull himself together. Of course if I had given this respite in the early days it would have only meant a more elaborated falsehood, with many witnesses to prove innocency.

Please do not imagine from this that the boys have given up lying altogether, but they have ceased to glory in it, and they have learnt that it pays better to speak the truth at school than to lie. Yet I can say this with truth, that I know of several old boys whose word I can accept with as much confidence as that of a Britisher.

And for the last few years in the school boys have actually blushed when they lied, which of course shows that they possessed a conscience. A great discovery for a Kashmiri.

CHAPTER XXII

A KASHMIR MISSION SCHOOL (*continued*)

TELLING tales of one another, generally known as "sneaking," was as troublesome as it was universal. It existed not only among the schoolboys but among the school staff; in the public offices; it was everywhere, the practice of doing your neighbour down, if there was any chance of benefiting yourself thereby.

A British officer who was head of a large State office told me one day that he had no less than forty anonymous letters in two weeks from his clerks, with evil tales of each other, and said that he did not know how to deal with the nuisance. This fact aroused me to action, for I felt at all costs I must tackle the matter properly in the school, as the only hope for the future. So I at once made it a penal offence for anyone to come to me with a tale against another unless he was prepared to fight with him in the playground with single-sticks. This order produced the desired effect in double-quick time, as it was found to be a somewhat painful experience to sneak.

This wholesome fear of the ordeal by battle produced some amusing scenes at times. Here is one. A strong Brahman youth, a member of the football team, complained to me that a certain Christian, who was a Pathan by race, had attacked him and his friends with his knife (the Pathans are handy men with their knives), and asked my protection. So I first called one of the Brahman teachers and asked him if he knew anything of this matter.

He said that he did, that it was true, but there was a reason for the Pathan's action. The Pathan being the only Christian in a class of thirty was harassed by them, and taunted for being a Christian, and when leaving school this class would add to their taunts by throwing stones and mud at him. The Pathan, having so many to deal with, drew his knife and went for them in true Pathan fashion. I called the Pathan, and asked him if it was true that he tried to knife his class-fellows, and he answered straight that it was perfectly true, as it was his only way of getting rid of so many adversaries at once. I answered that fists are the schoolboy's weapons, and not a knife, which I threw out of the window, to be out of harm's way, into the river. I then called up the Brahman accuser and said that as he had complained he must fight the Pathan himself.

So single-sticks were produced, and as I handed one to the Pathan I said: "Are you willing to fight this Pandit?" (Pandit, which means a learned man, is synonymous for Brahman in Kashmir.) He grasped the stick with zest, exclaiming: "I am!" I held out the second stick to the Pandit and asked if he was equally ready, but he would not take it, saying: "I am not a Christian. I do not know how to fight." So, as he would not stand up like a man, he was made to apologise in public, by taking off his pagri and placing his bare head at the feet of his adversary.

This ended all future trouble; in that class the Pathan was never molested again for being a Christian or anything else. The single-stick is a most excellent article for healing divisions and many other moral sicknesses.

One of the most difficult habits to correct was the

universal foul language, for there was no high ideal to which to appeal. To make a start, I naturally said to the boy: "You would not like your father to hear you use such language!" The boy simply smiled at my ignorance, and answered: "Why, my father always uses it." "Well," I answered, "anyway, your mother would not." Again a smile of compassion pervaded the boy's face as he answered: "Why, it was my mother who taught me." So then I said: "Does your religion sanction this foulness?" He answered: "Our priests always use this language." This last statement of the boy was corroborated by a Brahman judge, who, when I brought to him a case of gross immorality on the part of some priests, wishing to have them punished, said: "You must remember, Mr Biscoe, that the Hindu law sanctions a certain amount of impurity." On my pressing the case in point he allowed that it exceeded the leniency of Hindu law, so I congratulated him.

To alter the language of the boys meant raising the whole tone of Hindu morals, which was a large order. Later on you will see how we met this evil in a grave and more difficult form.

The Brahmans are a proud people, for besides being twice born they hold that they are part of God. The boys told me that they could not commit sin, and when they were caught at their various acts of transgression which I considered against the moral law they always said they were only following the custom of their fathers and forefathers, and therefore felt no shame.

How could one shame them? They felt no shame at their dirt of body, clothes and language, or of their lying or cowardice. They were Brahmans, and that was sufficient for all things.

I should say when I talk of boys that the top class consisted of beings from eighteen years of age to twenty-four years; many of them grew black beards, and were married, and therefore were fairly set in their ideas. Again, a very irritating idea they held, and that was their belief in their own superior knowledge. I could not get them to own that they did not know those things which they did not know. They always wished to argue, and would never own up when a fact was demonstrated to them. I had a brain-wave. I saw boxing-gloves—and these same boxing-gloves stopped argument, and all the rest of it, which nothing else would have done. It all began and ended in one morning.

A certain black-beard said that he knew everything. Did he know how to box? Yes, of course he did. So I asked him if he could prevent me hitting his nose if I wished to do so; he, of course, said yes, he could. So I said: "Prove it." The boxing-gloves were brought out, and I was able in a few seconds to demonstrate that for once he did not know.

So clearly had he learnt that lesson that when I expressed my wish to continue the demonstration he pleaded most forcibly that he could not defend his nose and knew nothing whatever of this painful game.

I had won through, for whenever in future any of the black-beards wished to argue I only had to say: "Can you box?" Would that one could have conquered all the other difficulties with such ease!

Rome was not built in a day, and these Brahmans were not made into self-respecting gentlemen in a day. What was needed to start with was self-respect instead of this self-conceit. Talking would never do it; it must be by action. So action they were to have, and plenty of it.

As I said before, we commenced with athletics, which were to be the precursor of social service, which would teach them unselfishness—after which all the rest would follow naturally. But how were we to begin athletic games with those who stoutly refused to play them?

"For," said they, "if we play football, or row, etc., we shall grow muscle on our bodies, and then we shall become low-caste folk like the boatmen and coolies. Moreover, if we play games we shall have to run about and be energetic, and people will laugh at us, for gentlemen must not hurry."

The story of how we commenced football will have to suffice to show how the difficulties of introducing athletics were overcome.

It was in the autumn of 1891, when I returned from Bombay with Mrs Tyndale-Biscoe, that amongst our luggage we brought a football, the first that our schoolboys had seen. I remember well the pleasure with which I brought that first football to the school, and the vision that I had of the boys' eagerness to learn this new game from the West. Well, I arrived at the school, and at a fitting time held up this ball to their view, but alas! it aroused no such interest or pleasure as I had expected.

"What is this?" said they.

"A football," said I.

"What is the use of it?"

"For playing with. It is an excellent game, and will help to make you strong."

"Shall we gain any rupees by playing it?"

"No."

"Then we do not wish to play the game. What is it made of?"

"Leather."

"Then we cannot play; we cannot touch it. Take it away, for it is unholy to our touch."

You will see that matters had not turned out as my optimism had led me to expect.

"All right," said I. "Rupees or no rupees, holy or unholy, you are going to play football this afternoon at three-thirty, so you had better learn the rules at once." And immediately, with the help of the blackboard, I was able to instruct them as to their places on the field, and the chief points and rules of the game.

Before the end of school I perceived that there would be trouble, so I called the teachers together and explained to them my plans for the afternoon. They were to arm themselves with single-sticks, picket the streets leading from the school to the playground, and prevent any of the boys escaping *en route*. Everything was ready, so at three o'clock the porter had orders to open the school gate. The boys poured forth, and I brought up the rear with a hunting-crop. Then came the trouble; for once outside the school compound they thought they were going to escape; but they were mistaken. We shooed them down the streets like sheep on their way to the butcher's. Such a dirty, smelling, cowardly crew you never saw. All were clothed in the long nightgown sort of garment I have described before, each boy carrying a fire-pot under his garment and so next to his body. This heating apparatus has from time immemorial taken the place of healthy exercise.

We dared not drive them too fast for fear of their tripping up (as several of them were wearing clogs) and falling with their fire-pots, which would have prevented their playing football for many days to come.

At length we are safely through the city with a goodly crowd following and arrive at the playground. Sides are made up, the ground is cleared and ready, the ball is in the centre, and all that remains is for the whistle to start the game.

The whistle is blown, but the ball does not move.

Thinking that the boys had not understood my order, I tell them again to kick off the ball immediately after hearing the whistle. I blow again, but with no result. I notice that the boys are looking at one another and at the crowd of spectators with unmistakable signs of fear and bewilderment on their faces.

On my asking them the cause, they say: "We cannot kick this ball, for it is an unholy ball and we are holy Brahmans." I answer them by taking out my watch and giving them five minutes to think over the situation: at the expiration of the time, I tell them, something will happen if the ball does not move. We all wait in silence, an ominous silence. The masters armed with their single-sticks are at their places behind the goals.

Time is just up, and I call out: "Five seconds left—four—three—two—one. Kick!" The ball remains stationary! My last card had now to be played, and I shout towards the right and left goals: "Sticks!"

Sticks won the day, for as soon as the boys see the sticks coming the ball bounds in the air, the spell is broken, and all is confusion. Puggarees are seen streaming yards behind the players, entangling their legs; their shoes and clogs leave their feet as they vainly try to kick the ball, and turn round and round in the air like catherine wheels descending on any and everybody's head. The onlookers who have followed us from the city are wildly excited, for they have never in their lives before seen anything like it—holy Kashmiri Brahman boys (in dirty nightgowns) tumbling over one another, using hands and legs freely to get a kick at a leather ball.

Well, as I said before, all was noise and excitement, when all of a sudden the storm is succeeded by a dead calm: the game ceases, the Brahmans, both players and onlookers, are all sucking their fingers for all they are worth (a Kashmiri way of showing amazement), and all eyes are turned towards one of the players who is a picture of misery. And no wonder, for this unholy piece of leather had bounded straight into this holy one's face, had actually kissed his lips. He had never before in his life felt the smack of a football, and certainly never dreamed of such a catastrophe. He thought all his front teeth were knocked out and that his nose was gone for ever. He would touch his mangled (?) features, but he dared not. Once or twice he essayed to do so, but his heart failed him. His face was defiled, so that he could not do what he would, and would not do what he could. He did the next best thing, which was to lift up his voice and weep, and this he did manfully. This moment was a terrible one for all concerned, and especially for me, for now all eyes were directed to the primary cause of all this misery.

What was I to do? I was not prepared for such a turn of events. I could "shoo" an unwilling school to the playground, I could make unwilling feet kick, but how could I make an unholy face holy? Fortunately the idea of water came into my distracted mind, and I said: "Take the fool down to the canal at once and wash him." Immediately the thoughts and the eyes of the victim's sympathisers were diverted to the cleansing waters and their magical effect on the outraged features of the body. On their return I placed the ball again in the centre, blew my whistle and the ball was kicked off. All was excitement once more, and the game was played with enthusiasm until I called "Time!"

Everyone left the field and scattered to various parts of the city, to tell their parents and neighbours of the great "tamasha" they had witnessed or in which they had taken part. The remarks made about me and the school in their homes over their curry and rice that night were, I expect, not all favourable.

I have been told more than twice that I behaved in an un-Christianlike manner, and that I had no business to force football or any other game upon boys against their will.

Well, we cannot all see alike, and it is just as well that we cannot, otherwise Rome would never have been built and there would not be much progress on this terrestrial sphere. That game introduced the leather ball to Srinagar and to the holy Brahman who lives therein, and although for the first year my presence was a necessity at every game, football came to stay.

Now all the various schools in the city have their football teams, and in all parts of the city you see boys playing this game with a make-shift for a football.

This year I watched an inter-class match, most keenly contested, the referee being not a teacher but a schoolboy. His decision was not once disputed, nor was there any altercation between any of the players; it was a truly sporting game.

Now for something more important than games.

Opportunities for social service in a city like Kashmir are endless, so we tackled the most obvious first—viz. the distress of the owners of houses when their property took fire; and in the early days of which we are writing I suppose there must have been as many fires in the city within twelve months as there are days in the year.

Before writing an account of our first fire I must say that amongst other things which militated against social service, besides it being considered coolie work and the like, the boys objected to giving up any of their time in school, for Eastern boys love books as the Western boys love games.

Then parents were also quite against what they call waste of time in sports. The boys were sent to school to pass examinations, and that is supposed to be the aim and end of school life. Most native schoolmasters have the same belief, and take no interest whatever in games. Games are useless to them, whereas passing examinations means Government employment and a rich wife.

Examinations have been the curse of education in India, for it has turned out, and is doing so still, a class of beings with swelled heads, who are a curse to the land, for they can talk and make speeches without end, and do all they can to pull down the ladder up which they climbed. Of true education and forming of character they know nothing and care less.

It seems strange to me that after all the educational authorities have not found a more suitable education for Indians. It has created a class which continues to despise manual labour, and panders to their desires for Government employment, in which there are not enough billets to satisfy them. Therefore the country is crowded with discontented half-educated men who give trouble to the Government which has given them this education at schools and colleges practically for nothing. Well, that same spirit which I found in the boys and parents of the boys, and which I have been trying to fight ever since, still remains, so until I can find anything better we are going in hard for "social service," to teach the youth of this country their duty towards their country and fellow-citizens. So I here describe our first attempt at fires.

On our looking out of the windows from our exalted position over the river we see crowds eagerly pressing towards the scene of fire, for on such occasions there is always a fair chance of profiting by a neighbour's loss. The trumpet-blower, a policeman's form, we see silhouetted against the sky, as he stands aloft on the roof of a house blowing for all he is worth. The owner of the burning house, and those of the houses touching it, are yelling, screaming and dancing, as is their custom on such occasions.

The scholars, having taken in the situation, are quite *blasé*, and squat down once more to continue their lessons, which to them are far more interesting than a dozen fires, for they have seen them often enough. But we of the West think differently from the East on such occasions. We understand that God has given us muscle as well as brains, and now is the time to make use of the former, so, choosing the biggest of the sucking scholars, we order books down and loins girt, and, on passing out, we arm ourselves with single-sticks, as they come in useful sometimes. We head for the fire, a party from thirty to forty strong. I shall never forget what I then saw; it has been impressed deep on my brain without any sucking or shouting. Such a woeful sight I never wish to see again.

There, straight in front of us, was a house in a blaze. The only occupants of it at the time were women, for the men were away. There stood, or rather danced, an old woman mad with excitement, imploring the bipeds around to help her save her property (no houses in the city are insured, so a fire means loss of everything). There were crowds of turbaned beings on all sides. Most of them had taken up positions so that they might enjoy thoroughly the sight, and see it through. The particular bipeds to whom this frantic woman was chiefly addressing her remarks were a bunch of things squatting on the ground with their mouths open, and with hands shading their eyes from the heat.

The woman implored these squatters to come to help her, and to show her agony she took hold of the upper part of her garment at the neck in both hands and rent it right down the centre, nearly dividing her garment in halves. These deaf adders took not the least notice; they simply looked beyond her. She then put both hands to her head, and with one lusty pull out came two large tufts of hair, which she held out theatrically towards the men, again imploring their help; but it was of no use. She then said: "I will give you money for every pot of water you will bring." Then, and not till then, did these bipeds show any intelligence. "How much will you give?" said they. She answered "So much," at which the bipeds relaxed once more into their vacant stare. The old woman roared, danced and screamed, doubling her price for a pot of water. That evidently satisfied them, for they moved at it. I suppose, they went off to find pots with which to make some money.

All this was enacted in shorter time far than it takes me to put it on paper.

The glare, the heat, the roar of the flames, the screams of the women, the boo-boos of the crowd in delight as the flames leap higher and higher, and the bonny, brave, *blasé*, blue-coated constable from his exalted position blowing, blaring and bellowing his brass braying bugle to let all good citizens know that there was something in the wind—it was a sight not easily to be forgotten. The thought in my mind, naturally, was how to procure pots with which to conduct the water from the river, which was close by, to the burning building. Now, as luck would have it, we saw a barge full of pots coming slowly up-stream, so I put some coin into the hands of the boys with which to secure the pots, but the boys returned to me immediately, saying that the bargee would not sell them any, and had steered his boat out into the stream to show his mind on the subject, no doubt hoping thereby to send up the price of his goods. But we were one too many for him. His boat was boarded, and we took all the pots we needed. The bargee relieved his feelings by giving tongue to his choicest vocabulary, giving us a list of all the great men in the land to whom he would report us for this gross act of brigandage. We told him that he was quite right, but at the present moment his pots were in great request, and that we had all that we required. We at once formed a line from the river to the house and passed up a grateful stream of water.

Having started the boys, I turned my attention to the crowd of sightseers, and asked them to lend a hand with the boys, naturally expecting that they would follow our lead. But no such thing—the crowd sat and stared at us, being highly entertained, and then commenced jeering. The Brahmans amongst them told our boys to desist, as they were lowering their position as nature's gentlemen, twice-born, and, what was more, dishonouring the Brahman name. I recall gratefully one exception, and that was an officer of a Gurkha regiment, a Hindu, who called out to some sepoys who were following him, "This is what I call Christianity," and he gave a word of cheer to the boys.

The boys stood the reproaches of their elders for some time, but a few, who valued their gentility more than their humanity, slunk away when I was not looking and joined the crowd at a respectful distance, some at a very respectful distance.

At last my patience gave out, and I collared several of the jeerers and put them in line with our lot, making them hand along the earthen pots. Here our single-sticks came into use, for I placed certain of the boys as officers over the impressed men to keep them going with their wands of office. Fortunately I had two Bengali Christians, two Parsees and the son of a major in his Highness' army, who were of different stuff to the Kashmiris; they made full use of their positions and kept the pots moving. After a while the Governor of the city arrived with some officials and a small manual fire-pump. They laughed heartily at seeing us at work, but nevertheless backed us up, which made the work easier for the boys. One of our self-imposed tasks was to protect the property that we had saved from being annexed by a certain class of citizens somewhat related to Sir Robert Peel, but not in a very direct line. These worthies had arrived on the scene with an empty barge, and were busy removing all movables into it, in order that they might be taken to a very safe place, out of the way of naughty men. Over these gallant gentlemen boys were placed, and the wands of office again proved useful.

Well, all things in this world have an ending, and this fire was no exception, for it got tired of blazing, not liking the water, and smoked instead. The woman and bipeds had yelled and danced themselves dog-tired, and settled down to mourn and weep as they sat and watched the ashes of their houses and the ashes of their gods vanish into smoke. Our boys, pretty well tired out, soaking with water and covered with grime, gradually found their way homewards to tell of their valour, and to receive in return pious lectures from their parents for the dishonour they had brought upon all self-respecting Brahmans and their own families in particular, while some, no doubt, came in for chastisement. Nevertheless seeds had been sown that day in their inmost souls which would never have got there had it been left to the classroom and book. However persuasive the preaching, or holy the book, duty to one's neighbours and duty towards God is most certainly not learnt practically through mouth and ear only. "Faith must be shown by works." Never was a day's schooling better lost; and many a school day has been lost since then, in so far as lectures and preachings are concerned, in our efforts to make budding bipeds into such men as we believe Almighty God wishes them to be.

I recount this episode at some length as it was one of those events which has helped to make history in this picturesque but dirty city. This first breaking up of a school day for social service was especially pleasing to me, for when at school myself in the seventies I, with a party of school-fellows, was standing in a similar line passing buckets of water from a horse-pond to a blazing farmyard, holding the fort till the fire-engine, from a town ten miles away, should arrive. We heard the school bell ring, plainly enough, and those of us who preferred social service to a master's wrath stuck to the buckets, and when the engine arrived we returned to school to be punished. We were not disappointed in this matter.

From that day to this I have always considered our punishment an error of judgment on the part of the master, and was therefore glad to have so excellent an opportunity of showing my belief by works.

We who live in this country have opportunities pretty well every day to stir the blood and awaken consciences to the life of service for our fellow-men, to which God calls all those who have ears to hear and eyes to see. Those who live in Christian countries have not the same golden opportunities as we have who live in non-Christian countries, for the Christianity of centuries, far from the ideal as it certainly has been, has produced men and not bipeds. For it may be within a rough or perhaps a haughty exterior there is, deep down, but which still can be reached, that innate kindness which is touched by weakness and sends through the veins blood red-hot at the sight of oppression and wrong, and always champions the weaker side. This spirit of chivalry comes from Christ, and Christ alone, whatever else men may say.

I am not talking quite through my hat, for before I came to this land I had had two strenuous years of service amongst the poor in the East End of London, under the guidance of the best of rectors, the Rev. A. J. Robinson. Grand times they were, and to them I always look back with thankfulness. While there I was obliged to know something of fallen humanity in doss-houses and elsewhere; but among these poor fallen creatures have I seen over and over again that spirit of chivalry which at once showed that there was hope for all men, and though many of them denied the existence of a God, that spirit of chivalry showed me that they still possessed a spark of that light which comes from the God whom they denied.

True, there were very many opportunities of service in that dark corner of a Christian country, but they were nothing, no, nothing, compared with needs and opportunities here. For instance, in the West it is the poor who usually steal from the rich and strong, but in the East it is the rich who squeeze the poor and helpless, and yet the man in the street here does not seem to notice that there is anything wrong or out of course.

This fact struck me very forcibly before I became accustomed to the manners and customs of Srinagar citizens. For example, in the winter-time, when the streets are covered with snow, and there is only a one-man path, one sees the women, children and old men all being shoved out into the snow by the strong and opulent. Again, year in and year out, one sees the women struggling up the steep, broken and slimy river ghats with the heavy earthenware water-pots; and again, as one watches the people going on their numerous pilgrimages to holy shrines in the country, the women are the beasts of burden, toiling the many weary miles loaded with brass cooking-pots and bedding, whilst the lord and master swaggers in front, every now and then looking behind and beckoning to his spouse to hurry up. All these and many other evils one has witnessed daily, but it is considered to be quite correct, for it is the custom of the East. It was not until some years had passed that I learnt of far greater evils, which are hidden from sight, the early marriage system and many other like evils that the women suffer uncomplainingly. These plague spots can only be tackled by women ministering to women, and such women as have come from the West, whose love and sympathy for their Eastern sisters enable them so to devote their lives to them that nothing can daunt them if they can in any way alleviate suffering.

CHAPTER XXIII

A KASHMIR MISSION SCHOOL (*continued*)

I HAD not been long in the country when I discovered the perils our boys were in from bands of immoral scoundrels. I had maps of the city on which I marked, in red, places of "refuge" for the hunted, with a deliverer in the person of a man who had learnt the noble art of self-defence, and, by the way, defence of others, who on call would come to the rescue.

These maps were hung up in each of the schools for the boys to study. So far so good. The next step was to catch these scoundrels red-handed. We had not to wait long.

On a certain afternoon when the boys were leaving the football ground in the outskirts of the city a gang of these scoundrels came down upon certain boys to carry them off. Fortunately some of the staff were near at hand and ran in to the rescue. During the fight which took place the leader of the gang was felled and secured, and from his pocket was taken a book which proved to be his undoing, for it was the club's information book. In it were the names of the president, secretary, treasurer and committee.

Then followed the names of 170 of the pretty boys in the city, their abode, and other information of use to the gang, but on this occasion it proved most useful for our purpose, when we were able to bring the criminals to justice, which proved to be a much more lengthy and difficult business than we had imagined, as we had yet to learn that this gang had strong backers.

I myself did not hear of this little scrap until I arrived at the school next morning, when I heard of the haul, and better still that the president of the gang was in the lock-up, my masters having handed the scoundrel to the police. I at once rode off to the thana (police station) in order to see the prisoner's face and to know that he was secure, but what was my disgust to be told by the police officer that the prisoner had escaped in the night; nor were the gentlemen in blue able to trace him. We were determined to have this scoundrel, as it was clear to us that the police did not wish to help us. It was a long hunt until about three months later, during another assault, he was captured and handed over to the police as it was evening-time. My men no doubt thought that the police would not dare to let him go a second time. As before, I was not told of the catch until my arrival at school next morning, when I immediately rode off to the thana, and was again told that the prisoner had escaped in the night. This news was decidedly riling, but did not disturb us as much as people not accustomed to the East and its ways might suppose. It only made us more determined to get the better of all concerned, for one is bound to win if one sticks to it. Again we watched, waited and also worked. After a month or two, for the third time the scoundrel fell into the hands of my fellows. It was, of course, after dark, so for the third time he was handed over for safe (?) keeping to the police.

For the third time I ride down to the thana, and for the third time hear that the guardians of the law have again been outwitted, for the prisoner escaped in the night.

I told the officer that I never forgive a third offence, also that I knew something of the customs of Kashmir in general and of his lot in particular. It was now ten o'clock, and I gave him two hours only in which to recapture the escaped prisoner, saying that I would be back at twelve o'clock punctually, and the prisoner must be in the thana, and if not I would ride him off at once to the British Resident. This was my last card, which I was loath to play, as one hates to bother hard-worked and often harassed British officials. Of course the officer said that I was demanding an impossibility, etc., etc. But I rode off saying that at twelve o'clock exactly I would be back. At twelve o'clock to the tick I was at the thana; the officer met me, and informed me that he had been successful and that the prisoner was in the thana. I asked him on what charge he had apprehended him, and he told me that his men had caught him stealing a tablecloth, which amused me not a little. However, the charge did not matter so long as he was in the lock-up on a police-recognised charge, for it would give us time to fix him up in the criminal court to stand his trial.

I will not pursue the story further, though I'm much tempted to do so because of the comic operas that followed one another so quickly, but conclude with the fact that the criminal was sentenced to two years' imprisonment with hard labour (the judge said that he ought to have given him seven years), and his accomplices received lighter sentences.

When the prisoner's time had expired he came to me to ask for forgiveness, thanking me for having put him in prison, and asking to be my servant, for he said he had, while in prison, learnt what a beast he had been.

To show that he meant it he has from that time to this thrown in his lot with us in fighting this evil. His knowledge and his help have been most valuable. He has suffered much in consequence from those who were his former friends and backers in the evil life. From this single slight peep behind the scenes those who are interested in true education in India may realise that something more is needed than preparing boys for examinations, and that the noble art of self-defence is really an art worth teaching.

I am glad to say that matters in this respect have improved in this city, and homes of refuge are no longer needed as in the days of old.

The various stages attained by the boys in their upward growth were illuminating. To start with, none of the boys would touch the gloves; they lay unused for three months, because Brahmans may not touch leather. However, one day I saw a Brahman boy wearing a black beard carrying his books in a leather cover, so I exclaimed: "You are carrying your books in a leather cover. I thought you said you could not touch boxing-gloves because they were made of leather." "Yes, Sahib, it is true; but, you see, this is the leather of books and that the leather of boxing-gloves." That day we commenced with the gloves, and the black-bearded youth was the first to lead the way.

The *first stage* produced much weeping, the gloves being thrown on the ground and the boy who was getting the worst of it running away; and when a nose was tapped and claret appeared the boxing stopped and the onlookers would shout, "Oh! Oh!" put their fingers in their mouths and suck them hard. The boy who was bleeding would cry aloud and know not what to do, as he might not touch blood, even his own. However, the application of some cold water soon settled the trouble. They usually, if not always, lost their tempers, and cried much, and wanted to finish off by scratching one another's faces.

Second stage.—They had learnt how to draw their adversaries' blood, so made those parts their objective;

the more they succeeded the more keen they became to shed more. They would try to knock their adversary on the ground, kneel on his chest and punch his head, the crowd around backing up the winner with shouts of "Give it him hard!" "Do not spare him!" "Thumbs down!"

Third stage, which has been reached but has taken many years of attainment. They now play the game, and the onlookers, unless the weaker one is unpopular, will always back up the weaker and prefer to see a well-matched pair, and if a boxer plays foul they will shout at him to play the game. And very rarely they lose their tempers, even when receiving punishment. I regard boxing as one of the quickest means for attaining that manly and sporting spirit which is needed in every country, and more especially in this lovely country of Kashmir, where self-respect is of so little account. I mean by boxing that which leads to chivalry, and not brutality, its use and not its misuse.

In the matter of social service in the city the qualities that have been attained in boxing have been of great help already to the oppressed, and especially in the case of ill-used animals.

I was astonished one day to see a curious beast come in through the arched gateway of the school playground. It certainly had a donkey's head, but I could not make out how it could be so tall, as its ears touched the arch, and as it moved into the light I saw that it was a man carrying a donkey, the donkey's fore-legs being over the man's shoulders. However, following the man-donkey came in my headmaster, a man beloved by the whole school from top to bottom, and respected or feared as the case might be by the whole city. He came in roaring with laughter. He had found this man riding a donkey far too small and weak for his weight, so he thought it more fitting for the donkey to ride the man. I would point out to the ignorant that a donkey is considered to be an unclean animal by Hindus, so for a Brahman to bother himself about the ill-treatment of an unclean animal shows that our headmaster's education in the Mission School has not been in vain, in that he believes in teaching kindness to animals by action, though the victim be the despised donkey, he himself leading the way. The life of a donkey in this land is not an enviable one. It is the usual custom to put loads on their backs before they are full grown, with the result that nearly every donkey in this country possesses bent hind legs, the hocks rubbing each other. Then they suffer from continual sore backs. There are sores at the various places where the pack-ropes grip their bodies. No one seems to care, for are they not donkeys?

In the winter-time, when it happens to be a severe one, the donkeys in the town as well as those in the villages near the city are let loose in the streets to find their own food with the pariah dogs. The owners of the village donkeys drive their animals into the city, because there is more filth there than in the villages. They have told me that they do not see why they should feed them in the winter as they are not doing any work. So one is continually horrified at the sight of these scores of starving animals wandering about the streets, nosing about in the snow for filth.

The boys took up the matter with zest as soon as they were told that they could bring these animals to school. Mohammedans and Hindus went out together to bring them in from the streets. The Hindus, not being able by their law to touch an unclean donkey, took off their pagris, made them into lassos, threw them over the necks of the donkeys and pulled, while the Mohammedan boys, who might touch donkeys, pushed behind, and thus it came to pass that the school playground became a donkey asylum for the winter. The staff and boys played up, and brought food every day and fed the animals. One winter, which was an especially hard one, our guests all through the winter numbered 100. When the spring came the owners came to claim them, but we would not give them up until the owners had paid two annas per day for their lodging. To this they objected, but as possession is nine-tenths of the law we stood our ground, and when they brought the law to bear upon us we said that we were willing to go to prison as a protest against this continued cruelty. Later on the State added to their statute book a law to prevent cruelty to animals, and appointed an inspector to see the law carried out. So quickly did the law take effect that for the last year or two our boys have had no donkeys or other animals to feed in the winter, and have only had to report half-a-dozen or so cases of cruelty to the lawful authorities—that is, in the city, for the law at present only applies to the city and the Jhelum Valley road, where Mr W. P. Appleford, the State engineer, sees that animals are not persecuted in his domain.

It is difficult to understand the attitude of Eastern people towards the suffering of animals. I saw a man riding along the main road on a small pony with its near fore-leg broken. It was a compound fracture: the bone of the upper part of the leg was sticking out through the skin, and the lower part swinging, as the poor beast hopped along. The rider evidently was happy, for he was whistling as he rode. To me the wonder was not that one man should act thus, but that from among the numberless people he must have passed not one of them had taken compassion on the pony and knocked the cruel beast off his mount. People say when the citizens are educated they will act differently, but I cannot say that I have found that the educated are any more humane than the uneducated. There is something wrong somewhere, and it is the business of those who have hearts to set wrong right.

Kashmir, being a land of rivers, lakes and canals, lends itself to many and various opportunities of social service. Kashmiris are not great swimmers, as one would naturally expect, so that many lose their lives from drowning during the year. Hence we soon set to work to teach swimming.

Unforeseen difficulties met us at once, for parents strongly objected. The Brahman parents said that their sons were gentlemen and therefore must not demean themselves, so to meet their case I made a law that every boy must pass the school swimming test by the age of thirteen, unless one of the doctors at the Mission Hospital should certify to physical weakness (for I knew the parents could get round their Indian doctors), or pay extra fees to the school according to scale, which would start with quarter fees at fourteen years, half fees at fifteen, double fees at sixteen, quadruple at seventeen, and so on. This ruling had the desired effect, so that practically every boy leaves the school a swimmer, and generally a strong swimmer. Each year we teach on an average two hundred boys to swim: a hundred will swim the Dal Lake, three and a half miles; about twenty will cross the Wular Lake, from four to five miles; a few will swim seven miles.

The result has far exceeded our hopes in practical usefulness, for those who have been saved from drowning have amounted up to twenty in a year. Some of these events have called forth great pluck and promptness. Then a further advantage has accrued to this country through the schools' activities. Other schools are following our example and turning out swimmers, and the public generally have learnt that gentlemen may swim without losing their dignity.

As an example: a Chief Minister's son, an undergraduate of the Lahore University, came to me to study English before going to Cambridge. Finding that he could not swim, I told him I would not teach him English unless he learnt to swim.

He said that this could not be for he came from a noble family.

I asked him a straight question. If he happened to be walking by the side of the river with his mother (it would have to be after dark, of course) and she fell in, what would he do, as he could not swim? "Oh, I would call a coolie and send him in after her." I said: "If there did not happen to be a coolie near at hand?" This closed the argument. "Anyway," I said, "before I teach you English you must first come to the lake with me," and we commenced forthwith. We were cycling to the lake when he called out: "My cycle is punctured, I cannot therefore go on to the lake." I said: "No matter, we will walk." And walk fast we did, no gentlemanly pace, that morning, for I knew he had stuck a pin into his tyre.

We never had another puncture, and the Chief Minister's son learnt not only to swim but to row, and eventually was in one of his college eights and thankful that he could say that he was a swimmer.

In the matter of swimming we have not won through yet with the parents, for in all the big swims we have, when one hundred to one hundred and fifty masters and boys will be swimming the lake, I have known only of two cases when parents have come to see their sons swim.

One of them was a Christian and a soldier who needed no pressure; the other was a Brahman who lived quite close to the water, and his son was making a very plucky effort to swim seven miles. He managed to swim only six miles that day. As a matter of fact, his parent had to be more or less pulled down to the water and put into a boat to accompany his son, and even then he would look only at me, and took no interest in his son's efforts. And when at the end the boys were crowding round to congratulate the swimmer the father came up to me, having first ascertained that I was in a happy frame of mind, and therefore it was an auspicious moment. He then informed me that he had an elder son who was out of employment, therefore, as his younger son had made me happy, would I in return help the elder son to obtain employment in a State office. Can a leopard ever change his spots, or an Ethiopian his skin?

This letter, written by a fond parent, may show how some superstitions die hard:

MOST RESPECTED SIR,—I most humbly and respectfully beg to bring to your kind notice that my son, Siri Bhan, student of the Lower School, is strictly prohibited by astrologers, who have examined his horoscope, from joining any playing party, etc. I would request you to kindly keep him exempt from joining the playing teams and boating, etc. I beg to remain, etc., etc.

CHAPTER XXIV

A KASHMIR MISSION SCHOOL (*continued*)

ANOTHER fact may seem inconceivable to those who do not know the Kashmiri—viz. that out of the many instances of our boys having saved life, which are well over 100, I have known only of two cases when the parents or relations have thanked the boys, and only one case where a parent tried to reward the boy for his brave deed. Anyway, it shows that the younger generation are changing their spots, for they are not only willing to risk their lives, but do it for honour and not for reward.

Never shall I forget on that memorable day in the summer of 1891 the shock I received when, having superintended the building of an English boat, and rowing it down to the school with the idea of making oarsmen of the boys, I was received with jeers as I rowed up to the school. Now they were quite convinced, they said, that I was a low-caste sahib, for only a low-caste man would handle an oar. They one and all refused absolutely to have anything to do with an oar, even the school staff taking the same attitude.

Fortunately my will proved the stronger, and so did other parts of my body, and I commenced teaching the art of propelling a boat with English oars that very day, and my pupils were two of the unwilling members of the staff. A young British officer who had been watching my efforts some weeks later said: "You will never teach these Kashmiris to row." (They were at that time still dressed in nightgowns, and looked an amusing crew.) "Why do you waste your time?"

A year later I was coaching a four-oar'd crew (they were swinging well together, but not dressed in nightgowns now), when another young officer said: "Of course you can teach them to row English fashion for they like that, but you will never get them into their own native boats nor teach them to paddle like the common boatmen."

Some years later I was in a Kashmiri boat being propelled by fifteen Brahman boys with paddles like the common Kashmiri boatmen, and a British officer said: "Yes, it is easy enough to get them to do this for it is after the custom of their country." I smiled inwardly, for as a matter of fact it took six years to persuade these Brahman schoolboys to get into a Kashmiri boat and propel it with Kashmiri paddles, and when they made their first trip they covered their heads with blankets to hide their identity so that they should not bring disgrace upon their families.

Time cures most things, and the Brahman antipathy to common boatman's work happened to be among the cures that time effected, so that every week, winter-time excepted, the school holds a regatta in which over 150 masters and boys take part, and crowds of boys walk or ride two or three miles to the lake-side to watch the crews and cheer on their particular classes and schools, while the school band plays a selection of airs during the intervals, and plays home the winners with plenty of drum. The last event is always the same: in the midst of the race home, at a given signal, all the boats sink. This is accomplished by the crew leaving their seats and running down to the bows of the boat: their weight puts the bows under the water, the stern mounts in the air and the boat disappears, leaving the crew on the surface of the water. When the boat reappears the boys swim to their respective sides and bale out the water with one hand while they swim alongside until it is fit for them to climb in one by one. The rest of the water is soon swished out with their paddles, and the boys paddle their boat to the winning-post. As soon as the last boat comes home the band strikes up the two national anthems, when all the crews stand up with paddles and oars erect and in dead silence honour their King Emperor and their Maharajah, and then race back to the city.

There are no prizes for winners, for all our sports and races are played and striven for for honour. We have this particular sinking race to prepare boys for catastrophes in storms, as it is not at all uncommon for boats to be swamped in squalls on the lakes, or by the current in the rivers, when it is the general rule for boatmen and passengers to lose their heads, which leads to the usual loss of life.

The following incident may show how the boys have learnt to be cool in disaster and so save life.

An American family consisting of a husband, wife, governess and little boy were travelling to their camp at night. It was about midnight when the boat capsized. The American party were asleep at the time, so they were all taken by surprise. The father grasped his little boy, the governess grasped the boat and climbed on to the upturned keel, to which also the boatmen were clinging. The wife was washed down-stream and would have certainly been drowned had not there been with the party one of our boys, who immediately swam after the lady, grasped her firmly and swam to shore with her. It all happened suddenly and in the dark, so that a cool head was a very necessary asset. The boy had always done well at our weekly upsettings, hence his smartness.

Use is made of the boats in various ways. It has been the practice now for some years to use the school boats for the sake of the sick in the city and hospitals. The boys, having found health and strength by their athletic life, wish to make use of it for the sake of those who have not.

I wish I could have photographed a particular scene on that beautiful afternoon in June. Allow me to try to describe what I saw. As I was passing a certain village on the banks of the lake I heard music and went in search of it. It led me to a boulder-strewn landing-place where a procession was forming, the school drum and fife band in front, with a crowd of twenty-nine bandaged and sick folk, and almost fifty boys, forming the crews of the fleet, who had just returned with their cargoes of hospital patients from a pleasant afternoon paddle on the lake, the band discoursing sweet music the while. Among this interesting crowd was a lame man with white bandages, supported under the arms by two boys who were helping him to walk. There was a strong boy with another cripple on his back. There were men with bandaged eyes being led by others, and told where to step, guided past holes or up steps. The villagers, of course, had flocked out of their houses and with mouths and eyes wide open were staring in wonder. Some were laughing. Was it from scorn or amusement? Mostly the latter, I think. Some few understood the scene that was being enacted before their eyes, and realised that this school party, which was for the most part composed of Brahmans, were helping Mohammedans. I feel sure some of that crowd will never forget that scene. I certainly shall not.

Now why do these boys spend many of their afternoons

with the sick, striving to brighten up the lives of those who need cheering? Are they paid for it? No.

Is it done to win my approval? Possibly some may do so for this reason.

Is it done because it is part of the Mission School effort? Yes, partly. There are no doubt many mixed motives, but when one has allowed for all these there is yet something more.

They have learnt to be sorry for those in trouble. They see the difference between their school spirit and the spirit of the city. They have realised that superstition, ignorance and stupid customs have drowned the nobler spirit. They realise that their country is down and needs lifting, and they will have their try at changing everlasting custom and the like.

Again, there are others who go deeper, and who have perceived that the daily teachings of the Gospel need expression in life. The life of Christ is speaking to them; it appeals to them as it does to all men in all nations in all times who have ears to hear and eyes to see.

Occasionally we have great floods. They happen when we have exceptionally heavy rain, which brings down the melting snow in the summer and fills up the river and overflows the embankments, when the country is from eight feet to ten feet under water. It all happens very quickly, so that those who have not reached high ground are on the roofs of houses or up trees crying for help. It is then the boatmen's harvest, for they can demand from the flood-stricken what they like, and the price of boats in these times is very much up. At such times the school fleet is very much to the fore.

Here is a coolie up a poplar-tree, where he has been standing all night, and a boatman is below demanding an exorbitant amount to take him home, when up comes a school boat and takes the man home free. The boatman curses. There is a school boat out on the search; they are led by the cries of women and children to a row of sweepers' houses, crowded with sweeper families. They have seen the houses around them disappear, and are in terrible dread lest their row of huts will soon disappear likewise. They have cried for help to many passing boats, but some of the boats had Brahman passengers, who do not like sweepers as near neighbours, and other boats are out for more moneyed folk. The school crew is proud to rescue them, though all the crew are Brahmans, except the cox, who is a Mohammedan.

One of the school staff who is walking towards a sheet of water sees several women on an island which is gradually growing smaller as the water rises. They are imploring a boatman who has brought his boat close to the island to allow them to enter; but they cannot, for his price is too high. The school teacher calls to the man to take the women in his boat, but he will not, so the master immediately dives into the water and comes up close to the boat. In less time than it takes to write the master was in and the boatman out of the boat, and the master ferried the women to a place of safety. That man had not learnt athletics for nothing. He also was a Brahman.

The knowledge of boat-craft has come in handy in many varied emergencies, and often the knowledge of united weight at the right time and place has been useful.

An English lady was in trouble, and she came to us for our help in the following matter:—

The house-boat in which she lived had a rotten plank in the flooring, which could not be repaired unless the boat could be taken out of the water. She tried to make arrangements with boatmen for hauling her big house-boat out of the river, but they asked an exorbitant price, so she appealed to us for aid. The masters and boys were delighted to give their help.

On a certain afternoon one hundred of our strongest masters and boys were on the bank of the river and close to the house-boat, ready to lend their muscles. Large beams of wood had been placed under the boat, on which she could slide. Tackle had been fastened from two large poplar-trees to the house-boat. A strong hawser had been passed between two pulleys; one end had been fastened to the boat and the other end was lying loose on the top of the bank waiting for power to be applied to it. At the word of command one hundred masters and boys seized the rope. At the words, "Are you ready? Go!" they threw their weight on the rope. There followed a loud report, as that from a cannon, and the one hundred pullers were deposited on their backs on the ground. The boatmen who had asked such extortionate wages had come to watch the proceedings; they jeered loudly when they saw the one hundred pullers sprawling on the ground. We now tied two hawsers to the boat and put fifty men at each rope, and again at the word "Go!" there was a report like two guns and the one hundred were again sprawling on the ground. The lookers-on were quite delighted, and showed their delight by their yells and taunts. The ropes were mended, and twenty-five men were put on to each rope, and at the word "Go!" there was no report this time, but a squeaking and creaking noise, and we saw the house-boat sliding up the beams. Then came our turn to cheer, for the school had won and the boatmen were defeated.

I have spoken of Srinagar with regard to its suffering by fires and floods, but there is another trouble which is more dreaded than either—viz. cholera, which always visits Kashmir in epidemic form every four or five years. It always finds the city ready to receive it, and makes full use of its opportunities of taking toll from the inhabitants. The epidemic of 1902 was my first experience of this terrible visitation. The people were terribly scared; offices and schools were closed, and the people sat in their houses, as they said, waiting to die. They would only take the medicine of their "hakims"—*i.e.* native doctors—or trust to the prayers and incantations of the priests. The priests would write some sacred words on pieces of paper which the patients would swallow. They would take no precautions, for they did not believe they were of any use. You would see a man washing in the river the clothes of a relation who has just died of cholera, and a few feet down-stream a man would be drinking the water of the river. It was useless remonstrating, for your words had no meaning to them. Cholera was the will of Allah, or of the gods, what had water or anything else to do with it? Ten thousand deaths were reported in the city, but there must have been hundreds more unreported.

I am thankful to say that superstition and ignorance on this matter is giving way before education, so much so that our masters and boys are welcomed in the houses of the stricken, and they will take from us the medicine of the West, so that in the last epidemic our staff and boys saved seventy-three lives out of the hundred and three cases they took up. When cholera appears in the city we immediately stock bottles of medicine in the schools. Masters and boys come on duty for regular watches night and day; bicycles and lanterns are ready so that they may start the instant the call comes, for in cholera it is all-important to reach the case at once, for all may be over in three hours, though the patient generally succumbs after nine or twelve hours.

We did not win the confidence of the people at once, you may be sure; it has taken years to win it. Often the parents insisted on the masters drinking the medicine before allowing the patient to touch it. One master had to drink so much medicine in this way that he had to go to hospital to be cured of the cholera cure.

In the last two epidemics we have used the simple remedy of permanganate of potash, giving the patient a drink of this, and as much of it as he can manage to get down, and we have found this most efficacious so long as we secured the patient before he had reached the second stage; if in the third stage we called for medical aid and used the hypodermic syringe.

This incident may show how keen our men are in their self-imposed tasks of fighting the cholera.

One of the staff was struck down with cholera, but his parents called in the hakim and priests to use their arts, and it was not until he had entered the third stage that the parents let us know. At once our men were at the house; they had divided themselves into watches two and two for the day and night.

At ten P.M. I visited him, and found four of our party massaging his arms and legs, for he was in great pain from cramp. Seeing that he was *in extremis*, I poured a little brandy down his throat. The man who was holding his head whispered to me to leave the room. I thought he asked me to do this as there were many women in the room and they objected to my presence, so I left.

Next morning early the same man came to tell me that our friend had passed away. "When?" I asked. "At the moment you put the brandy into the patient's mouth." I asked why he had asked me to leave the room, and why he did not tell me that he had died. "Because," said he, "if the people in the room had thought that he had died then they would have said that you had poisoned him; and also we did not wish the women to know that he was dead, for women can bear bad news better in the light than they can in the darkness, so we continued massaging the corpse all through the night, until the morning, and then when the sun arose we broke the news to them, when they would be better able to bear it."

We can employ only a restricted number of masters and boys in nursing the cholera-stricken, but we can make use of many of them to help the city in another way.

I mentioned how frightened the people become when cholera visits the city; this is, of course, bad, as fear predisposes people to the epidemic. So the school tries to counteract the blues by attracting their attention. They bring their boats from the lake to the river, and have races up and down the river in the middle of the city, making as much noise as they possibly can, to show the people that they at any rate do not intend to die. Of course some do die, but their places are filled up by those who live, and they go on racing, and so help the people to transfer their thoughts from deaths and funeral pyres to young life enjoying itself. It also keeps our boys in good spirits, and thus enables them to cheer up their own families.

I expect I have already wearied my readers with this account of education in action, so I will spare them from further talk on the subject.

Finally, I end with the school motto, which has proved an inspiration to many, and is the Alpha and Omega of our teaching and aspirations while in this land of beauty and humour.

THE SCHOOL MOTTO & CREST

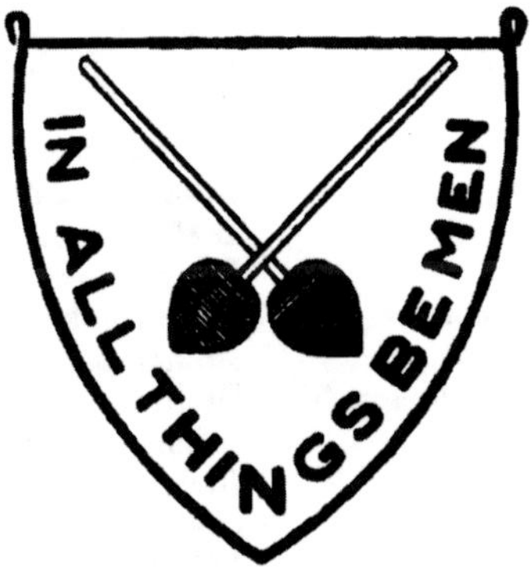

By the term Man is meant one who combines in his nature both strength and kindness, the idea of which is borne out by the crest. The paddle indicates hard work or strength, and the heart-shaped blade betokens kindness. The crossed paddles express self-sacrifice, and are a reminder to all men of Him who taught that great lesson, and all that His Cross meant to the world.

INDEX

Adgonand, Raja, 68
Afghan coolies, a rough lot of, 30
Afghan and the subaltern, the, 151
Afghans, Kashmir under the, 26
Ahmad Shah Durani, 74
Akbar the Great, 72, 87
Albruni the historian, 69
Ali Kadal, 116
Ali Shah, 71
Amar Nath, 146
Amritsar station, 18
Anglo-Indians, 60
Ankhor tree, the poisonous, 54
Appleford and the Afghan, 31
Asoka, introducer of Buddhism, 69
Athletics, 275
Aurangzeb, 74

Baramulla, 30, 36, 55, 192
Barbers, 130
Barges, State, 90
Barges, the building of, 170
Barr, Col. D., 264
Bathe, an uncomfortable, 201
"Batish," the, 133
Batta Mazir, 75
Bears, 43
Bedding, 17
Beggars, 130
Besant, Mrs Annie, 110
Beyond the Pir Punjal, Dr E. Neve's, 248
Bhishties or water-carriers, 22, 107
Bicycling episodes, 121
Birch bark for roofs, 87
Birds, fortunate and unfortunate, 158
"Black art," the, 165
Black bear and carpenter, the, 46
Boat, an Oxford-built, 174
Boat-building, 169
Boat club, the European, 173
Boat people, morals of the, 96
Boatmen, 94, 97
Boats, 89, 92
Boland, Father, 84
Brahman carpenters, 261
Brahman clerk in his home, the, 143
Brahman, dress of the, 142
Brahman holy man or Sadhu, 144
Brahman restrictions, 265
Brahmani sacred bull, the, 123
Brahmans at prayer, 101
Brahman's thread, the, 140
Brahman's toilet, a, 139
Brass pots of the Hindus, 101
Bridges, 89
British and natives, 20
British Resident, the, 75
Bud Shad, 115
Buddhism in Kashmir, 69
Buffalo, origin of the, 41
Buffaloes, 41
Bugle, the driver's, 24
Bulbul, the, 158
Bulbul Shah, 70
Burial ceremonies, 163
Burial custom, a curious, 203
"Burka," the, 150
Burma and Kashmir contrasted, 106

Caravans, 207
Caste marks, 140
Cataract, operations for, 232
Cavalcade, an imposing, 219
Central Asia, travellers from, 134
Ceremonial ablutions, 101
Champion liars, 270
"Chang" or beer, 210

Index

Chang Chenmo, 203
Children, 156
Cholera, 63, 306
Chowkidar and the milk, 80
Christian, Capt., 231
C.M.S., the, 239
C.M.S. High School, 110
Clark, Rev. R., and the "black art," 165
Complexion of Kashmiri women, 60
Consumption, 63
Coolies, 20, 33, 82
Copper work, 133
Coverdale, Miss, 258
Cow-killing, penalties for, 123
Cremation, 160
Cruelty to animals, 124

Dailyas, 85
Dal Lake, 55, 85
Dal, an unrehearsed effect on the, 176
Damudhar Udar, 159
Danudar, Raja, 69
Death, ceremonies at, 156, 163
Delivery, ceremonies before and after, 153
Demons, exorcising, 167
Dentists, 131
Dhobi or washerman, the, 104
Dirty habits of the Kashmiris, 106
Display, love of, 61
Dogras, the, 77
Domel, 30
Doongas and house-boats, 96
Downes, Dr E., 240
Dras, 202
Dress, bright colours in, 141
Dress of the Brahman, 142
Dress, men's and women's, 138
Dress, picturesque, at Ladakh, 213
Dudh Ganga, the, 187
Duni Chand, Col., 251
Durga, 85

Eagles, 190
Eclipses, 159
Egg collecting, 190
Elmslie, Dr, 240
Embroidery work, 132
Epidemics, 62
Evil eye, the, 107
Examinations, 256
Expeditions, 182

Family life in winter, 64
Fateh Kadal, 113
Fires, 88
Fitze, Miss, 259
Flattery, adepts at, 143
Fleas, 198
Floods, 303
Football game, the first, 277
Foul language, 274
Fruits, 56

Gada Bata, rite of, 68
Gadhi, 76
Games, the value of, 268
Ganger, a dishonest, 31
Ganges, the, 157
Genge, Lieut., 232
Gharis, 21
Ghat or yaribal, the, 105
Ghi, 42
Ghost in a mosque, story of a, 117
Ghusal or professional washer, 163
Gilgit, 55
Gilgit road, forced labour on the, 236
Girls, the education of, 257
Glacier, crossing a, 231
Glacier, at the foot of a, 224
"Gog Sahib," 260
Graduates and State appointments, 259
Grasping officials, 241
Grenfell, Dr W., 246
Griffith, Padre, 23
Gujars or cow-herds, 42
Gulab Singh, Maharajah, 26, 75
Gulmarg, 39

Index

HADOW, Mr C. M., 47
Hangi fights, 95
Hanuman, temple of, 116
Hari Parbat, 85
Hatti bungalow, 34
Hazrat Bal mosque, 113, 244
Health officer and Brahman priests, the, 63
Heber, Dr and Mrs, 223
Hemis monastery, 224
Henna ceremony, the 154
Himalayas, the, 17
Hindus at prayer, 101
Horoscope, the, 153
Hospitality, 21
House-boats, 178
Houses of Srinagar, 87, 108, 132
Humour of the Kashmiris, 80
Humour and tragedy, 135
Huns in Kashmir, 69

ID GAH, 117
Ill-treatment of animals, 294
Immorality of the river people, 96
Insanitary conditions, 114
Islamabad, 59
Islamabad, Mrs Bishop's hospital at, 252
Ismalia the boatman, 98
Itch, prevalence of, 59

JACKALS, 52
Jahangir, 72
Jaluki, Raja, 69
Jhats or Sikh farmers, 19
Jhelum river, 35, 84
Joseph, 221
Jumma Musjid mosque, 134
Jummu, 75

KALI GHAT, the, 114
Kangri or fire-pot, the, 139
Kardang Pass, 223
Kargil, 203
Karma, the law of, 157
Kashmir: and Afghans, 26; Sikhs, 26; Rajputs, 26; Gulab Singh, 26; Ranbir Singh, 26; Pratab Singh, 26; views in, 55; fruits and exports, 56; industries, 59, 115, 132; epidemics, 59, 62, 248, 396; people, 60; women, 60, 101; sanitation, 60; Srinagar, 38, 83, 87; villages, 64; history, 67; geology, 68; Huns, 69; Tartars, 69; Mohammedans, 69, 72, 100, 234; religion, 69; Mogul, 72; cession to England, 75; humour, 80, 135; character, 77; habits, 106, 114; immorality, 96; Rajas, 242; customs, 131, 161, 203; Brahmans, 101, 139, 142, 144, 265; education, 151, 253, 256, 259, 261
"Kashmiri," a term of abuse, 78
Kashmiri Sadhus, 149
Kashmiri women, 60
Kashmiris, the, 60
Kawa Punim, rite of, 68
Kechi Mavas, rite of, 68
Kennard, Mr, 178
Khos, 75
Kinaras, 171
Kindergarten system, 261
Kishen Ganga, the, 29
Kites, daring, 123
Knowles, Rev. J. H., 260, 263
Kohala, 26
Konsar Nag Lake, 191
Kotitirtha, 56

LACUSTRINE deposits, 68
Ladakh, 215
Lamayuru, 216
Landslips, 32
Lawrence, Lord J., 84
Lawrence, Sir W., 80
Legends and traditions, 67
Leh, 218
Leper hospital, 248
Lepers, 129
Leprosy, 248

Index

Liquor shops, 127
Locusts, 22
Lunatics, 129
Lynx, the, 52

McCormick, Miss Lucy, 243
Maha Ganisha, the elephant god, 86
Maha Shri, temple of, 115
Maharajah Gulab Singh, 87
Maharajah of Kashmir, generosity of the, 251
Maharajahs, attitude of the, 242
Maharajah's temple, the, 109
Mahmud of Ghuzni, 69
Mahseer, the, 57
Mail runners' shelter, 200
Maina, the, 85
Malodorous river, the, 106
Manisbal Lake, 184
Margs, 39
Marmots, 231
Marriage middleman, the, 161
Marriages, arrangement of, 155, 161
Marsa Lake, 186
Marx, Dr, 222
Massage among coolies, 65
Mastiffs, savage, 228
Match-maker, or marriage go-between, 131
Maxwell, Dr T., 240
Maypole dance, a, 208
Medal, a Brahman's fateful, 140
Medical aid in Kashmir, 251
Mehrakula the Hun king, 69
Middleman, the marriage, 161
Milkmen, 134
Mir Sayid Ali of Hamdan, 113
Mission Hospital, the, 84, 244
Mission at Leh, the, 222
Mitchell, Mr W., 40
Mogul Subadars, 74
Mohammedan invasions, 69
Mohammedan kings, oppression of the, 72
Mohammedans, oppression of, by Hindus, 234
Monasteries and lamas, 211
Monastery band, a, 210
Monastery of Lamayuru, 216
Monkeys, Himalayan, 52
Monks and nuns, 218
Mos Deen Khan, story of, 235
Mosques and temples of Srinagar, 84
Mosquitoes, 57
Mountain dwellers, 65
Mountain road, story of a, 29
Mourners, professional, 161
Mulbek monastery, 208
Mullah Khan, 74
Munshi, the, 61
Munshi Bagh, the, 84
Murree, 26
Mussulman at prayer, the, 100
Mussuth band, 74

Nadir Shah, 74
Nanga Parbat, 41
Naseem Bagh, 58
Nawa Kadal, 116
Nedou & Sons, 40
Nestorian Christians, 213
Neve, Dr, 146, 197
Neve, Dr A., 241, 248
Neve, Dr E. F., 242
Neve, Miss Nora, 243
Newman, Miss, 197, 252
Nicholson, Gen. J., 84
Nisbet, Col. Parry, and the mountain road, 27, 29
Nur Jahan, 115

Officers and panther, 58
Oppressed people, an, 79
Oppression, native, 20
Ordeal by battle, 272

Paddles, stolen, 178
Pagodas, 212
Pagri, the uses of a, 137
Pandits, 72
Pang Gong Lake, 203
Panthers, 47

Index

Paper making, introduction of, 72
Pariah dogs, 124
Pathans, 31
Patthar Masjid mosque, 115
Pestle and mortar, the family, 65
Petrie, Miss Irene, 223
"Pheron," the, 138
Physique of Kashmiri, 62
Pigs, wild, 51
Pine-martens, 52
Pipe, an improvised, 230
Pir Punjal Mts, 84
"Pirak," a, 214
Play, a religious, 225
Policemen, 18
Political Officer, the, 27
Polo, 210
Polo at Leh, 220
Polyandry, 224
Ponies, cruelty to, 28
Poonch state, the, 78
Pratab Singh, Maharajah Sir, 27, 75
Pravarasena, 86
Prayer flags, 212
Prayers, 99
Praying wheels, 212
Prideaux, Colonel, 27
Public examinations, candidates for, 151

Qazi, 161
Qutub-ud-Din, 70

Racing eight, a, 176
Railway carriages, 18
Railway passengers, native, 19
"Raja Kat," the, 158
Raja Sandiman, 83
Raja Sir Amar Singh, 256
Rajas of Kashmir, 68
Rajputs, Kashmir under the, 26
Ram Chand, a holy man, 147
Ranbir Singh, Maharajah, 27
Ranjit Singh, 75
Rawal Pindi, 18
Rice, husking, 65
Rites and ceremonies, 68
River scenes, 92
Red beards, 120
Redslop, Dr, 222
"Refuges," 289
Religious rites and ceremonies, 68
Renchan Shah, 69
Rest-houses, 200
Robinson, Rev. A. J., 287
Roofs, 87
Rope bridges, 35
Rowing, 299
Russia, menace of, 30

Saddles, 132
Sadhu, a chivalrous, 149
Sadhu and the Mission School, 148
Sadhus, 146
Saffa Kadal, 116
Sakhi Muni Gaotam, or Buddha, 69
Sangi Safed, 187
Sartorius, Colonel, 173
Schools, indigenous, 253
Servants, the custom of, 229
Shah Hamdan, 70
Shah Hamdan, mosque of, 113
Shah Jahan, 74
Sharika, the hill of, 86
Shawl industry, the, 115
Shawl weavers, pitiable condition of, 238
Shawl weaving, introduction of, 72
Sheep as carriers, 207
Sheikh Bagh, the, 84
Shergol monastery, 230
Shikara, the, 89
Shops, 126
Shroud for the dead, 163
Sikh fort, the, 85
Sikhs, the, and Kashmir, 26
Sindh Valley, the, 197
Single-sticks for healing divisions, 273
Small-pox, 62, 132
Snakes, 198

Index

"Sneaking," 272
Sneezing, superstition about, 158
Snow-clad mountains, 133
Social service, 280
Sona Marg, 198
Sopor, 38, 57
Spedding, Mr, contractor, 30
Srinagar, 38, 83, 87
Staff, the school, 262
Stages in the boys' education, 292
Stamps, Kashmiri, 91
State schools, 255
Storrs, Rev. W. J., 238
Street episodes, annoying, 119
Sulphur springs, 59
Sundri, our pet monkey, 53
Superstitions, 158, 167
Suru, R., 230
Swimming, 296

"Taffy," 111
Takht-i-Suliman, 83
Tamerlane and the poor man, 70
Tarsa Lake, 186
Tartars, invasion by, 69
Tati Kuti, 188
Tears and laughter, 247
Technical school, 256
Telegraph Office, State, 90
Temperance Society, a, 127
Textile industries, 59
Thirty Years in Kashmir, Dr Neve's, 236
Thorp, Lieut. R., 234, 239
Thread ceremony, the, 154
Tibetan Buddhists, 213
Timber, 56
Tollman and bicycle, the, 27
Tonga, the, 23
Trade marks on clothes, 141
Transmigration, theories about, 157
Trees in Leh, 220
Trench, Capt. C., 197, 203
Trips, the value of, 187
Turban as a sign of vocation, 137
Typhoid, 63

Uniformed robbers, 135

Vaccination and small-pox, 158
Valleys of Kashmir, 39
"Van," 161
Varaha, temple of, 56
Varamul or Baramulla, 56
Vaughan, Dr Janet, 252
Villages, 64
Vishnu, 56

Wade, Rev. T. R., and the "black art," 165, 240
Wardwan Valley, 232
Water-carriers, women as, 107
Wedding parties, boatmen's, 118
Weddings and wedding feasts, 155
Well and the horse, the, 25
Wives, duties of, 156
Woodwork, 59
Woman's place in Hinduism, 101
Women of Ladakh, status of the, 214
Wular Lake, 38, 57, 192

Yadhus, the, 69
Yarkandi, Serai, 117

Zain-ul-Abidin, 72
Zana Kadal, 115
Zenana Hospital, 252
Ziarats or shrines, 86
Zoji La, 199

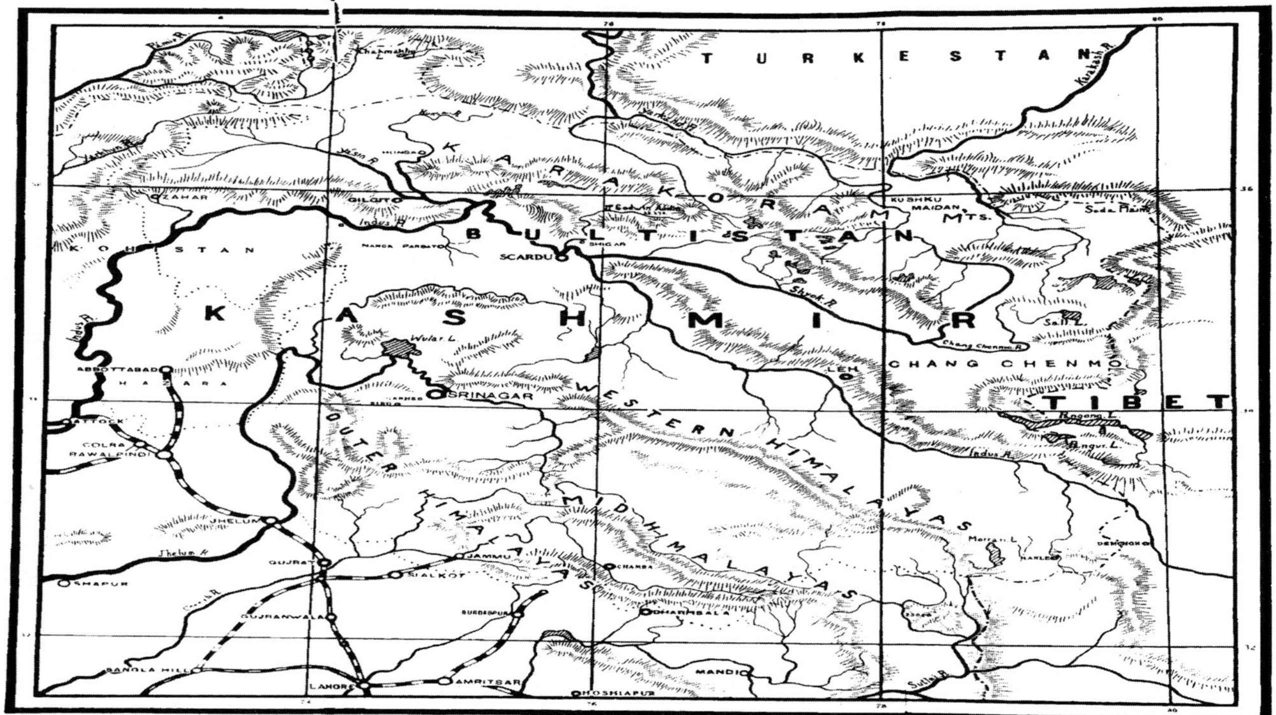

Scale = 1:2,636,500

KASHMIR